W9-BAT-396

RIVER COTTAGE
VEG

*200 inspired
vegetable recipes*

Hugh Fearnley-Whittingstall

Photography by Simon Wheeler
Illustrations by Mariko Jesse

TEN SPEED PRESS
Berkeley

For Louisa

Hugh Fearnley-Whittingstall *is an award-winning British writer, broadcaster, and food campaigner with an uncompromising commitment to seasonal, ethically produced food. He has been presenting programs for Channel Four in the UK for over fifteen years, and this is the seventh River Cottage book he has written. His previous work includes* The River Cottage Cookbook, *for which he won the Glenfiddich Trophy and the André Simon Award;* The River Cottage Meat Book, *which won the André Simon Award and the 2008 James Beard Cookbook of the Year Award;* The River Cottage Fish Book, *which also won the André Simon Award;* The River Cottage Family Cookbook, *which was the Guild of Food Writers Cookery Book of the Year; and* River Cottage Every Day. *He also writes a weekly recipe column for the* Guardian. *Hugh and his family live in Devon, not far from River Cottage HQ, where Hugh and his team teach and host events that celebrate their enthusiasm for local, seasonal produce.*

Published in the United States by Ten Speed Press, an imprint of the Crown Publishing Group, a division of Random House, Inc., New York.
www.crownpublishing.com
www.tenspeed.com

Ten Speed Press and the Ten Speed Press colophon are registered trademarks of Random House, Inc.

Originally published in slightly different form in hardcover in Great Britain as *River Cottage Veg Everyday* by Bloomsbury Publishing Plc, London, in 2011

First Ten Speed Press printing, 2013

Library of Congress Cataloging-in-Publication Data is on file with the publisher.

Hardcover ISBN: 978-1-60774-472-6
eBook ISBN: 978-1-60774-473-3

Printed in China

Project editor: Janet Illsley
Cover design by Sarah Adelman
Interior design by Lawrence Morton
Illustrations by Mariko Jesse
Photography by Simon Wheeler

10 9 8 7 6 5 4 3 2 1

First United States Edition

All recipes are vegetarian. Those marked 🗘 are suitable for vegans, provided optional nonvegan ingredients are excluded and vegan options for ingredients such as mustard and wine are used.

introduction

This is a vegetable cookbook. Whether or not it's a *vegetarian* cookbook depends perhaps on your point of view and your food politics. It's not written by a vegetarian, or with the intention of persuading you or anyone else to become a vegetarian. But in the sense that not one of the recipes here contains a scrap of meat or fish, then it is indeed quite strictly vegetarian. I certainly hope that many vegetarians will buy it, use it, and enjoy it.

And it is also, I would like to think, evangelical. Call me power-crazed, but I'm trying to change your life here. The object of the exercise is, unambiguously, to persuade you to eat more vegetables. *Many* more vegetables. Perhaps even to make veg the mainstay of your daily cooking. And therefore, by implication, to eat less meat, maybe *a lot* less meat, and maybe a bit less fish, too. Why? We need to eat more vegetables and less flesh because vegetables are the foods that do us the most good and our planet the least harm. Do I need to spell out in detail the arguments to support that assertion? Is there anyone who seriously doubts it to be true? Just ask yourself if you, or anyone you know, might be in danger of eating *too many* vegetables. Or if you think the world might be a better, cleaner, greener place with a few more factory chicken or pig farms or intensive cattle feedlots scattered about the countryside. Surely it's close to being a no-brainer.

So, to be absolutely clear, all the recipes that follow are suitable for vegetarians. Since I have used dairy products and eggs, they are not all appropriate for vegans. But over a third of them are (those marked ⓥ), and another third easily could be if suitable substitutes for butter and milk were used. If you're a vegan, you'll know what to do.

I can certainly appreciate that if you've used my books, you may be feeling a bit baffled to be holding in your hand a near-as-damn-it vegetarian cookbook written by that notorious carnivore Hugh Fearnley-Whittingstall. But if you know my work a little more intimately, if you've probed and dabbled beyond the recipes and into the more discursive text, this should come as no great surprise – I've visited this territory before. Only now I'm at the vegetable end of the meat argument, and it's a very refreshing place to be.

But let me recap my core thinking on this subject anyway – I'll try and keep it pithy. In my meat book, I argued that we eat far too much meat in the West – too much for our own health, and far too much for the welfare of the many millions of animals we raise for food. I believe that factory farming is plain wrong – environmentally and ethically. So it saddens me to say that, despite some recent significant gains in the UK on poultry and pork welfare, the problems associated with the industrial production of meat are, globally speaking, as bad as ever. I've been similarly forthright about fish. I believe it's a wonderful food, which I like to catch and love to eat. But I have also pointed out that we are in ever-increasing danger of eradicating this amazing source of food altogether.

Good reasons, you might think, for becoming an out-and-out vegetarian. But that isn't my plan. I still believe in being a selective omnivore, casting a positive vote in favor of ethically produced meat and sustainably caught fish. However, I now understand that in order to eat these two great foods in good conscience, I have to recognize, control, and impose limits on my appetite for them.

But why, I hear some of you remonstrating, given that I still eat meat and fish, would I want this book to exclude them *entirely*? What's wrong with a soupçon of meat and fish? Perhaps, like me, you've already become adept at making a little meat go a long way. You've embraced the notion that a few shards of bacon, or a sprinkling of chorizo crumbs, or some scraps of leftover chicken, are a perfect way to give a lift to a big salad or add interest, spice, and texture to a creamy vegetable soup; and that an anchovy here and there gives a lovely salty tang (especially, as it happens, to vegetables).

So why will I not allow such sound and thrifty strategies, where a modest amount of meat is used as a perk or spice in a dish, to season and punctuate the vegetable recipes in this book? Because it would be a cop-out, that's why! That approach, useful though it is at times, is ultimately the wrong mindset for serious change. It suggests you're *clinging on* to meat; that you feel any meal is incomplete without it. And that's the feeling I think we all need to let go of.

The way I see it, if we are remotely serious in our commitment to eat less meat and fish, we will want to make plenty of meals – perhaps even the majority of them – *completely without* meat and fish. For many of us, this is quite a big concept to swallow, but I want to tackle it head-on. We may be increasingly aware of the good reasons to eat less meat, but our cooking culture is still largely based around flesh. The idea of a fridge entirely free of sausages, bacon, chops, or chicken can strike fear into the heart of many a cook – even a resourceful one. Meat is so familiar, so convenient; it's the easy route to something that we instantly recognize as a "proper meal." I want to show you how straightforward it can be to embrace vegetables in the same way.

Changing your prime culinary focus from meat to veg will require a shift in attitude – but not, I would argue, a very big or difficult one. It's true that if you eschew meat and fish, you have to look at other ingredients with fresh eyes. You have to take a new, more creative approach to them. But once you become accustomed to cooking vegetables as main meals it will soon seem like the most natural thing. This book is your starter pack on that mission.

I have to admit that when making my own commitment to cook and eat more veg, and indeed to write this book, I found it a little hard to shake off the meat lover's niggling prejudices. But I can honestly say that my own anxieties – about cooking without meat being somehow less satisfying, less flavorsome, or less easy – have proved groundless. I have actually found it all to be very liberating. I think the kind of vegetable cookery I've embraced here is more democratic – there's no longer a tyrannical piece of meat dominating the agenda, making everything else feel like a supporting act.

In contrast, the recipes that follow are often a harmonious blend of several different vegetables; a meal based on veg often gives equal weight to several different dishes. Much as I enjoy the generous one-pot or one-plate vegetarian curries, hotpots, or lasagnes (of which plenty are coming up), I find there's something *particularly* enticing and satisfying about a meal made up of several "small" dishes, such as you get with Middle Eastern meze or Spanish tapas. Vegetable cookery really lends itself to such delicious, mix-and-match spreads, where you can try a little (or a lot) of whatever takes your fancy. I love the slight lawlessness of this way of eating. It's all so much less predictable and more fun than being a slave to meat.

If you *are* a vegetarian and a keen cook, I'm sure you'll already have your own repertoire of favorite dishes. Perhaps you're wondering whether this book is for you. Well, I hope I can offer you something new, too. My view is that vegetarians have not been as richly served in the cookbook market as they deserve. Ironically, I think there's

been a little too much emphasis (consciously or unconsciously) on *replacing* meat, whereas I think that when we turn our attention to veg, we should feel pretty relaxed about simply *ignoring* meat. Then we can get on with the life-enhancing business of enjoying the extraordinary range of fresh seasonal vegetables we can buy (and indeed grow), by cooking them in a whole range of new and exciting ways. Much as I see the vital food value and great culinary potential of legumes and grains, I've little time for veggie patties and textured vegetable protein. I'd rather break that mold and muddle my chickpeas, kidney beans, and quinoa with fresh leaves, crunchy roots, and sun-ripened fruits: squashes, peppers, eggplants, and tomatoes, to name but four.

The truth is, I really don't need to be talked into a conversation with vegetarians. I've been having that conversation, and enjoying it, for years. I have a lot of time for vegetarians (though apparently not *all* of them have a lot of time for me), and that's because I respect anyone with principles about food. One of the silliest spectacles I have ever seen in the brash world of TV chefs is that of colleagues who really should know better than to goad vegetarians as if they were somehow not to be taken seriously in the kitchen. (Or even out of it – one chef actually said that if any of his children grew up to be vegetarians, he'd shoot them. I'm secretly hoping that one of them does, so I can see their dad eat his words.)

In some quarters, it's even been assumed I might harbor similar feelings toward vegetarians. Of course I don't. In fact – and I can't say this without smiling – *some of my best friends are vegetarians.* When it comes to the recipes in this book, I hope it's very much a two-way street, not least because I learned some of my favorite dishes from my vegetarian friends. I also feel I am a better cook now than I was when I set out to write this book. I feed my family better – with more vegetables – than I did before. I am less reliant on that freezer full of homegrown meat and self-caught fish (fantastic as those ingredients are) than I used to be. I enjoy my cooking, and my eating, more than ever. And that feels wonderful.

So here you are: more than two hundred River Cottage veg recipes. And for those who just love to get on and cook, here's the best bit: the philosophizing and moralizing is done. I'm climbing down off my soapbox. Because this is not a book of caveats and cautions. It's not an argumentative case for not eating something bad, or rare, or threatened. In fact, it's not a book about problems at all. Quite the opposite: it's full of solutions. And the main solution is, quite simply, to eat more vegetables!

Comfort food
& feasts

With this chapter, right from the start, I want to lay to rest any fears you may have about vegetable-based meals being insubstantial, lacking in flavor, or somehow not "proper food." These recipes are the first to turn to if you want to eat less meat but are a little bit wary about the prospect – perhaps because you can't help feeling some degree of sensory deprivation may ensue. It needn't. Pile into these recipes and your tummy will be filled, your craving for flavor fully satisfied. They are fulfilling in every sense – they will not only sate your hunger, but their tastes, scents, and textures will both tempt and gratify you.

The dishes here are multilayered and multifaceted, with strength and depth of both flavor and texture. You'll find saucy, sweet, and spicy curries and stews; crisply crusted pies and tarts; starchy staples enlivened with unexpected twists; and a host of tempting vegetarian classics from around the world – reinterpreted for the busy modern family. This is where your decision to serve up more meals without meat really takes root – with a bunch of reliable regulars you'll always be proud to present and delighted to share.

These recipes all meet the important criterion of being able to stand up comfortably as main courses in their own right. That doesn't necessarily mean you would want to serve them entirely on their own (although in some cases, you most certainly could). But each of them can clearly be the principal offering of a meal. They are, dare I say it, among the "meatier" dishes of the book. Indeed many of them can be brought out as the kind of abundant, generous, celebratory centerpieces you might choose to serve for a Sunday lunch, a birthday supper, a bonfire night party, or any other kind of festive gathering. Yes, it really is possible to celebrate such occasions without cooking flesh!

This chapter also bears out a truth you'll find me repeating more than once through these pages: that if you decide to eat less meat, and at some meals no meat, then you have to take a fresh look at all the other ingredients you're cooking with. Many of them will need to appear center stage, where the meat used to be. Don't worry about it. Root vegetables, beans and legumes, fleshy stems, and even full-flavored green leaves can all take the strain, holding their own in stews, hotpots, curries, and pies. The recipes that follow have been chosen to prove the point.

I'll also be asking you to reassess a certain style of dish that you might previously have regarded as a complement to, rather than a replacement for, meat. You may be used to eating comforting things like a classic potato dauphinoise (see page 60), or the more quirky sweet potato and peanut gratin (see page 63) "on the side." However, if you shunt them into the middle of your plate and build around them with a few simple accompaniments, they will satisfy in a whole new way.

If you doubt this, ask yourself how often is it that the lovely potato and celery root gratin, or even the perfect roasted spud or tender, sweet parsnip is actually the most delicious thing on a plate that it just happens to be sharing with some not-so-great meat and less-than-inspired gravy? Now imagine what is possible when, from the outset, you aim to make that gratin, or those roasted roots, the focal point of the feast. A bit of extra spice perhaps; a cheesy, nutty, crumby topping; something unexpected hiding in the middle . . . As soon as you lavish a bit of attention on the veg, you'll find you're richly rewarded.

As you might expect, there are plenty of what could be called cold weather dishes in this section – lots of lovely, bubbling root gratins; beany chilis and curries; and rich savory lasagnes. But food doesn't have to be wintry to be comforting and filling, and you'll also find a roughly equal number of summery dishes, such as the lettuce, green onion, and cheese tart (see page 44), or the gorgeous tomato and pepper stew known as chachouka (see page 20). These will help to convince you, I hope, that vegetable-based meals can deliver top-notch contentment at any time of year.

I've given suggestions for how to serve the dishes at the end of most of the recipes, but they are just ideas. Common sense and your own personal tastes will prevail. Sometimes you might feel that a helping of pasta or rice, or perhaps a baked potato or a pile of creamy mashed potatoes – is required in order to soak up the sauce, round out the dishes, and make a meal of them. Conversely, you might hanker for a crisp, light salad to cut their richness. It'll depend on your mood, the weather, who you're feeding, and how hungry you all are. This is the kind of food where I hope the lion will sit down and tuck in with the lamb, the old with the young, the hungry with the light of appetite. In other words, there's elasticity here to cater to all comers on all occasions. And they will all be special occasions, I promise.

Eggplant parmigiana

This is one of my favorite ways to cook large eggplants, and it's one of those dishes with few ingredients that seems to be greater than the sum of its parts. It is one to take your time over – ideal for a rainy afternoon in the kitchen – but once assembled, it can be chilled or even frozen and cooked later on.

SERVES 6

4 medium eggplants
(about 2 pounds / 1kg)

Sea salt

4 to 5 tablespoons olive oil

2 balls of buffalo mozzarella
(about 4 ounces / 125g each),
torn into pieces

About 1¼ ounces / 35g
Parmesan, hard goat cheese,
or other well-flavored hard
cheese, finely grated

FOR THE TOMATO SAUCE

2 tablespoons olive oil

2 onions, chopped

3 garlic cloves, chopped

4 (14-ounce / 400g) cans plum
tomatoes, coarsely chopped,
any stalky ends and skin
removed

1 bay leaf

Sea salt and freshly ground
black pepper

A little sugar

Trim the eggplants and slice lengthwise into ⅛-inch-thick / 3mm-thick slices. Layer the slices in a colander, sprinkling each layer with a little salt. Leave to drain for an hour or so.

Meanwhile, make the tomato sauce. Heat the 2 tablespoons of olive oil in a very large, wide pan over medium heat. Add the onions and garlic and sauté gently for about 10 minutes, stirring occasionally, until soft. Add the tomatoes with their juice and the bay leaf. Bring to a simmer, then simmer briskly, stirring often, for about half an hour, or until the sauce is thick and rich. Season well with salt and pepper and a little sugar to taste.

Quickly rinse the eggplant slices and pat dry thoroughly with a kitchen towel or paper towels. Heat a large frying pan over medium-high heat and add 1 tablespoon of the oil. When the oil is hot, fry a batch of eggplant slices for about 2 minutes each side, until golden and tender. Remove and set aside. Repeat with the remaining eggplant slices, adding a little more oil to the pan before you fry each batch.

Preheat the oven to 350°F / 180°C. Lay a third of the eggplant slices in the bottom of an ovenproof dish, 8 by 10 inches / 25 by 20cm and at least 2 inches / 5cm deep. Cover with a third of the tomato sauce. Dot a third of the mozzarella over the sauce, then scatter a thin layer of grated cheese over that. Repeat with the remaining ingredients so you have three layers in the dish.

Bake for 30 to 40 minutes, until bubbling and golden on top. Serve with lots of fresh green salad – and bread, if you like.

Chachouka

This spicy North African pepper and tomato stew with eggs baked on top makes a lovely, lazy supper. The classic Italian peperonata (see variation) is prepared in the same way but without eggs or spices – it is equally good.

SERVES 4

3 tablespoons olive oil

1 teaspoon cumin seeds

1 large onion, halved and thinly sliced

1 garlic clove, crushed

1 red bell pepper, cored, seeded, and thinly sliced

1 yellow bell pepper, cored, seeded, and thinly sliced

1/2 teaspoon hot smoked paprika

A pinch of saffron strands

1 (14-ounce / 400g) can plum tomatoes, coarsely chopped, any stalky ends and skin removed

Sea salt and freshly ground black pepper

4 large eggs

Heat the olive oil in a large, preferably ovenproof, frying pan over medium heat. Add the cumin seeds and let them fry gently for a couple of minutes. Add the onion and cook gently for 8 to 10 minutes, or until soft and golden.

Add the garlic and peppers and continue to cook over low heat for at least 20 minutes, stirring often, until the peppers are soft and wilted. Add the paprika and crumble in the saffron, then add the tomatoes with their juice and some salt and pepper. Cook gently, stirring from time to time, for 10 to 15 minutes. Preheat the oven to 350°F / 180°C.

Taste the mixture and adjust the seasoning if necessary. If your frying pan isn't ovenproof, transfer the mixture to a baking dish. Make 4 hollows in the surface and carefully break an egg into each one. Sprinkle with salt and pepper. Bake for 10 to 12 minutes, until the egg white is set and the yolk still runny.

VARIATION

Peperonata ᵛ

Simply leave out the cumin, paprika, saffron, and eggs, serving the stew after simmering with bread and/or a crisp green salad.

Pinto bean chili⍌

You can adapt this easy, fiery chili to the seasons, swapping summer's zucchini and peppers for autumn's mushrooms and winter squash, for instance. And you can easily double or triple the quantities if you want to feed a crowd (it's perfect for bonfire night), or freeze some for later.

SERVES 4 OR 5

2 tablespoons olive, sunflower, or canola oil

3 onions, chopped

2 or 3 green chiles, to taste, seeded and finely chopped

2 garlic cloves, finely chopped

2 teaspoons ground cumin

1 teaspoon cayenne pepper

1/4 teaspoon allspice

2 zucchini, cut into 1/2-inch / 1cm dice

1 red bell pepper, cored, seeded, and cut into 1/2-inch / 1cm dice

2 tablespoons tomato paste

1 (14-ounce / 400g) can plum tomatoes, coarsely chopped, any stalky ends and skin removed

1 (14-ounce / 400g) can pinto beans, drained and rinsed

A scant 1/2 cup / 100ml red wine

A good handful of parsley, finely chopped

A good handful of cilantro, finely chopped, plus extra to serve

A handful of oregano, finely chopped

Sea salt and freshly ground black pepper

TO SERVE

Lemony guacamole (see page 296)

Shredded lettuce

Sour cream (optional)

Grated cheddar (optional)

Heat the oil in a large saucepan over medium-low heat, add the onions, and sweat, stirring from time to time, until very soft and just starting to take on some color. Add the chiles, garlic, cumin, cayenne, and allspice and stir for a minute.

Add the zucchini and red pepper and stir to coat with the spices. Add the tomato paste, canned tomatoes with their juice, pinto beans, red wine, parsley, cilantro, and oregano. Pour over about 3/4 cup / 200ml of water and add some salt and pepper. Simmer gently for 25 to 30 minutes, stirring from time to time, until all the vegetables are tender and everything is thick and saucy. Taste and adjust the seasoning, adding a little more salt and/or pepper if you think it needs it.

To serve, put the guacamole, shredded lettuce, sour cream, and cheese, if using, into small serving bowls. Scatter more chopped cilantro over the chili and accompany with the various toppings and rice and/or flat breads (see page 176) or tortillas, for everyone to help themselves.

Chard and new potato curry

This hearty curry is fantastic in late summer or early autumn. If you want to make it ahead of time and refrigerate or freeze it, leave out the yogurt and add it at the last minute, just before serving.

SERVES 4

About 1 pound / 500g Swiss chard

2 tablespoons sunflower oil

1 onion, halved and thinly sliced

3 garlic cloves, peeled

1 green chile, seeded and finely chopped

1 (1-inch / 2.5cm) piece of ginger, peeled and chopped

1 teaspoon garam masala

1/2 teaspoon mustard seeds

1/2 teaspoon ground cumin

1/4 teaspoon ground turmeric

3 cardamom pods, bashed

12 ounces / 350g new potatoes, quartered

1 cup / 250g plain full-fat yogurt

1 1/2 tablespoons tomato paste

A small bunch of cilantro, coarsely chopped

Sea salt and freshly ground black pepper

A small handful of almonds, cashews, or pistachios, toasted and chopped

Separate the chard leaves from the stalks. Cut the stalks into 1-inch / 2.5cm pieces and coarsely chop the leaves.

Heat the oil in a large saucepan over medium heat, add the onion, and fry until just golden. Meanwhile, pound together the garlic, chile, and ginger with a pinch of salt to a paste. Add the paste to the onion and cook, stirring, for a couple of minutes. Tip in the rest of the spices and stir for a minute or two.

Add the potatoes and chopped chard stalks and fry, stirring frequently, for 5 minutes, so that they are well coated with the spice mixture. Pour in about 1²/₃ cups / 400ml of water – enough to just cover the vegetables. Bring to a simmer, cover, and cook for 10 to 12 minutes, until the potatoes are just tender. Add the chard leaves, stir, and cook until just wilted.

In a bowl, whisk together the yogurt, tomato paste, and some of the hot liquid from the curry. Remove the curry from the heat, stir in the yogurt mixture, return to the heat, and warm through very gently (if it gets too hot, the yogurt will curdle). Stir in most of the cilantro.

Taste and add salt and pepper if needed. Scatter over the toasted nuts and remaining cilantro, then serve with rice and naan or chapatis.

VARIATIONS

Spinach and new potato curry
Use about 1 1/2 pounds / 600 to 700g spinach in place of the chard. Remove any tough stems and add the leaves to the curry once the potatoes are done. Cook for a minute or two before adding the yogurt mixture.

Winter kale and potato curry
Use medium or large potatoes, peeled and cut into bite-sized chunks, rather than new potatoes, and replace the chard with kale. Discard the kale stalks, coarsely shred the leaves, and add them when the potatoes are nearly done. Simmer for 2 to 3 minutes, or until tender.

Cauliflower and chickpea curry ❧

This beautifully simple, light curry is closely based on a wonderful recipe from chef Angela Hartnett. It's always preferable to use some carefully selected ground and whole spices in a recipe like this, but if you're in a hurry, use a ready-made curry powder instead of the dry spices.

SERVES 4 TO 6

1 medium-large cauliflower (about 1³/₄ pounds / 800g), trimmed

Sea salt

2 tablespoons sunflower oil

3 onions, chopped

4 garlic cloves, chopped

1 teaspoon freshly grated ginger

2 teaspoons ground coriander

2 teaspoons ground cumin

A large pinch of dried chile flakes

2 star anise

1 (14-ounce / 400g) can plum tomatoes, chopped, any stalky ends and skin removed

1 (14-ounce / 400g) can chickpeas, drained and rinsed

2 teaspoons garam masala

A good handful of cilantro, chopped

Sea salt and freshly ground black pepper

Cut the cauliflower into medium florets. Put into a large pan, cover with cold water, add some salt, and bring up to a rolling boil. This will partly cook the cauliflower. Take off the heat right away, drain well, and keep warm in the pan.

Heat the oil in a second large saucepan over medium heat. Add the onions, garlic, and ginger and sauté for about 10 minutes, stirring often.

Add the ground coriander, cumin, chile flakes, star anise, and some salt and pepper and cook for a further 5 minutes.

Add the tomatoes with their juice and the chickpeas. Stir well, then add the parcooked cauliflower. Pour in enough cold water to almost but not quite cover everything (¹/₃ to ³/₄ cup / 100 to 200ml) and bring to a simmer. Simmer for 5 to 10 minutes, stirring once or twice, until the cauliflower is tender.

Stir in the garam masala and half of the chopped cilantro, then check the seasoning. Serve scattered with the remaining cilantro and accompanied by rice, flat breads (see page 176), or naan.

Eggplant and green bean curry ^v

This gorgeously rich curry uses my roasted tomato sauce as a base, though a good-quality canned sauce would work well, too. I've deliberately made twice as much curry paste as you need for the recipe – partly because it's easier to blend that way, but also because it's so useful to have a second batch either to make this again or for any other veg curry. Alternatively, use a well-sautéed blob of it as the base for a simple noodle soup. You can keep the paste, covered, in the fridge for up to a week, or freeze it.

SERVES 6 TO 8

5 large eggplants (about 4 pounds / 1.8kg)

Sunflower oil

1¼ cups / 300ml roasted tomato sauce (see page 366)

1 (14-ounce / 400ml) can coconut milk

10 ounces / 300g green beans

Sea salt and freshly ground black pepper

A good handful of cilantro, chopped

⅔ cup / 75g cashews or almonds, toasted and coarsely chopped (optional)

FOR THE CURRY PASTE

5 or 6 shallots or 2 medium onions, finely chopped

6 garlic cloves, coarsely chopped

2 thumb-sized pieces of ginger, peeled and coarsely chopped

2 lemongrass stalks, tough outer layer removed, thinly sliced

5 or 6 medium green chiles (medium-hot), seeded and coarsely chopped

2 teaspoons ground cumin

2 teaspoons ground coriander

1 teaspoon ground turmeric

TO SERVE

Lime wedges

Put all the curry paste ingredients into a blender with 2 tablespoons of water and whiz to a coarse paste. Stop a few times to scrape down the sides if necessary.

Halve the eggplants lengthwise. Cut each half lengthwise into thirds, then halve each piece so that you have 12 wedges from each eggplant.

Heat 2 to 3 tablespoons of oil over medium-high heat in a large nonstick frying pan. Sauté the eggplant wedges in batches until lightly browned, adding more oil as needed. As you remove the wedges from the pan, lay them on paper towels to drain.

Heat 1 tablespoon of oil in a large, deep saucepan and add half of the curry paste (refrigerate the rest for another use). Fry over medium heat, stirring constantly, for 3 to 4 minutes. Add the eggplants to the pan and stir for a minute or two until coated with the curry paste.

Now add the tomato sauce and coconut milk. If the tomato sauce is very thick, you can add a little water now, too. Simmer, partially covered, for 10 minutes. Add the green beans and simmer until they are tender, about 5 minutes.

Season well with salt and pepper and stir in the chopped cilantro. If using the toasted nuts, scatter them over the curry, then serve with lime wedges and accompanied by rice.

North african squash and chickpea stew

This richly spiced combination of squash, tomatoes, and legumes is based on a traditional Moroccan recipe, harira. That dish is actually a soup, but whenever I make it, I find myself veering toward such a thick and chunky texture that "stew" seems a more appropriate description. It hardly matters – it's a delicious, belly-filling one-pot dish.

SERVES 6

2 tablespoons sunflower oil

2 large onions, diced

2 garlic cloves, finely chopped

1 celery stalk, finely diced

1 teaspoon ground turmeric

1/2 teaspoon ground cinnamon

1/2 teaspoon ground ginger

Sea salt and freshly ground black pepper

1/2 cup / 100g red lentils

1 (14-ounce / 400g) can chickpeas, drained and rinsed

8 saffron strands, toasted and crushed

2 cups / 500ml roasted tomato sauce (see page 366) or canned tomato sauce

A good handful of parsley, coarsely chopped

A large bunch of cilantro, coarsely chopped

10 ounces / 300g winter squash or pumpkin

5 cups / 1.2 liters vegetable stock (see page 130)

1 bay leaf

2 ounces / 60g orzo or other small pasta

Dates, to serve (optional)

Heat the oil in a large saucepan over medium heat. Add the onions and sauté until just starting to turn golden. Turn down the heat to medium-low and add the garlic, celery, turmeric, cinnamon, ginger, and 1 teaspoon pepper. Sauté for a couple of minutes.

Now add the lentils, chickpeas, saffron, tomato sauce, parsley, and about half of the cilantro. Cook over low heat for 15 minutes.

Meanwhile, peel and seed the squash and cut into large cubes. Add to the pan with the stock and bay leaf. Cover and simmer gently for about 30 minutes. Add the pasta and simmer until it is cooked. Season with salt and pepper to taste.

Serve immediately, scattered with the remaining cilantro leaves and with a few dates on the side, if you like.

Squash and fennel lasagne

There are endless versions of vegetarian lasagne and many of them are disappointing, being over-reliant on legumes and tomato sauce. I think this unusual recipe is really special, proper comfort food and just what you need on a chilly autumn night: lots of earthy flavors, plenty of creamy béchamel sauce, and a good dose of melting cheese.

SERVES 6

2 pounds / 1kg winter squash

6 tablespoons canola or olive oil, plus extra to trickle

Sea salt and freshly ground black pepper

1 fat garlic clove, finely chopped

A few sprigs of thyme, leaves only, finely chopped

1 1/2 pounds / 750g fennel (3 large bulbs)

5 ounces / 150g blue cheese or goat cheese, crumbled

4 ounces / 125g lasagne noodles (fresh is best, but dried is fine)

3/4 ounce / 20g Parmesan, cheddar, or other well-flavored hard cheese, grated

FOR THE BÉCHAMEL SAUCE

1 quart / 1 liter whole milk

1 bay leaf

1 onion, coarsely chopped

1 celery stalk, coarsely chopped

A few black peppercorns

3 1/2 tablespoons / 50g unsalted butter

6 1/2 tablespoons / 50g all-purpose flour

2 teaspoons Dijon mustard

Sea salt and freshly ground black pepper

Preheat the oven to 350°F / 180°C. For the béchamel, heat the milk in a saucepan with the bay leaf, onion, celery, and peppercorns until just below simmering. Remove from the heat and set aside to infuse.

Peel and seed the squash and cut into 1-inch / 2.5cm cubes. Toss with 4 tablespoons of the oil in a roasting dish, season well with salt and pepper, and roast for 30 minutes, or until tender. Remove from the oven, toss immediately with the garlic and thyme, and set aside.

Trim the fennel, removing the tough outer layer, then cut the bulbs into roughly 1/4-inch / 5mm slices. Heat the remaining 2 tablespoons oil in a large frying pan over medium-low heat. Add the fennel and sauté for 10 to 15 minutes, or until tender. Set aside.

Gently reheat the infused milk, then strain. Heat the butter in a large saucepan over medium heat. Stir in the flour to form a smooth roux and cook gently for a minute or two. Remove from the heat. Add about a quarter of the hot milk and beat well until smooth. Repeat with the remaining milk, adding it in 2 or 3 lots, until you have a smooth sauce. Return to the heat and cook, stirring often and allowing the sauce to bubble gently for a few minutes, until thickened. Stir in the mustard and season with salt and pepper.

Spread a third of the béchamel sauce over the bottom of a 9 by 11-inch / 28 by 22cm (or thereabouts) ovenproof dish. Layer half the lasagne noodles in the dish, then scatter the roasted squash evenly over it. Trickle over another third of the sauce. Layer in the remaining lasagne, then the fennel. Scatter the crumbled cheese over the fennel, then spoon on the remaining béchamel.

Sprinkle with the grated cheese and add a trickle of oil. Bake for about 30 minutes, until golden. Serve at once, with peas or a green salad.

Kale and mushroom lasagne

This is what I call a good weekender: a dish that requires a little bit of preparation, but one you can put together in a relaxed way over an hour or two, and that results in something truly warming and delicious.

SERVES 6

About 10 ounces / 300g curly or Lacinato kale, tough stalks removed

2 tablespoons / 30g butter

1 pound / 500g mushrooms, sliced

Sea salt and freshly ground black pepper

2 garlic cloves, finely chopped

A few sprigs of thyme, leaves only, chopped

6 ounces / 175g lasagne noodles (fresh is best, but dried is fine)

³/₄ ounce / 20g Parmesan, hard goat cheese, or other well-flavored hard cheese, grated

A little canola or olive oil

FOR THE BÉCHAMEL SAUCE

3 cups / 750ml whole milk

1 bay leaf

1 onion, coarsely chopped

1 celery stalk, coarsely chopped

A few black peppercorns

3¹/₂ tablespoons / 50g unsalted butter

6¹/₂ tablespoons / 50g all-purpose flour

2 teaspoons Dijon mustard

Sea salt and freshly ground black pepper

Preheat the oven to 350°F / 180°C. For the béchamel, heat the milk in a saucepan with the bay leaf, onion, celery, and peppercorns until just below simmering. Remove from the heat and set aside to infuse.

Roughly shred the kale. Put into a large saucepan and just cover with cold water. Add salt. Bring to a boil, lower the heat, and simmer for 2 to 3 minutes, until just tender. Drain well and set aside.

Heat half of the butter in a large, wide frying pan over medium heat. Add half of the mushrooms and some salt and pepper. Increase the heat and fry, stirring often, for 5 to 10 minutes, until the liquid released by the mushrooms has evaporated and they are starting to shrink, concentrate, and caramelize. Stir in half of the garlic and half of the thyme, cook for a minute longer, then remove to a bowl. Repeat to cook the remaining mushrooms and set aside.

Gently reheat the infused milk, then strain. Heat the butter for the béchamel sauce in a large saucepan. Stir in the flour to form a smooth roux and cook gently for a minute or two. Remove from the heat. Add about a quarter of the hot milk and beat vigorously until smooth. Repeat with the remaining milk, adding it in 2 or 3 lots, until you have a smooth sauce. Return to the heat and cook for a few minutes, stirring often, allowing the sauce to bubble gently until thickened. Stir in the mustard, then add some salt and pepper.

Stir about half of the béchamel sauce into the kale; put to one side.

Spread half the remaining béchamel over the bottom of a 9 by 11-inch / 28 by 22cm (or thereabouts) ovenproof dish. Layer a third of the lasagne noodles in the dish, then spoon the kale over the top. Add another layer of lasagne, then the mushrooms. Finish with a final layer of pasta and the remaining béchamel.

Scatter over the cheese and add a trickle of oil. Bake for about 30 minutes, until golden. Serve straight away.

Chiles stuffed with beans

I like to use fat, mildly piquant, poblano chiles or piquillo peppers for this dish. But if you can't get hold of stuffable large chiles, you can use small red or yellow bell peppers instead.

**SERVES 6 AS A STARTER,
2 OR 3 AS A MAIN COURSE**

6 large, fresh poblano chiles

1 tablespoon canola or olive oil

2 or 3 shallots or 1 medium onion, finely chopped

2 garlic cloves, finely chopped

6 ounces / 150 to 200g fresh, ripe tomatoes

1 (14-ounce / 400g) can beans, such as borlotti, pinto, or lima beans, drained and rinsed

A bunch of cilantro, chopped

1 teaspoon ground cumin

1 teaspoon hot smoked paprika

Sea salt and freshly ground black pepper

FOR THE GARLICKY YOGURT (OPTIONAL)

6 tablespoons / 90g plain full-fat yogurt or sour cream

½ garlic clove, crushed

Preheat the broiler to high. Lay the chiles on a baking sheet and broil, turning from time to time, until the skins begin to char. Leave until cool enough to handle, then carefully peel away the skins, taking care to keep the chiles whole. Cut around and remove the stalks and a flap of flesh to form a "lid." Carefully scrape out all the seeds and membranes from inside the chiles and lids, and tip out any juice.

Preheat the oven to 350°F / 180°C. Heat the oil in a frying pan over medium-low heat, then gently sauté the shallots and garlic until soft, about 10 minutes. Slice the tomatoes in half and grate their flesh straight into the pan, holding back the skin. Simmer for a minute or two to reduce slightly. Remove from the heat.

Add the drained beans to the pan and coarsely mash some of them with a fork so they break up a little – don't overdo it, you want plenty of them to stay whole. Add the chopped cilantro, cumin, and paprika, mix well, and season with salt and pepper to taste. Carefully stuff the mixture into the chiles and top with the lids. Lay the stuffed chiles in a lightly oiled ovenproof dish and bake for 20 minutes.

While the chiles are in the oven, combine the yogurt with the crushed garlic and some salt and pepper, if serving, and set aside.

Serve the stuffed chiles hot, with a spoonful of garlicky yogurt if you like, and a crisp, green salad.

Stuffed cabbage leaves

This is a great dish for a special occasion. It may not be quick, but it's one to prepare when you have a willing accomplice in the kitchen, as in, "You make the sauce, I'll make the stuffing, and we'll roll the parcels together."

SERVES 4

12 outer leaves from a large savoy cabbage

¼ cup / 60g sour cream, plus extra to serve (optional)

FOR THE TOMATO SAUCE

2 tablespoons olive oil

1 onion, chopped

1 bay leaf

A couple of sprigs of thyme

1 carrot, chopped

1 celery stalk, chopped

2 garlic cloves, finely chopped

1⅓ pounds / 600g fresh, ripe tomatoes, peeled and chopped, or 1 (14-ounce / 400g) can plum tomatoes, coarsely chopped, any stalky ends and skin removed

Sea salt and freshly ground black pepper

A pinch of sugar (optional)

FOR THE FILLING

⅔ cup / 120g pearled spelt, rice, or pearled barley

1 tablespoon olive oil

1 onion, chopped

1 or 2 garlic cloves, finely chopped

⅓ cup / 50g currants

⅓ cup / 50g walnuts, coarsely chopped

Finely grated zest of 1 lemon

A bunch of parsley, chopped

A handful of dill, chopped

¼ teaspoon dried chile flakes

1 large egg, lightly beaten

First make the tomato sauce. Heat the olive oil in a saucepan over medium-low heat and sweat the onion, bay leaf, and thyme for about 10 minutes, until the onion is soft. Add the carrot and celery and sauté for a further 5 minutes, then stir in the garlic and cook for a minute. Add the tomatoes with their juice, some salt and pepper, and a pinch of sugar if you like. Simmer gently until thickened, about 15 minutes.

Preheat the oven to 350°F / 180°C. If the ribs of the cabbage leaves are thick, pare down the thickest part a bit with a vegetable peeler. Bring a saucepan of lightly salted water to a boil and blanch the cabbage leaves for 2 to 3 minutes. Drain and refresh under cold water, then pat the leaves dry with a kitchen towel or paper towels.

To make the filling, cook the spelt, rice, or barley according to the package instructions. Heat the olive oil in a small frying pan, add the onion, and sweat over low heat until soft but not colored. Add the garlic and stir for a minute. Tip the onion and garlic into a bowl and add the cooked grain, currants, walnuts, lemon zest, chopped herbs, and chile flakes. Season very generously with salt and pepper, stir until well mixed, then add the egg and stir again until combined.

Lay out the blanched cabbage leaves on a clean surface. Place a big spoonful of the filling mixture in the center of each leaf, fold over the sides, and roll up from the stalk end so you have 12 neat packages. Place them in an ovenproof dish seam side down.

Spoon the tomato sauce over the stuffed leaves, dot some sour cream on top, and sprinkle with pepper. Bake for 30 to 35 minutes, until piping hot. Serve with more sour cream, if you like.

VARIATIONS

Instead of cabbage, you can use large fresh or preserved grape leaves, blanching fresh ones for 1 minute only; preserved leaves just need to be rinsed well. Alternatively, you can use the leaves of winter greens such as Swiss chard and kale; remove any coarse stalks and blanch the leaves for a minute or two to soften.

Squash stuffed with leeks

These tempting baked stuffed squash make for an impressive and substantial meal. The scent of thyme, leeks, and cheese that wafts up as you lift the lid off is so very alluring. Small gem or acorn squash are ideal; you could even use a squat butternut. Those around 14 ounces / 400g will serve one; larger squash can be shared.

SERVES 4

2 tablespoons / 30g butter

2 large leeks, trimmed and thinly sliced

1 teaspoon English mustard

¼ cup / 60g crème fraîche

About 4 ounces / 125g Gruyère or other well-flavored hard cheese, finely grated

Sea salt and freshly ground black pepper

2 to 4 smallish squash (14 ounces to 1¾ pounds / 400 to 800g each)

A handful of thyme sprigs

Preheat the oven to 375°F / 190°C. Heat the butter in a saucepan over medium heat and add the leeks. As soon as they begin to sizzle, turn the heat right down and cover the pan. Sweat the leeks gently for about 10 minutes, until very soft. Remove from the heat and stir in the mustard, crème fraîche, and cheese. Season the mixture well with salt and pepper, as it will be surrounded by a good amount of squash.

Cut a small slice off the base of each squash so it will stand up on a baking sheet without wobbling. Carefully slice a "lid" off the top of each one, too, and set aside. Now, with a small, sharp knife, cut into the center of each squash, then use a teaspoon to scoop out all of the seeds and fibers.

Fill the squash cavities with the leek mixture – they should be about two-thirds full. Tuck a few thyme sprigs into the center of each. Put the lids back on top and stand the squash on a large baking sheet – there should be plenty of room for hot air to circulate around them.

Bake for 50 to 60 minutes – possibly longer if the squash are large – until the flesh feels very tender inside. Serve right away.

Spinach, penne, and cheese "spouffle"

I love using pasta to turn a light, puffy spinach soufflé into a sustaining one-pot supper, or "spoufflé," as I call it. The zucchini version (below) is equally good.

SERVES 4

1¼ cups / 300ml whole milk

1 bay leaf

½ onion

A few black peppercorns

3½ ounces / 100g penne or similar-shaped pasta

A little canola or olive oil

9 ounces / 250g spinach, tough stems removed

3½ tablespoons / 50g unsalted butter

6½ tablespoons / 50g all-purpose flour

3 ounces / 75g mature cheddar, finely grated

A little freshly grated nutmeg

Sea salt and freshly ground black pepper

3 large eggs, separated, plus 1 egg white

Preheat the oven to 375°F / 190°C and put in a baking sheet to heat up. Liberally butter a 6-cup / 1.5-liter soufflé dish or fairly deep ovenproof dish of similar capacity.

Put the milk, bay leaf, onion, and peppercorns into a small saucepan and bring to just below a simmer. Turn off the heat and leave to infuse.

Bring a saucepan of well-salted water to a boil. Add the penne and cook until al dente. Drain well, then toss in the oil to stop the pasta from sticking together.

Cook the spinach, with only the water clinging to it after washing, in a large covered saucepan over medium heat until wilted – just a few minutes. Drain well. When cool enough to handle, squeeze out the liquid with your hands, then coarsely chop the spinach.

Reheat the infused milk, then strain. Heat the butter in a saucepan over medium heat, stir in the flour to form a roux, and cook for a few minutes. Remove from the heat, add the milk to the roux a third at a time, beating well. Return to the heat and cook, stirring, for a couple of minutes; you will end up with a thick béchamel sauce. Remove from the heat and stir in the cheese, nutmeg, spinach, and some salt and pepper – the mixture should be well seasoned. Beat in the egg yolks, then fold in the penne.

In a clean bowl, whisk the egg whites to firm peaks. Stir a spoonful into the béchamel mixture to loosen it, then carefully fold in the rest. Tip into the buttered dish and place on the hot baking sheet in the oven. Bake for 25 to 30 minutes, until well risen and golden. Serve right away.

VARIATION

Zucchini penne "spoufflé"
Instead of the spinach, use 1 pound / 500g thinly sliced zucchini. Heat about 2 tablespoons olive oil in a large frying pan over medium heat, add the zucchini along with a thinly sliced garlic clove and a good pinch of salt, and fry gently for 15 minutes, tossing regularly, without browning. As the zucchini slices soften, break them up a bit with your spatula to form a very coarse, creamy purée. Fold into the béchamel mixture along with the cooked penne and continue as above.

Lettuce, green onion, and cheese tart

Cooked lettuce can be absolutely wonderful, combining sweet and slightly bitter flavors. Mixed with fresh-tasting green onions and a creamy, savory custard, it makes a very lovely tart – perfect for an early summer lunch.

SERVES 6 TO 8

FOR THE PASTRY

2 cups / 250g all-purpose flour

A pinch of sea salt

1/2 cup plus 1 tablespoon / 125g chilled unsalted butter, cut into small cubes

About 1/3 cup / 75ml cold whole milk

FOR THE FILLING

1 tablespoon canola or olive oil

4 Little Gem lettuce hearts, trimmed and quartered

Sea salt and freshly ground black pepper

1 tablespoon / 15g butter

2 bunches of green onions (about 9 ounces / 250g), trimmed and cut into chunky slices

3 1/2 ounces / 100g Lancashire, medium cheddar, or hard goat cheese

2 large eggs, plus 2 egg yolks

Scant 1 cup / 200ml heavy cream

Scant 1 cup / 200ml whole milk

To make the pastry, sift together the flour and salt, or give them a quick blitz in a food processor. Add the butter and rub in with your fingertips, or blitz in the food processor, until the mixture resembles fine bread crumbs. Mix in the cold milk little by little, until the pastry just comes together, then turn out onto a work surface and knead briefly to bring it into a ball. Wrap and chill for 30 minutes.

Preheat the oven to 350°F / 180°C. On a lightly floured surface, roll out the pastry quite thin and use to line a 10-inch / 25cm tart pan. Leave the rough edges of the pastry hanging over the sides of the pan. Line with foil, fill with baking weights, and blind bake for 15 minutes. Remove the foil and weights, prick the pastry in a few places with a sharp fork, and bake uncovered for a further 10 to 15 minutes, or until the pastry is just starting to color. Using a small, sharp knife, trim away the excess pastry from the edge. Leave the oven on.

To make the filling, heat the oil in a frying pan over medium heat. Add the quartered lettuce hearts, sprinkle with salt and pepper, and cook for about 5 minutes, turning once or twice, until the cut surfaces are golden brown. Add the butter toward the end of cooking, letting it melt in the pan, then spooning it over the lettuces. Using a slotted spoon, remove the lettuce hearts and arrange in the tart shell.

Reduce the heat under the frying pan a little. Add the green onions and sauté gently for 5 minutes, then scatter in the tart shell over and around the lettuce hearts. Crumble or grate the cheese over the top.

Lightly beat together the eggs, egg yolks, cream, and milk in a bowl and season generously with salt and pepper. Carefully pour this mixture into the tart shell (depending on the depth of your pan, you might not need all of it). Bake for about 35 minutes until golden. Serve warm or at room temperature.

Beet greens (or chard) and ricotta tart

If you come by bunches of baby beets with the leaves and stems still attached, this is a great use for them. Fine-stemmed varieties of chard, such as red or rainbow, are ideal too. You can use any ricotta for this, but a delicate, crumbly sheep's milk ricotta is particularly good.

SERVES 6 TO 8

FOR THE PASTRY

2 cups / 250g all-purpose flour

A pinch of sea salt

1/2 cup plus 1 tablespoon / 125g chilled unsalted butter, cut into small cubes

About 5 tablespoons / 75ml cold whole milk

FOR THE FILLING

Greens from a bunch of beets or a bunch of red or rainbow Swiss chard (about 10 ounces / 300g in all)

1 tablespoon canola or olive oil

1 large onion, halved and sliced

A handful of thyme sprigs, leaves only, chopped

1 garlic clove, finely chopped

Sea salt and freshly ground black pepper

3½ ounces / 100g ricotta salata, finely crumbled

2 large eggs, plus 2 egg yolks

Scant 1 cup / 200ml heavy cream

Scant 1 cup / 200ml whole milk

Make the pastry, let rest, then use to line a 10-inch / 25cm tart pan and blind bake following the method on page 44. Leave the oven on after baking the tart shell.

To make the filling, chop the stalks from the beet tops or chard and shred the leaves. Heat the oil in a large frying pan, add the onion with the thyme, and sweat gently for about 10 minutes, until softened. Add the garlic and chopped beet or chard stalks. Cook, stirring often, for about 10 minutes, until the stalks are tender. Add the shredded leaves and cook for another 5 minutes or so, until the leaves have wilted right down. Season well with salt and pepper.

Spread the leafy mixture in the tart shell. Scatter the crumbled ricotta over the top. Lightly beat together the eggs, egg yolks, cream, and milk in a bowl and season well with salt and pepper. Carefully pour this mixture into the tart shell. Bake the tart at 350°F / 180°C for about 35 minutes until golden. Serve warm or cold.

VARIATION

Samphire and spinach tart

Salty, succulent marsh samphire, which is at its best in June and July, makes an unusual and delicious alternative filling for this tart – it's especially good combined with fresh spinach. Wilt down about 8 ounces / 250g spinach, drain well, and squeeze out all water, then chop coarsely. Thoroughly wash about 5 ounces / 150g marsh samphire and remove any woody ends. Cook the onion as above, adding the thyme and garlic, and seasoning with pepper but no salt, as the samphire is already salty. Distribute the onion, chopped spinach, and samphire around the tart shell, then scatter over the ricotta. Add the custard and bake as above.

Baby beet tarte tatin

The classic tarte tatin is made, of course, with apples. But the principle of caramelizing some delicious, round, sweet things, topping them with puff pastry, then flipping it upside down, works equally well in this savory interpretation. The shallot/green onion vinaigrette finishes off the tart a treat, but if you fancy ringing the changes, it's also very good topped with crumbled feta and coarsely chopped parsley.

SERVES 4

8 ounces / 250g rough puff pastry (see page 52) or all-butter puff pastry (ready-made)

A knob of butter

1 tablespoon canola or olive oil

2 teaspoons cider vinegar

2 teaspoons brown sugar

Sea salt and freshly ground black pepper

10 to 14 ounces / 300 to 400g baby beets (the size of a golf ball or no bigger than a small apple), scrubbed and halved

FOR THE VINAIGRETTE

1 or 2 shallots or 3 or 4 green onions, trimmed and very finely chopped

1 teaspoon English mustard

1 tablespoon cider vinegar

¼ cup / 60ml canola oil

A pinch of sugar

A handful of parsley leaves, finely chopped

Preheat the oven to 375°F / 190°C. Roll out the pastry on a lightly floured surface to a thickness of about ¼ inch / 5mm. Take an ovenproof frying pan (or a tarte tatin dish) roughly 8 inches / 20cm in diameter, place it upside down on the pastry, and cut around it. Wrap the pastry disk and place it in the fridge.

Melt the butter with the oil in the frying pan (or tarte tatin dish). Add the cider vinegar, sugar, and some salt and pepper, stir well, then add the halved beets and toss to coat. You want the beets to fill the pan snugly, so add a few more if you need to. Cover the pan with foil, transfer to the oven, and roast for 30 to 40 minutes, until the beets are tender.

Take the pan from the oven and rearrange the beet halves neatly, placing them cut side up. Lay the pastry disk over the beets, patting it down and tucking in the edges down the side of the pan. Return to the oven and bake for 20 minutes, until the pastry is fully puffed up and golden brown.

Leave the tarte to cool in its pan for about 15 minutes, then turn it out by putting a plate over the top and inverting it. Pour any juices left in the pan back over the beets.

Put the ingredients for the vinaigrette into a screw-topped jar, season well with salt and pepper, and shake to combine. Trickle over the tarte tatin and serve.

Zucchini and rice filo pie

This is based on an intriguing, delicious Greek dish that I came across in a battered old copy of Mediterranean Vegetable Cookery by Rena Salaman. The rice steals the water from the grated zucchini and plumps up as the two cook together inside the pie. It's as tasty as it is cunning.

SERVES 4

1 pound / 500g zucchini, coarsely grated

1/3 cup / 75g long-grain white rice

1/2 medium red onion, finely chopped

2 1/2 ounces / 75g hard goat cheese or mature cheddar, grated

2 large eggs, lightly beaten

2 tablespoons olive oil

A handful of dill, chopped

A good handful of flat-leaf parsley, chopped

Sea salt and freshly ground black pepper

8 ounces / 250g ready-made filo pastry

5 tablespoons / 75g unsalted butter, melted

Preheat the oven to 375°F / 190°C. Mix the zucchini, rice, onion, cheese, eggs, olive oil, and chopped herbs together in a large bowl. Season with plenty of salt and pepper.

Take a sheet of filo pastry, brush with a little melted butter, and use it to line a smallish ovenproof dish, about 6 cups / 1.5 liter capacity, placing the pastry buttered side down. Let any excess hang over at the ends. Add another buttered sheet on top and continue until you've used all but one sheet of the pastry.

Tip the filling into the pastry-lined dish. Fold over the pastry ends to enclose the filling, dabbing with a little more melted butter to keep the pastry together. Take the remaining sheet of pastry, crumple it lightly in your hands to give a nicely textured finish, and place it on top of the pie, tucking in the edges around the side.

Dab a little more butter over the surface and bake for 45 minutes, until golden. Serve hot or warm.

Rutabaga and potato pasties

Generously seasoned root vegetables make a hearty pasty filling. These are delicious served hot, but are great cold too – in packed lunches or as a sustaining snack. You can use ordinary piecrust or a store-bought puff pastry, but the pasties are particularly good with the easy-to-make rough puff pastry I suggest here. The cheese is optional. Being a bit of a rutabaga purist, I like it without, but it does give an extra dimension of savoriness.

SERVES 4

FOR THE ROUGH PUFF PASTRY

2¹/₃ cups / 300g all-purpose flour

A pinch of sea salt

¹/₂ cup plus 2¹/₂ tablespoons / 150g chilled unsalted butter, cut into small cubes

Ice water

FOR THE FILLING

8 ounces / 225g potato

4 ounces / 125g rutabaga

3 ounces / 75g carrot

1 small onion, grated

A handful of parsley, finely chopped

A few sprigs of thyme, leaves only, chopped

1 teaspoon vegetable bouillon powder

¹/₂ teaspoon freshly ground black pepper

¹/₂ teaspoon sea salt

1¹/₂ ounces / 45g strong cheddar, grated (optional)

2 tablespoons / 30g butter, melted

TO FINISH

1 large egg, lightly beaten with 1 teaspoon milk, to glaze

To make the pastry, mix the flour with the salt, then add the cubed butter and toss until the pieces are coated in the flour. Stir in just enough ice water (about ²/₃ cup / 150ml) to bring the mixture together into a fairly firm dough.

On a well-floured surface, shape the dough into a rectangle with your hands and then roll it out in one direction, away from you, so you end up with a rectangle about ¹/₂ inch / 1cm thick. Fold the far third toward you, then fold the nearest third over that (rather like folding a business letter), so that you now have a rectangle made up of 3 equal layers. Give the pastry a quarter turn, then repeat the rolling, folding, and turning process 5 more times. Wrap the pastry in plastic wrap and rest in the fridge for about 30 minutes or up to an hour.

Preheat the oven to 375°F / 190°C. For the filling, peel the potato, rutabaga, and carrot and cut into ¹/₈-inch / 3mm dice. Mix together with all the other ingredients in a bowl, adding the butter last of all to bind.

Roll out the pastry on a lightly floured surface to approximately a ¹/₈-inch / 3mm thickness. Using an 8-inch / 20cm plate as a template, cut out 4 circles; you may have to gather up the trimmings and then reroll them to get your fourth circle.

Spoon the vegetable mixture onto one half of each circle. Brush the pastry edges with a little water, fold the other half of the pastry over the filling to form half-moon shapes, and crimp the edges well to seal.

Place the pasties on a baking sheet lined with parchment paper and brush with the egg glaze. Bake for 35 to 40 minutes, until the pastry is golden brown. Eat hot or cold.

Corner shop spanakopita

This spinach pie is a pretty loose take on the classic Greek spanakopita. It came about in response to a challenge laid down by a friend: could I cook up a menu using only ingredients available from the average convenience store? I bit the bullet, and this is one of the recipes I came up with. I can't say frozen spinach is an ingredient I use often, but you can now get decent frozen whole-leaf stuff, and it works well here. Of course, you could use fresh spinach, wilted, drained, squeezed, and chopped, if you prefer.

SERVES 4

1 (2-pound / 1kg) bag frozen whole-leaf spinach

2 tablespoons olive oil

1 teaspoon cumin, fennel, or caraway seeds (whichever is handy)

1 large onion, halved and thinly sliced

$^1/_2$ teaspoon dried thyme or a few sprigs of fresh thyme, leaves only, chopped

A squeeze of lemon juice

Sea salt and freshly ground black pepper

2 large eggs, lightly beaten

$3^1/_2$ ounces / 100g soft goat cheese or feta, broken into small chunks

$^1/_4$ cup / 35g pine nuts, toasted (or coarsely chopped cashews)

13 ounces / 375g all-butter, ready-made puff pastry (ideally ready-rolled)

Preheat the oven to 400°F / 200°C. Put the frozen spinach into a saucepan with a splash of water. Cover and heat gently, stirring from time to time, until completely defrosted. Tip into a colander or sieve to drain off all water, pressing with a wooden spoon to help it along.

Meanwhile, heat the olive oil in a frying pan over medium heat. Add the spice seeds and let them cook for a minute or two, shaking the pan frequently, then add the onion and sauté for 5 to 10 minutes, or until soft and golden. Add the thyme. Remove from the heat.

When the spinach has cooled a little, squeeze as much liquid out of it as you can with your hands, then chop it coarsely. Combine it with the onion, along with a squeeze of lemon juice and plenty of salt and pepper. Set aside 2 to 3 tablespoons of the beaten egg for glazing and stir the remainder into the spinach and onion mixture.

Spoon half the spinach mixture into an 8 by 10-inch / 25 by 20cm (or thereabouts) ovenproof dish. Scatter over the cheese and toasted pine nuts, then top with the remaining spinach. Brush a little of the reserved beaten egg around the rim of the dish.

On a lightly floured surface, roll out the pastry to a thickness of about $^1/_4$ inch / 5mm (unless, of course, it's ready-rolled). Lay the pastry over the dish and trim off the excess overhanging the rim. Press down the edge of the pastry so that it sticks to the rim of the dish. Brush the pie with the reserved beaten egg and bake for about 25 minutes until the pastry is puffed and golden brown. Serve immediately.

Mushroom ragout with soft polenta

This is very easy to put together, and pretty quick, too. Use a mix of well-flavored mushrooms, such as cremini and portabello; add wild or exotic mushrooms if you have some on hand. If you have any polenta left over, let it go cold, then cut it into chunks or cubes and fry it.

SERVES 4

FOR THE POLENTA

1²/₃ cups / 400ml milk

1 bay leaf

A sprig of thyme

A few black peppercorns

½ onion and/or 2 garlic cloves, bashed

1¼ cups / 150g quick-cooking polenta

4 teaspoons / 20g butter

1 teaspoon finely chopped rosemary

¾ ounce / 20g Parmesan, hard goat cheese, or other well-flavored hard cheese, grated

Sea salt and freshly ground black pepper

FOR THE RAGOUT

2 tablespoons canola or olive oil

A large knob of butter

1½ pounds / 650g mushrooms, thickly sliced

Sea salt and freshly ground black pepper

1 large garlic clove, chopped

A few sprigs of thyme, leaves only, chopped

²/₃ cup / 150ml red wine

²/₃ cup / 150ml vegetable or mushroom stock (see page 130)

TO SERVE (OPTIONAL)

A trickle of top-notch olive oil

Extra Parmesan or other hard cheese, shaved

For the polenta, put the milk and 1²/₃ cups / 400ml of water into a saucepan. Add the bay leaf, thyme, peppercorns, and onion/garlic. Bring to just below a boil, then set aside to infuse for 20 minutes.

Meanwhile, make the ragout. Heat 1 tablespoon of the oil and half of the butter in a large, wide frying pan over medium heat. Add half of the mushrooms and some salt and pepper and turn the heat up to high. Cook, stirring often, to encourage the mushrooms to release their juices. Continue to cook until most of the juices have evaporated and the mushrooms are starting to concentrate and caramelize. Add half of the garlic and thyme and cook for a minute more, then tip the contents of the pan out onto a plate. Repeat with the remaining mushrooms, using the rest of the garlic and thyme. Return the first batch of mushrooms to the pan. Add the wine and stock, lower the heat, and simmer for about 15 minutes, until the liquid has reduced by about half. Check the seasoning.

To cook the polenta, strain the infused milk mixture into a clean saucepan (or just scoop out the flavorings with a slotted spoon, as I do). Bring to a simmer, then pour in the polenta in a thin stream, stirring as you do so. Stir until the mixture is smooth and then let it return to a simmer. Cook for just 1 minute, then remove from the heat. Stir in the butter, rosemary, and cheese, then season generously with salt and pepper (adding at least ¼ teaspoon of salt).

Immediately scoop the polenta into warmed dishes, top with the juicy mushroom ragout, and serve, with a trickle of best olive oil and a few slivers of shaved cheese, if you like.

Chile, cheese, and rosemary polenta with tomato sauce

This is a really great way to cook polenta: well flavored, well seasoned, and nicely caramelized. The simple sauce, based on canned tomatoes, is a mainstay in my kitchen and is used in many different ways – with pasta or roasted vegetables, or on a pizza crust (see page 180), for example.

SERVES 4

FOR THE POLENTA

4 tablespoons olive oil

1 garlic clove, chopped

1 fresh red chile, seeded, and finely chopped, or a good pinch of dried chile flakes

1 tablespoon finely chopped rosemary

1¼ cups / 150g quick-cooking polenta

3½ ounces / 100g strong cheddar, hard goat cheese, or other well-flavored hard cheese, grated

Sea salt and freshly ground black pepper

FOR THE TOMATO SAUCE

2 tablespoons olive oil

2 garlic cloves, finely slivered

2 (14-ounce / 400g) cans plum tomatoes, any stalky ends and skin removed

1 bay leaf (optional)

Sea salt and freshly ground black pepper

A pinch of sugar

To make the polenta, heat 2 tablespoons of the olive oil in a frying pan over medium-low heat. Add the garlic and chile and sweat gently for a couple of minutes – don't let the garlic color. Add the rosemary and remove from the heat.

Pour 3½ cups / 800ml of water into a saucepan and bring to a boil. Now pour in the polenta in a thin stream, stirring all the time. When smooth, allow it to return to a simmer. Cook for 4 to 5 minutes, stirring often, then remove from the heat. Stir in the garlic, chile, and rosemary mixture, then add the grated cheese and a generous amount of salt and pepper. Mix well.

Tip the polenta onto a cold surface, such as a plate or a marble slab, and spread it smoothly into an even disk, about 1 inch / 2cm thick. Leave to cool completely.

To make the tomato sauce, heat the olive oil in a wide frying pan over medium-low heat. Add the garlic and sweat gently for a couple of minutes; don't let it color. Put the tomatoes into a large bowl with their juice and crush them with your hands. Tip the lot into the frying pan, adding a bay leaf if you have one handy. Bring to a simmer, then cook for 20 to 30 minutes, stirring often and crushing the tomatoes with a fork until you have a thick, pulpy sauce. Season with salt, pepper, and a pinch of sugar.

When the polenta is cool and firm, cut into slices or wedges. Heat the remaining 2 tablespoons of olive oil in a nonstick pan over medium-high heat and fry the polenta pieces for 2 to 3 minutes each side, until they have a light golden brown crust. Serve with the hot tomato sauce.

Potato dauphinoise

This classic potato dish with its glorious caramelized top and rich, melting interior will always be one of my favorites. Something magical happens when you bake potatoes, thinly sliced, in garlic-scented cream. I tend to use whichever starchy variety I have on hand, but you can also make it with large new potatoes. The texture is a bit different but still very good. I love a dauphinoise with a green salad and plain-cooked green lentils (see page 237).

(see page 237)

SERVES 6

2 tablespoons / 30g butter

2 pounds / 1kg starchy potatoes

1²/₃ cups / 400ml heavy cream

2 large garlic cloves, crushed

¹/₄ teaspoon freshly grated nutmeg

Sea salt and freshly ground black pepper

Preheat the oven to 325°F / 160°C. Rub a large gratin dish liberally with the butter.

Peel the potatoes and slice them thinly, either with a sharp knife or a mandoline. In a large bowl, whisk together the cream, garlic, and nutmeg and season well with salt and pepper. Toss the potatoes in the cream mixture, then layer them in the gratin dish, spreading them as flat and evenly as you can. Pour over any remaining cream.

Bake for 1¹/₄ to 1¹/₂ hours, pressing down with a spatula every 15 minutes or so to compress the potatoes and stop them from drying out. The gratin is ready when the top is golden and bubbling and the potatoes are tender. You may want to turn up the oven to 350°F or 375°F / 190°C or 200°C for the last 5 minutes to achieve a bit of extra bubbling crispness. Leave to stand for 5 minutes or so before serving.

VARIATIONS

Half-and-half dauphinoise

For something a little more virtuous, you can substitute half-and-half for the cream. That goes for the following variations, too.

Celery root and potato dauphinoise

A wonderful combination. Replace a quarter to half of the potatoes with celery root, peeled and thinly sliced. It's very good with about 1 ounce / 30g grated Parmesan or Gruyère sprinkled on top before baking.

Potato and turnip dauphinoise

Peel 2 small turnips (about 7 ounces / 200g) and slice very thinly, using a mandoline or sharp knife. Use roughly 1³/₄ pounds / 800g potatoes and toss with the cream as above. Layer half of the cream-coated potato slices in the bottom of the gratin dish, followed by a thin layer of turnips and the rest of the potatoes. Bake as above.

Sweet potato and peanut gratin

Although sweet potatoes are not much grown in the UK, I do enjoy them every now and then. They're extremely good for you, and spiked with a little garlic and chile to cut their sweetness, they make a tempting gratin. Here I've added a seam of slightly salty, crunchy peanut butter with a touch of lime, which brings a hint of satay-like flavor to the whole thing, but you can leave this out if you prefer. A bitter-leaved salad is a good accompaniment.

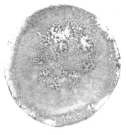

SERVES 4

About 2 pounds / 1kg sweet potatoes

2 tablespoons sunflower oil

1 fresh red chile, seeded and finely chopped, or 1 teaspoon dried chile flakes

3 garlic cloves, finely chopped

1 cup / 250ml heavy cream

Sea salt and freshly ground black pepper

1/2 cup / 150g crunchy (no-sugar-added) peanut butter

Finely grated zest of 1 lime, plus about 2 teaspoons juice

Preheat the oven to 375°F / 190°C and lightly oil a large gratin dish. Peel the sweet potatoes and cut them into slices a bit thinner than 1/8 inch / 3mm. In a large bowl, toss the sweet potato slices with 1 tablespoon of the oil, the chile, garlic, cream, and some salt and pepper.

Arrange half the sweet potato slices evenly in the gratin dish. You do not have to layer them piece by piece, but try to ensure that the slices are mostly lying flat.

Beat the peanut butter with the remaining 1 tablespoon of oil, the lime zest, and the lime juice. Spread this mixture in dollops over the sweet potatoes in the dish. Cover evenly with the remaining sweet potato slices. Pour over any cream remaining in the bowl.

Cover the dish with foil and bake for about 20 minutes, then remove the foil. Bake for a further 30 minutes or so, until the sweet potatoes are completely tender and the top is browned and crisp. For extra crispness, you can finish under the broiler for a couple of minutes, but watch carefully. Serve hot, with a crisp, leafy salad to balance the sweet richness of the gratin.

Three-root boulangère

One could hardly call this dish "light," but it's certainly less rich than a creamy, dauphinoise-style gratin, and it's a lovely way to enjoy the flavors of some seasonal roots. You don't have to stick to the ones I suggest here: try substituting Jerusalem artichokes, carrots, or rutabagas, for example – they all work well. I like to serve this with big, flat mushrooms simply baked with some butter, garlic, and cheese (see page 385) and some good bread.

SERVES 4

2 tablespoons / 30g butter

2 onions, halved and thinly sliced

2 garlic cloves, sliced

1 small celery root

2 large potatoes

3 large parsnips

Sea salt and freshly ground black pepper

A couple of sprigs of thyme, leaves only, chopped

3 sage leaves, finely chopped

About 5 cups / 1.2 liters vegetable stock (see page 130)

Preheat the oven to 350°F / 180°C. Melt the butter in a heavy-bottomed frying pan and use some of it to grease a large gratin dish. Add the onions to the pan and sauté over medium heat for about 10 minutes, until nice and soft, then add the garlic and cook gently for a further minute or two.

Meanwhile, peel the celery root, potatoes, and parsnips and cut into slices a little thinner than ⅛ inch / 3mm, slicing the parsnips lengthwise.

Spread out the celery root in the gratin dish, season generously with salt and pepper, then sprinkle with half of the onions and half of the herbs. Layer the parsnips on top, then scatter the remaining onions and herbs on top and finish with a layer of potatoes.

Bring the stock to a simmer and add some salt and pepper, then pour it over the vegetables to barely cover them (you may not need all of it). Cover the dish with foil and bake for 30 minutes, then uncover and continue to bake for another 30 minutes or so, until the vegetables are tender.

At this point, if there is still liquid covering the potatoes, spoon off a little and return the dish to the oven for 15 minutes or so to brown the potatoes on the top. You can use the broiler to get a darker, crisper top if you like. Serve piping hot.

Hearty salads

If you normally think of "salad" as just a bit of greenery on the side of your plate – more a garnish or afterthought than a meaningful offering to a hearty appetite – then that needs to change. Because the less you are relying on meat and fish, the more you will find that "salad" is no longer merely a euphemism for limp lettuce served up to offset the flesh you've just consumed. It's a meal.

In a "hearty salad," a well-tuned mixture of the raw and the cooked, the chunky and the leafy, perhaps the nutty and the cheesy, creates an enticing, self-contained plateful. Big, gutsy salads like these are fun to eat, full of color, with lots of different flavors and textures competing for attention. You can taste the ingredients one at a time, or make each forkful an original cocktail. Each mouthful will be different, but all will be good.

These substantial salads need not be bound by any particular conventions – you can play around with all sorts of ingredients, many of which may never have struck you as "salady" at all. If you're a Yotam Ottolenghi fan – and I certainly am – you may be familiar with this highly eclectic, rule-bending approach to "salads," in the broadest sense of the word. And if you want to extend your reach into this highly rewarding style of cooking, you should definitely check out his work.

There is, however, a certain logic to the composition of these salads. Generally they are built around a delicious and sustaining trinity of starch, protein, and fresh seasonal vegetables. What makes a salad truly "hearty" is often a carbohydrate element – most obviously potatoes, pasta, bread, or a grain such as rice or spelt. But the addition of some kind of protein – cheese or eggs, say – can also boost their heft. And legumes such as chickpeas or lentils, being both carb and protein, can do either or both jobs as well as or instead of another "hearty" element. The fresh, green, raw, leafy, and/or crunchy veg that we more conventionally think of as "salad" are there too, but often in a supporting role.

What really tickles up many of these salads is the deployment of vegetables that we don't usually eat cold at all – the ones that, all too often, tragically, we boil to oblivion. Here, though, we may emphasize their character, and sweeten and darken their edges, by roasting, grilling, or frying them. In particular, I like to roast roots from the more colorful and aromatic end of the spectrum – parsnips, beets, carrots, Jerusalem artichokes, and squashes (which are fruits, I know, but with honorary root status). I also like to fry, grill, and broil those Mediterranean high-summer fruit-vegetables –

eggplants, zucchini, peppers, and chiles – along with young leeks and green onions. What gives them their newfound "salad" status is a process of gentle assembly, the tumbling or layering together of the still warm, often slightly caramelized pieces with some of the aforementioned items: leaves, legumes, nuts, or grains, perhaps some crumblings or shavings of cheese, maybe a final scattering of herbs.

Finally, there are the various "finishing touches," hinted at already – the dressings and sprinkles that make the salad sing. My dressings often depart from the straight-up vinaigrette, not just with the use of more characterful oils and vinegars, but through the addition of chopped herbs, or a hint of honey, or a spike of chile. By "sprinkles," I mostly mean seeds, nuts, and (whole) spices, often toasted (dry-fried in a hot pan for a minute or two) to make them more intense and fragrant. They crackle on the tongue or pop between the teeth and add an irresistible snap that puts a real spring into a salad.

The beauty of these hearty salads is that they are endlessly mutable. Almost always, each element can happily be replaced with something else. Don't like blue cheese? Use goat cheese. No canola oil? Olive will be fine. Or try a dash of walnut oil for a change. And don't think twice about replacing hazelnuts with pumpkin seeds, or basil with parsley. The fact that each combination will inevitably be slightly different each time you make it is a strong part of their appeal.

When it comes to serving these salads, you can relax, too. They are substantial enough to be the main event – perhaps with bread on the side – and that's what I had in mind when putting them together. However, they'll also make a zesty opener to a meal. So, if I've said "serves 4," you can interpret that as serving 6 or even 8 as a starter or a complement to something else. While I quite often plate them individually – especially as a starter – most work extremely well on a big, generous platter placed in the center of the table for everyone to help themselves. Three or four of these lovely combinations are a great way to feed a crowd, or a couple of these and one or two dishes from another chapter, especially Meze and Tapas (pages 292–327) and Side Dishes (pages 370–99).

Whether you're entertaining guests with a lavish spread or just sitting down to a simple family supper, these hearty salads will always bring a riot of seasonal color and impeccable good taste to your table. This is the kind of food that will make you think, "I really must do this more often." And I'm really hoping you will.

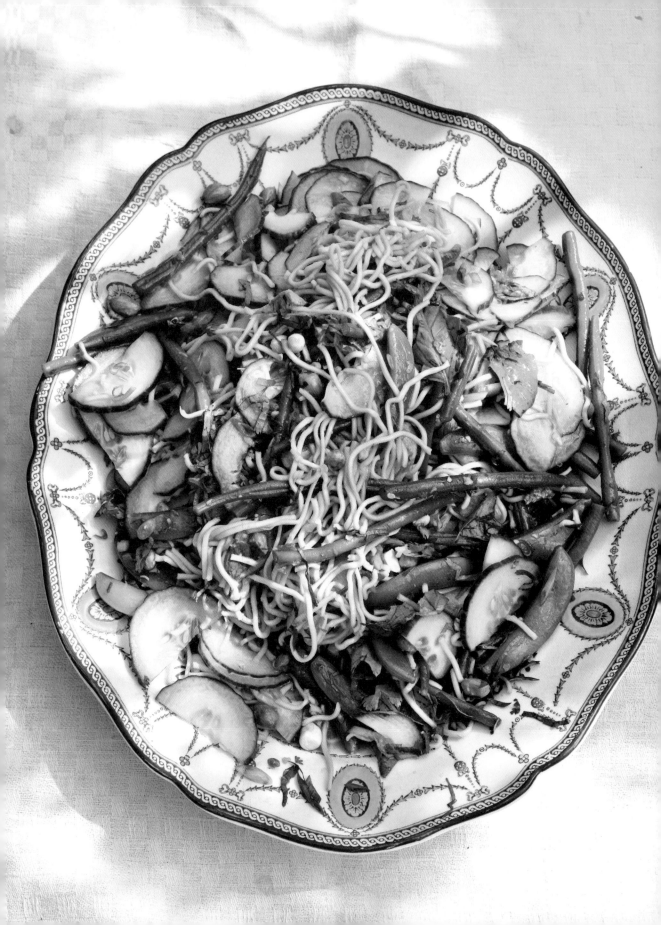

Herby, peanutty, noodly salad

A bright and zingy dressing, handfuls of herbs, and crunchy peanuts pack loads of flavor into simple, easy-to-cook noodles. If you can only find salted peanuts, rinse off the salt and pat them dry. When it comes to the fresh herbs, the mint's pretty much a must; the other two are desirable but optional.

SERVES 4

$1/2$ cup / 75g raw or roasted unsalted peanuts

7 ounces / 200g fine egg noodles or rice vermicelli

5 ounces / 150g green beans or snow peas, or a combination

$1/2$ cucumber

6 green onions, trimmed

About 12 basil leaves (ideally Thai basil), coarsely torn

A small bunch of mint, coarsely chopped

A small bunch of cilantro, coarsely chopped (optional)

FOR THE DRESSING

2 tablespoons rice vinegar

Grated zest and juice of 1 lime or $1/2$ lemon

$1/2$ to 1 small fresh red chile, finely chopped

1 garlic clove, finely chopped

1 teaspoon brown sugar

1 teaspoon toasted sesame oil

$1/2$ teaspoon soy sauce, plus extra to serve

If using raw peanuts, roast on a baking sheet in the oven (at 350°F / 180°C) for 8 to 10 minutes, until golden brown. Leave to cool, then lightly bash the nuts to break them up a bit.

For the dressing, whisk together all the ingredients in a large bowl.

Cook the noodles according to the instructions on the package. Drain and rinse under cold water. Add to the dressing and toss until well coated. Leave to cool completely in the dressing.

Cook the beans and/or snow peas in a saucepan of lightly salted boiling water until just tender and still a bit crunchy, 3 to 5 minutes for beans, 2 to 3 minutes for snow peas. Drain, refresh in cold water, and drain well.

Halve the cucumber lengthwise and slice thinly. Finely slice the green onions on the diagonal.

Toss the cooled noodles with the peanuts, cucumber, green onions, beans, and/or snow peas and herbs. Serve with soy sauce on the side, for everyone to help themselves.

Spelt salad with squash and fennel

This substantial grainy salad makes a lovely autumn/winter lunch or supper. By all means, replace the fennel with chunks of leek, red onion wedges, or halved shallots. Indeed you can improvise a spelt salad along these lines for all seasons.

SERVES 4

1 smallish butternut squash (about 1⅓ pounds / 600g), peeled, seeded, and cut into ¾-inch / 2cm chunks

4 or 5 tablespoons olive oil

Sea salt and freshly ground black pepper

2 to 3 fennel bulbs, trimmed (any feathery fronds chopped and reserved)

1 garlic clove, finely chopped

2 ounces / 60g walnuts

7 ounces / 200g pearled spelt (or pearled barley), rinsed

Juice of ½ lemon

¾ ounce / 20g Parmesan, hard goat cheese, or other well-flavored hard cheese, grated, plus extra to serve

A small handful of parsley, coarsely chopped

Preheat the oven to 375°F / 190°C. Scatter the squash chunks in a large roasting pan. Trickle over 2 tablespoons of the olive oil and season well with salt and pepper. Toss well and put the pan into the oven. Meanwhile, cut each fennel bulb lengthwise into 6 or 8 wedges.

After 15 minutes, add the fennel and garlic to the roasting pan, toss with the squash, and add another tablespoon of olive oil. Roast for a further 20 minutes or so, until the vegetables are soft and starting to caramelize around the edges. Scatter over the walnuts and cook for another 8 to 10 minutes. By the end, the vegetables should be tender and caramelized, and the walnuts lightly toasted and fragrant. If you're serving the salad warm, the vegetables can go into the spelt straight from the oven; if serving it cold, let the vegetables cool completely.

While the vegetables are roasting, cook the spelt (or barley) in plenty of well-salted boiling water until tender, but still with just a bit of nutty bite; spelt should take about 20 minutes (allow a bit longer for barley). Drain well and leave to cool a little (or completely, if you're assembling this in advance as a cold salad). Toss with the roasted vegetable mixture and any oil in the roasting pan, the remaining 2 or 3 tablespoons of olive oil, the lemon juice, cheese, parsley, and fennel fronds. Taste and season with salt and pepper. Shave over some more cheese and serve warm or cold.

VARIATION

Summer spelt salad♥

Cook and drain the spelt or barley as above and then add 2 tablespoons canola or olive oil and the grated zest and juice of ½ lemon, season with salt and pepper, and leave to cool. When cool, toss with about 7 ounces / 200g blanched and cooled baby vegetables, which could include baby lima beans, baby carrots, and peas. Add about 10 ounces / 300g cooked and cooled new potatoes, cut into cubes, and a shredded handful of mint. Taste and add more oil, lemon juice, salt, and/or pepper as needed. I like to finish this with green onions gently fried in olive oil for a couple of minutes until they're tender and sweet.

Tahini-dressed zucchini and green bean salad

This lovely dish is as much about the dressing as the salad. It's the kind of thick, trickling dressing that Yotam Ottolenghi does so well. It's particularly good whenever zucchini or eggplants – grilled, broiled, or fried – are part of the mix, hence this salad and the serving suggestion for chargrilled summer vegetables on page 332. It works with lentils, other legumes, spelt, and quinoa, too. And its coating consistency makes it ideal to use as a dip-cum-dressing for crudités and rolled-up lettuce leaves.

SERVES 4

FOR THE TAHINI DRESSING

½ garlic clove, crushed with a little coarse sea salt

2 tablespoons light tahini (stir the jar well first)

Finely grated zest and juice of ½ lemon

Juice of ½ orange

½ teaspoon clear honey

Sea salt and freshly ground black pepper

2 tablespoons olive oil

FOR THE SALAD

2 tablespoons olive oil

3 medium zucchini (about 14 ounces / 400g), sliced into ⅛-inch / 3mm rounds

Sea salt and freshly ground black pepper

Juice of ½ lemon

1 fresh red chile, seeded and finely chopped

About 4 ounces / 125g green beans, trimmed

4 good handfuls of salad greens

12 to 18 oven-dried tomatoes (see page 304; optional)

A handful of mint, finely shredded (optional)

To make the tahini dressing, put the crushed garlic into a small bowl with the tahini, lemon zest and juice, orange juice, honey, and a grind of black pepper, and stir together well. The dressing may thicken and go grainy or pasty, but don't worry. Just thin it down by whisking in a little water, 1 tablespoon at a time, until you get a creamy, trickling consistency. Finally, gently stir in the olive oil. Taste and add a little more salt and pepper if needed. The dressing is now ready to use.

For the salad, heat the olive oil in a large nonstick frying pan over fairly high heat and cook the zucchini slices in batches, tossing them occasionally, for a few minutes until tender and browned on both sides, transferring them to a bowl once cooked.

When the zucchini are all cooked, season generously with salt and pepper, add the lemon juice and chile, and toss together well.

Bring a saucepan of salted water to a boil. Tip in the green beans, return to a boil, and blanch for 1 minute. Drain, then dunk in cold water to refresh. Drain again, pat dry with a clean kitchen towel, and toss the beans with the zucchini.

To assemble the salad, spread the salad greens in a large, shallow serving bowl and scatter over the dressed zucchini and beans, tomatoes, and shredded mint, if using. Trickle the tahini dressing generously over the whole lot and serve.

New potato, tomato, and boiled egg salad

This rich, yolky dressing, made by combining chopped "soft hard-boiled" eggs with a vinaigrette, is one of my favorites. It works brilliantly with new potatoes and sweet, ripe cherry tomatoes.

SERVES 4

About 14 ounces / 400g new potatoes

Sea salt and freshly ground black pepper

4 large eggs, at room temperature

About 9 ounces / 250g cherry tomatoes, halved

A good handful of chives

FOR THE VINAIGRETTE

6 tablespoons canola or olive oil

4 teaspoons cider vinegar

1 teaspoon English mustard

A pinch of sugar

Sea salt and freshly ground black pepper

Cut the potatoes into chunks if they are large. Put them in a saucepan, cover with water, add salt, and bring to a boil. Turn down the heat and simmer for 8 to 12 minutes, or until tender. Drain well and leave to cool.

Meanwhile, to cook the eggs, bring a saucepan of water to a boil. Add the eggs, return to a simmer, then cook for 7 minutes. Remove the eggs from the pan, lightly crack the shells, and run the eggs under cold water for a minute or two to stop the cooking. Leave until cool, then peel the eggs.

For the vinaigrette, put the oil, vinegar, mustard, and sugar into a screw-top jar with some salt and pepper and shake until emulsified.

Chop the boiled eggs very coarsely and put them into a large bowl. Pour on the vinaigrette and mix well, breaking down the eggs a bit as you go. Add the potatoes and cherry tomatoes and toss together well. Taste and adjust the seasoning if you need to, then snip over the chives and serve.

New potato salad "tartare"

A simple, deconstructed version of good old tartar sauce is used to dress freshly cooked, earthy little new potatoes. Serve as a starter or light lunch.

SERVES 4

2 pounds / 1kg small new or waxy potatoes

Sea salt and freshly ground black pepper

2 tablespoons capers, rinsed

1 tablespoon chopped gherkins

A handful of chives, finely chopped

A good handful of flat-leaf parsley, finely chopped

A handful of dill, finely chopped

3 soft hard-boiled large eggs (see page 76), peeled

FOR THE VINAIGRETTE

1 tablespoon cider vinegar

1½ teaspoons Dijon mustard

3 tablespoons canola or olive oil

Sea salt and freshly ground black pepper

Make sure the potatoes are all roughly similar in size (cut up larger ones if necessary). Put the potatoes in a saucepan, cover with water, add salt, and bring to a boil. Lower the heat and simmer for 8 to 12 minutes, or until tender.

Meanwhile, for the vinaigrette, put the cider vinegar, mustard, oil, and a little salt and pepper in a screw-top jar and shake to emulsify.

Drain the potatoes and place in a large bowl. While they are still warm, pour on the vinaigrette and toss to mix. Leave until cool.

Add the capers, gherkins, herbs, and some salt and pepper and toss again. Quarter the boiled eggs lengthwise, gently mix into the salad, and serve.

Lettuce, egg, and fried bread salad

Many a salad is improved by the addition of croutons – and what is a crouton if not a big, chunky, golden cube of lovely fried bread? Of course fried bread is fantastic with eggs – and not just in a breakfast fry-up. In this summery salad, the pairing enhances crisp lettuce leaves, while a garlicky dressing brings the whole thing deliciously together. Try it . . .

SERVES 3 OR 4

4 large eggs, at room temperature

1 romaine lettuce

2 Little Gem lettuces

1 small butterhead lettuce

A handful of chives

FOR THE CROUTONS

2 large slices of coarse, robust bread, such as sourdough

3 tablespoons olive or canola oil

FOR THE DRESSING

½ teaspoon Dijon mustard

½ garlic clove, crushed with a little coarse sea salt

5 tablespoons canola or olive oil

1 tablespoon cider vinegar

A pinch of sugar

Sea salt and freshly ground black pepper

Start with the croutons. Cut the bread into chunky cubes. Heat the oil in a large nonstick pan over medium heat. Add the bread cubes and fry for a few minutes, turning often, until crisp and golden all over. Set aside to cool.

To cook the eggs, bring a saucepan of water to a boil. Add the eggs, return to a simmer, then cook for 7 minutes. Remove the eggs from the pan, lightly crack the shells, then run the eggs under cold water for a minute or two to stop the cooking. Leave until cool, then peel the eggs.

Separate the lettuce leaves and put them all into a large bowl.

For the dressing, put all the mustard, garlic, oil, vinegar, and sugar into a screw-top jar, season well with salt and pepper, and shake until emulsified.

Tip about half of the dressing over the lettuce leaves and toss gently to dress. Coarsely chop the boiled eggs and combine with the remaining dressing.

Arrange the dressed leaves on a large serving platter and distribute the egg over the top. Scatter the croutons over the salad, snip over the chives, and serve.

Arugula, fennel, and green lentil salad ♥

Arugula has become such a ubiquitous leaf, so often thrown into generic mixes of salad leaves, that it's easy to forget how well it shines solo, or nearly solo. Combined with the delicate aniseed note of fennel, some earthy lentils, and a lemony dressing, it really comes into its own. With some good bread, this simple assembly is a supper in itself. It also makes a great starter.

SERVES 4

²/₃ cup / 125g French green lentils

1 bay leaf

½ small onion

A few parsley stems (optional)

1 large or 2 small fennel bulbs

2 to 3 ounces / 75g arugula, or arugula mixed with a few other peppery leaves such as mizuna

FOR THE DRESSING

½ cup / 120ml canola or olive oil

2 tablespoons lemon juice

2 teaspoons Dijon mustard

Finely grated zest of 1 lemon

A pinch of sugar

Sea salt and freshly ground black pepper

Put the lentils in a saucepan and add plenty of water. Bring to a boil and simmer for a minute only, then drain. Return the lentils to the pan and pour in just enough water to cover them. Add the bay leaf, onion, and parsley stems, if using. Bring back to a very gentle simmer and cook slowly for about half an hour, until tender but not mushy.

Meanwhile, to make the dressing, put the oil, lemon juice, mustard, lemon zest, and sugar in a screw-topped jar, season with salt and pepper, and shake until emulsified.

When the lentils are done, drain them well and discard the herbs and onion. While still warm, combine with a good half of the dressing. Leave until cool, then taste and adjust the seasoning; you could add a little more salt, sugar, pepper, or lemon juice if needed.

Trim the fennel, removing the tough outer layer (unless the fennel is young and very fresh). Halve the bulb(s) vertically, then slice as thinly as you can, tip to base.

Divide about two-thirds of the lentils among wide serving bowls. Scatter over the arugula and fennel and trickle over the rest of the dressing. Scatter the remaining lentils over the top and serve.

Fish-free salad niçoise

Without any tuna or anchovies, I guess you might upset the good people of Nice a bit with this one, but it is an exceptionally delicious and substantial salad – with plenty going on. I like to cook the eggs so they are hard-boiled but with the yolks still quite soft and sticky.

SERVES 4

1 pound / 500g new potatoes

Sea salt and freshly ground black pepper

7 ounces / 200g green beans, cut into roughly 1-inch / 2.5cm lengths

4 large eggs, at room temperature

2 or 3 Little Gem or similar lettuces

A handful of small black olives

About 12 large basil leaves, torn (or use small ones whole)

FOR THE DRESSING

½ small garlic clove, crushed with a little coarse sea salt

3 tablespoons olive oil

1 tablespoon cider vinegar

1 teaspoon Dijon mustard

A pinch of sugar

Sea salt and freshly ground black pepper

You can cook small new potatoes whole, but cut larger ones in half or smaller so the pieces are all roughly the same size. Put the potatoes in a saucepan, cover with cold water, add salt, and bring to a boil. Reduce the heat and simmer for 8 to 12 minutes until tender, adding the beans for the last 4 minutes of cooking. Drain, tip into a bowl, and leave to cool.

To cook the eggs, bring a saucepan of water to a boil. Add the eggs, return to a simmer, then cook for 7 minutes. Remove the eggs from the pan, lightly crack the shells, and run the eggs under cold water for a minute or two to stop the cooking. Leave to cool, then peel and quarter the eggs.

To make the dressing, put the garlic, oil, vinegar, mustard, and sugar into a screw-top jar, season with salt and pepper, and shake until emulsified.

Halve, quarter, or thickly slice the cooked potatoes. Put them back with the beans, add some of the dressing, and toss together gently.

Separate the lettuce leaves and gently toss in a bowl with a little of the dressing. Arrange the lettuce, potatoes, and beans on a serving platter and distribute the olives and eggs over the salad. Scatter with the torn basil, trickle over the remaining dressing, and grind over some pepper. Serve right away, with bread.

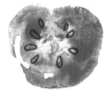

Panzanella ♥

*This classic Italian combination of tomatoes
and stale bread, pepped up with onion, olives,
capers, and basil, is hard to beat for a summer
lunch. There are various approaches to this dish,
but I like to "sacrifice" about two-thirds of the
tomatoes by sieving them into a fresh pulp that
soaks into the bread with the rest of the dressing.
Then I add more tomatoes, perhaps a different
variety, along with the rest of the ingredients.
The tomatoes must be sweet and ripe.*

SERVES 4

About 1½ pounds / 700g large,
very ripe tomatoes

¼ cup / 60ml extra-virgin
olive oil

2 tablespoons cider vinegar

Sea salt and freshly ground
black pepper

10 to 14 ounces / 300 to 400g
(about ½ loaf) slightly stale
sourdough, ciabatta, or good
country bread

About 25 black olives, such as
Kalamata (2 ounces / 60g or so)

1 small cucumber, peeled,
seeded, and cut into thick
half-moons

1 small red onion, halved and
thinly sliced

About 12 ounces / 350g cherry
tomatoes, halved (or a larger
variety, cut into chunks)

1 tablespoon capers, drained
and rinsed

A handful of basil leaves, torn

Put the 1½ pounds / 700g of large, ripe tomatoes into a large bowl
and crush them with your hands. Tip them into a sieve set over a
bowl and rub the pulp through the mesh. Discard the skin and seeds.
Add the olive oil, cider vinegar, and plenty of salt and pepper to the
tomato juice.

Tear the bread into bite-sized chunks, put into a large bowl, and pour
over the tomatoey dressing. Add the olives, cucumber, red onion,
cherry tomatoes, capers, and basil and season well with salt and
pepper. Toss everything together well with your hands.

If you can, leave the salad to stand for 20 minutes or so to allow the
flavors to develop, then toss one more time and leave for a few
minutes before serving.

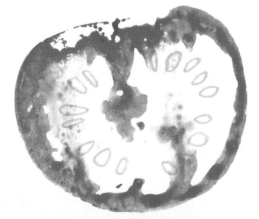

Couscous salad with herbs and walnuts ✿

For this salad, I like to use a type of "giant" whole-wheat couscous. ("Giant" couscous is also known as Israeli couscous in the U.S.) The salad would also work well with brown rice, quinoa, or bulgur wheat instead of the couscous.

SERVES 4

2 teaspoons cumin seeds

1 teaspoon fennel seeds

4 to 5 tablespoons extra-virgin olive oil

1 onion, chopped

2 celery stalks, chopped

1 fennel bulb, chopped

2 garlic cloves, chopped

Finely grated zest and juice of 1 lemon

7 ounces / 200g whole-wheat Israeli couscous

A bunch of flat-leaf parsley, chopped

A handful of chives, chopped (optional)

A handful of tarragon, chopped (optional)

3/4 cup / 75g walnuts, lightly toasted and coarsely chopped

Sea salt and freshly ground black pepper

Put the cumin and fennel seeds in a dry frying pan and toast over medium heat, shaking the pan often, for a few minutes until fragrant. Tip into a mortar and, when cool, grind with the pestle to a powder.

Heat 2 tablespoons of the olive oil in the frying pan and sauté the onion, celery, fennel, and garlic over medium heat for 5 minutes or so, until softened but still with a bit of bite. Remove from the heat and add the ground spices and lemon zest.

Cook the couscous in salted water following the package instructions. Drain well and mix with the onion and spice mixture. Allow to cool.

Stir in the lemon juice, herbs, walnuts, and plenty of salt and pepper. Before serving, add more oil to lubricate the couscous to your taste – you might want a little more lemon juice, too.

VARIATION

Summer couscous salad ✿

Use standard, fine-grained couscous instead of the big whole-wheat variety and cook in vegetable stock or water according to the package instructions. Meanwhile, blanch 3½ ounces / 100g each peas or petite peas and fava beans in boiling water until just tender. Drain and refresh in ice water. If you have the patience, slip the fava beans from their outer skins. You could also include about 3½ ounces / 100g small zucchini, cut into ½-inch / 1cm dice and fried in a little olive oil for a few minutes until lightly colored. For the dressing, whisk together the finely grated zest and juice of 1 lemon, ¼ cup / 60ml olive oil, a finely chopped garlic clove, and some salt and pepper. Trickle the dressing over the warm couscous and toss with a fork until fluffy. Allow to cool, then toss with the vegetables and 7 ounces / 200g or so of halved cherry tomatoes, if you like. Add a finely chopped handful each of parsley, basil, mint, and cilantro. Taste and add more lemon juice and/or salt and pepper if required, then serve.

Roasted parsnip, green lentil, and watercress salad

This is a great, if unexpected, three-way combination of lovely flavors and textures, all held together by the nutty canola oil dressing – a perfect autumn salad.

SERVES 4

5 medium parsnips

Sea salt and freshly ground black pepper

2 tablespoons canola oil

²/₃ cup / 125g French green lentils

1 bay leaf

½ onion

A few parsley stems (optional)

A large bunch of watercress, tough stems removed

FOR THE DRESSING

¼ cup / 60ml canola oil

1 tablespoon lemon juice

2 teaspoons clear honey

1 teaspoon English mustard

1 garlic clove, crushed with a little coarse sea salt

Sea salt and freshly ground black pepper

TO SERVE (OPTIONAL)

Parmesan, hard goat cheese, or other well-flavored hard cheese

Preheat the oven to 375°F / 190°C. Peel the parsnips and halve them crosswise. Cut the wider top parts in half again; the aim is to get chunky pieces roughly all the same size. Put the parsnips into a roasting pan, season with some salt and pepper, and toss with the oil. Roast for 40 minutes, stirring halfway through, or until tender and starting to caramelize.

Meanwhile, put the lentils in a saucepan, add plenty of water, and bring to a boil. Simmer for a minute only, then drain. Return the lentils to the pan and pour in just enough water to cover them. Add the bay leaf, onion, and parsley stalks, if using. Bring back to a very low simmer and cook slowly for about half an hour, until tender but not mushy.

For the dressing, thoroughly whisk together the oil, lemon juice, honey, mustard, and garlic and season with some salt and pepper.

Drain the lentils and pick out the bay leaf, parsley stems, and onion. While still hot, toss the lentils with the dressing. Taste and make sure they are well seasoned.

Scatter the warm lentils, roasted parsnip chunks, and watercress on serving plates and finish with a few cheese shavings, if you like. Serve warm.

Roasted baby beets with walnuts and yogurt dressing

Fold the beets very gently into the dressing to maintain a dramatic marbled look.

2 pounds / 1kg small red beets (about the size of golf balls), scrubbed, or halved or quartered larger beets

4 garlic cloves (skin on), bashed

4 sprigs of thyme

3 bay leaves

Sea salt and freshly ground black pepper

5 tablespoons olive oil

¾ cup / 75g walnut halves

Juice of ½ lemon

A small handful of dill or chives, coarsely chopped

FOR THE DRESSING

¼ cup / 60g plain full-fat yogurt

2 tablespoons sour cream

1 small garlic clove, crushed with a little coarse sea salt

Sea salt and freshly ground black pepper

TO FINISH

A couple of handfuls of watercress or arugula

First, roast the beets. Preheat the oven to 400°F / 200°C. Put the beets into a baking pan and scatter with the garlic, thyme, and bay leaves. Season with salt and pepper and trickle over 3 tablespoons of the olive oil. Shake the pan so everything is well mingled, then cover with foil, sealing it tightly. Roast until tender – about an hour, though it could take longer, depending on the size of the beets. They are cooked when a knife slips easily into the flesh.

Turn down the oven to 350°F / 180°C. Scatter the walnuts on a baking sheet and toast in the oven for 5 to 7 minutes, until just fragrant.

Leave the beets until cool enough to handle, then top and tail them and remove their skins. Cut the beets into halves or quarters and place them in a large bowl. While still warm, toss with the lemon juice, the remaining 2 tablespoons of olive oil, and some pepper. Allow to cool.

For the dressing, in a small bowl, whisk together the yogurt and sour cream. Whisk in the garlic and salt and pepper to taste.

Lightly toss the cooled beets and about two-thirds of the toasted walnuts in the dressing along with most of the dill or chives. Pile the beet salad into serving bowls and scatter over the remaining walnuts and dill or chives. Finish with the watercress or arugula.

Warm salad of mushrooms and roasted squash

This substantial salad is something of a River Cottage classic, and a great way to bring together two of autumn's finest ingredients: mushrooms and squash. Blue cheese is quite delicious here, but you could use other cheeses – shavings of Parmesan, a hard goat cheese such as Ticklemore, or a firm sheep's milk cheese such as Berkswell would also work well.

SERVES 4

1 small squash, such as butternut, acorn, or red kuri, or ½ larger one (about 2 pounds / 1kg)

12 sage leaves, bruised

4 garlic cloves, thickly sliced

7 tablespoons / 100ml canola or olive oil

Sea salt and freshly ground black pepper

About 1 tablespoon butter

10 ounces / 300g open-cap mushrooms, thickly sliced

A small bunch of arugula

5 ounces / 150g blue cheese, crumbled

FOR THE DRESSING

3 tablespoons canola or olive oil

1 tablespoon balsamic vinegar (ideally apple balsamic)

Sea salt and freshly ground black pepper

Preheat the oven to 375°F / 190°C. Peel, halve, and seed the squash. Cut into 1-inch / 2.5cm chunks and put into a roasting pan with the sage leaves, garlic, 6 tablespoons of the oil, and a generous seasoning of salt and pepper. Roast for about 40 minutes, stirring once, or until the squash is soft and colored at the edges.

Put the remaining 1 tablespoon of oil in a frying pan with the butter and place over medium heat. Throw in the mushrooms along with a little salt and pepper and fry for 4 to 5 minutes, or until the mushrooms are cooked through and any liquid they release has evaporated.

For the dressing, in a small bowl, whisk together the oil and balsamic vinegar and season with some salt and pepper.

In a large bowl, combine the still-warm (but not hot) cooked squash and mushrooms with the arugula and cheese. Add enough dressing to lightly coat the ingredients (you may not need it all), toss together, and serve.

Raw assemblies

There's no question in my mind that most of us don't eat enough raw food. Fond as I am of the art of cooking, the application of heat to vegetables doesn't always do them a favor. And all too often it isn't a great deal for the person dining on them either. Cafeteria carrots: need I say more? So right now I want to extol those dishes that illustrate that sometimes the best thing you can do for the fine, fresh produce in front of you is next to nothing.

The dishes that follow are certainly salads, of a sort, but quite different from the earlier "hearty salads." These recipes are for vegetables at their simplest: fresh, raw, and barely tinkered with. With the exception of the odd toasted nut or whizzed-up dressing, most of the ingredients require just a little peeling, slicing, or grating before bringing together. The result is some really elegant, delicious dishes that will add a resounding crunch of rude health to any meal. If, for instance, you're indulging in one of the greedier, starchier, or creamier offerings in the book, stick one of these dishes alongside, and your virtue will be saved. Alternatively, put one at the beginning of a meal, and your dinner party could be made: these are stylish dishes, for the most part, that look lovely on the plate. Serve the kohlrabi "carpaccio" (see page 116) or the shaved summer vegetables (see page 100) to your most discerning foodie friends, and you'll see what I mean.

This chapter draws on a lesson I've learned when trying to encourage my kids (and other peoples') to eat more fresh fruit and veg: namely, that preparation and presentation count for a lot. Youngsters, in my experience, are so much more likely to gobble that apple, carrot, or stalk of celery if you cut it into handleable wedges or batons first. I got my kids to eat lettuce by serving the salad dressing as a dip and encouraging them to roll up their leaves and plunge them in. And I found I could get even more roots and fruits inside them by grating and dressing them.

So a little deft knife-work applied to raw vegetables, aimed at pleasing the eye and turning on the taste buds, can make all the difference. However, these are not mere tricks of presentation – they change the whole experience of eating the vegetables in question. The idea of biting into a whole bulb of fennel probably doesn't appeal, but trimmed, finely sliced, and dressed with a little peppery oil and fresh lemon juice, it's a vastly more alluring prospect. Cut your vegetables the right way, jumble them up with a dressing or dip, and you have a more unexpected – and tempting – plate of food, but also one that is much more enjoyable to eat. Try offering my cauliflower with toasted seeds (see page 108) to a cauli-phobe or – and this is one of my favorite tests – the brussels sprouts, apple, and cheddar (see page 108) to a sprout-hater, and you could be amazed at the response.

There are dishes here that may raise a few eyebrows. Raw carrots and tomatoes are well embedded in our culinary culture, but raw celery root, beets, and parsnips? All I can say is: don't knock them until you've tried them. If you have a fresh, young example of almost any vegetable (potatoes being a rule-proving exception), there's almost always the potential to eat it raw – indeed, to enjoy it raw. This way of preparing veg is another string in the bow of the vegetable cook because it opens up a whole new area of texture and flavor. The difference between a boiled carrot and a raw one (cafeteria carrot versus one just pulled from the ground) can be so great as to make them seem two different vegetables. The same goes for cabbage or zucchini. In short, open your mind to the potential of raw veg and you're pretty much doubling your vegetable repertoire.

This leads me on to an important point, which is that the care you take over preparing your lovely veg is never of greater importance than it is here. So have a decent peeler and a sharp knife standing by. You'll also need a sturdy box grater (you'll get most use out of the coarse setting), and you might want to think about acquiring a mandoline (the plastic V-cutter kind with various different slide-in slicing trays are the best, I think, as well as the cheapest). Provided you take care of them, and of yourself while you're using them, they'll last you many years. These tools also exist, of course, as attachments for most modern food processors. Get the hang of them and you can knock out dinner-party quantities of these raw assemblies in very little time.

Such equipment, whether handheld or automated, is useful because it can give precision to your work without adding effort, stress, or time. I don't like being pedantic about food preparation, and usually when I say "chop finely" or "slice thinly," I'm happy to allow a good margin for error. It rarely matters when veg is going to be cooked. But with these recipes, accuracy doesn't go amiss – the dishes will actually taste better for it.

And finally, though this probably goes without saying, the quality of the vegetables is crucial. Young, tender, and snappingly fresh is the order of the day. The rewards for being picky here are, as you're about to find out, really very great. And the best kind of picky, I hardly need tell you, is picking your own.

Shaved summer vegetables

*Wafer-thin slices of sweet root vegetables, kohlrabi, and zucchini
make for a deliciously crunchy and gorgeously colorful salad.
The rich dressing ties the lot together nicely – it uses canola
oil, honey, and mustard, all of which marry particularly well
with root vegetables. You don't have to stick to these veg –
you can try carrots, fennel, or cucumber in the mix as well.*

But always shave or slice as thinly as you possibly can.

SERVES 4

1 medium or 2 small beets
(3½ to 5 ounces / 100 to 150g),
any color you like

1 medium or 2 small kohlrabi
(3½ to 5 ounces / 100 to 150g)

3½ to 5 ounces / 100 to 150g
radishes

1 medium zucchini
(about 5 ounces / 150g)

FOR THE DRESSING

¼ cup / 60ml canola oil

1 tablespoon lemon juice

2 teaspoons clear honey

1 teaspoon English mustard

Sea salt and freshly ground
black pepper

Trim all the vegetables and peel the beets and the kohlrabi. Use a mandoline, a vegetable peeler, or a very sharp knife to shave/slice the vegetables as thinly as you can. (Trying to shave radishes with a vegetable peeler is quite high risk – take care!) Mix them together and divide among serving plates.

For the dressing, put the oil, lemon juice, honey, and mustard in a screw-top jar, season with salt and pepper, and shake to mix and emulsify. Trickle generously over the salad and serve.

Radishes with butter and salt

This is a simple, time-honored way of serving radishes, and it is hard to beat. My one caveat, as with all radish recipes, is that it's really only worth doing this with very fresh little roots because radishes quickly lose their crunch and peppery flavor. It's essential to use a good, sweet sea salt, too, such as Maldon, Cornish, or Halen Môn.

SERVES 4

About 14 ounces / 400g radishes

A pat or two of unsalted butter, at room temperature but not too soft

A little dish of best-quality flaky sea salt

Arrange everything on the table and make sure each diner has a butter knife. To eat, just smear a little of the butter on the end of a radish, sprinkle with the tiniest pinch of salt, then pop the radish into your mouth.

Fennel and goat cheese

A simple but lovely way to enjoy very fresh, crisp fennel.

SERVES 4

2 large or 3 medium fennel bulbs, trimmed (any feathery fronds chopped and reserved)

½ lemon

2 to 3 tablespoons canola or extra-virgin olive oil

Sea salt and freshly ground black pepper

About 1 ounce / 30g soft, fresh goat cheese

Remove and discard the tough outer layer of the fennel bulbs (unless they are young and very fresh). Cut the bulbs in half vertically. Now, using a large, sharp knife, slice the fennel as finely as you can from tip to root.

Put the fennel into a large bowl, squeeze over the juice of the lemon half, trickle over the oil, and add some salt and pepper. Toss everything together with your hands, then cover and set aside for 30 minutes to allow the fennel to macerate in its dressing. Taste and add a little more lemon, oil, and/or salt and pepper if you like.

Transfer to a serving dish, then crumble the cheese over the top. Finish with a scattering of fennel fronds, if you have them, then serve.

Crudités with tarator sauce

That's really not a misprint for "tartar." Tarator is a rich and very garlicky walnut sauce that works brilliantly as a dip for fresh, crunchy crudités. It's lovely summer party food, and a brilliant way to show off the harvest from your garden.

SERVES 6

FOR THE TARATOR SAUCE

1 cup / 100g walnuts or blanched almonds

2 slices of good white bread (about 3½ ounces / 100g), crusts removed

1 fat garlic clove, crushed

⅔ cup / 150ml olive oil

Juice of ½ lemon or 2 tablespoons red wine vinegar

Sea salt and freshly ground black pepper

Paprika, to finish

FOR THE CRUDITÉS

A selection from:

Cucumber batons

Firm, young zucchini, halved lengthwise

Baby carrots or carrot batons

Small beets, peeled and cut into wedges or sticks

Baby fennel

Kohlrabi batons

Green onions, halved lengthwise

Sugar snap peas

Preheat the oven to 300°F / 180°C. Scatter the nuts on a baking sheet and toast for 5 to 7 minutes, giving them a shake halfway through. Leave to cool.

Soak the bread in water to cover for a minute or two, then squeeze out most of the water.

Blitz the toasted nuts and garlic in a food processor until quite finely ground. Add the bread and pulse until fairly smooth. With the motor running, add the olive oil in a thin stream through the feeder tube. Finally, add the lemon juice or vinegar and season to taste with salt and pepper. Dollop into a small bowl and dust with a little paprika.

Arrange a selection of crudités around the tarator sauce to serve.

Carrot, orange, and cashews ᵛ

This sweet-nutty combination is an ideal starter before something fairly substantial, such as my lettuce, green onion, and cheese tart (see page 44). It's also great with a potato salad, a green salad, and some good bread.

SERVES 2

½ cup / 50g cashews

1 teaspoon cumin seeds

2 oranges

2 or 3 large carrots, peeled

A dash of canola or olive oil

A few drops of cider vinegar

Sea salt and freshly ground black pepper

Toast the cashews in a hot, dry frying pan over medium heat for about 5 minutes, until lightly browned, tossing frequently and adding the cumin seeds for the last minute or so. Tip onto a plate to cool.

Finely grate the zest from one of the oranges and set aside. Using a small, sharp, serrated knife, slice the peel and pith off both oranges. Working over a serving bowl, carefully cut out each segment from between the membranes, letting it fall into the bowl. Squeeze the remaining membrane to extract all the juice and add the zest.

Cut the carrots into thick matchsticks using a mandoline or by hand. Add to the oranges with the oil, cider vinegar, and some salt and pepper. Toss well, check the seasoning, and scatter over the cashews and cumin seeds to serve.

Celery root with apple, raisins, and parsley ᵛ

I like to serve this with French green lentils – cooked as in the recipe on page 90. It's important to use a good, fresh, firm celery root, ideally an early season one. Big, old roots can be woody and a bit spongy in the middle.

SERVES 4

7 ounces / 200g celery root (peeled weight)

1 eating apple

⅓ cup / 50g raisins

A good handful of flat-leaf parsley, coarsely torn

FOR THE DRESSING

2 tablespoons sunflower or canola oil

2 tablespoons olive oil

1 tablespoon cider vinegar

1 teaspoon English mustard

1 teaspoon sugar

Sea salt and freshly ground black pepper

For the dressing, put the sunflower oil, olive oil, vinegar, mustard, and sugar in a screw-top jar, season with salt and pepper, and shake to emulsify. Tip the dressing into a bowl.

Cut the celery root into matchstick-sized pieces. The easiest way to do this is with a mandoline, but you can use a large, sharp knife. Immediately transfer to the bowl of dressing and toss to coat, so the celery root doesn't get a chance to brown.

Peel, quarter, core, and thinly slice the apple, and add to the salad with the raisins. Taste and adjust the seasoning if you need to.

If serving right away, toss in the parsley. Or leave for an hour or so, which will allow the celery root to soften slightly, and add the parsley just before serving.

Brussels sprouts, apple, and cheddar

Fresh young brussels sprouts, sliced thinly and served raw, can be a revelation – crisp, earthy, and not bitter at all. I love them paired with sweet apple and nutty cheddar in this raw salad.

SERVES 2

½ cup / 50g hazelnuts, pecans, or almonds (optional)

5 ounces / 150g very fresh, small brussels sprouts, trimmed of outer leaves

A good squeeze of lemon juice

2 tablespoons extra-virgin olive oil

A few sprigs of thyme, leaves only, coarsely chopped

Sea salt and freshly ground black pepper

1 tart, crisp eating apple

1 ounce / 35g cheddar

If using nuts, preheat the oven to 350°F / 180°C. Scatter the nuts on a baking sheet and toast in the oven until fragrant and browned, 8 to 10 minutes. If they are skin-on, wrap in a clean kitchen towel and leave for a minute, then rub vigorously in the towel to remove most of the skins. Chop the nuts coarsely, or leave whole if you prefer.

Cut the trimmed brussels sprouts lengthwise into fairly thin slices. Put them into a bowl and add a good squeeze of lemon juice, the olive oil, thyme, and plenty of salt and pepper. Toss together well.

Quarter and core the apple, and thinly slice straight into the bowl, then toss together with the sprouts. Crumble in the cheddar and toss lightly again.

Serve the salad right away, scattered with the toasted nuts, if using.

Cauliflower with toasted seeds ᵛ

Sumac lends a lovely, lemony-sweet tang to this salad of thinly sliced raw cauliflower, but if you can't get hold of this bright red spice, use the finely grated zest of half a lemon instead.

SERVES 4

1 small, firm cauliflower (about 1⅓ pounds / 600g), broken into florets

4 tablespoons pumpkin seeds

2 tablespoons sesame seeds

A small handful of parsley leaves, coarsely chopped

3 tablespoons canola oil

2 lemons

½ teaspoon sumac, plus a little more to finish

Flaky sea salt and freshly ground black pepper

Using either a sharp knife or a mandoline, slice the cauliflower florets thinly lengthwise, about ⅛ inch / 3mm thick.

In a small frying pan, toast the pumpkin seeds over medium heat until they are fragrant and just beginning to take on some color. Tip into a bowl and set aside. In the same pan, toast the sesame seeds until they just begin to crackle and turn golden. Tip into the bowl with the pumpkin seeds.

Whisk together the canola oil, the juice of 1 lemon, and the sumac. Toss the sliced florets and the seeds in the dressing and season well with salt and pepper. To serve, arrange on serving plates, squeeze over more lemon juice, and scatter a few pinches of sumac over the top.

Red cabbage, parsnip, orange, and dates

This salad is perfect for a winter starter or light lunch. It's quick to prepare, looks stunning, and is adaptable, too: try using unsulfured dried apricots instead of dates, for instance; leave out the parsnip for a lighter salad; or substitute a large carrot if you like. Chervil and parsley both work well in place of the thyme.

SERVES 2

1 large or 2 small oranges

¼ small red cabbage, core removed, finely shredded

1 small-medium parsnip, peeled and coarsely grated or cut into julienne

2 tablespoons extra-virgin olive oil

Sea salt and freshly ground black pepper

2 Medjool dates, pits removed, sliced lengthwise

A couple of sprigs of thyme, leaves only, chopped

Slice off the top and bottom from the orange(s). Stand the fruit upright on the board and work your way around it with a sharp knife, cutting off the skin and all the pith. Cut out the segments from between the membranes, working over a bowl to save the juice and letting the segments fall into the bowl. When you've finished, squeeze the juice from the remaining membrane into the bowl, too.

Put the shredded cabbage and grated parsnip into another bowl, add most of the orange juice (not the segments yet), and trickle over the olive oil. Add a little salt and pepper, toss the lot together with your hands, then transfer to serving plates.

Scatter the orange segments and date slices over the red cabbage and parsnip, then finish with a scattering of thyme. Serve right away.

Beets with walnuts and cumin[♥]

This is a lovely way to use raw beets that balances their rooty sweetness with a touch of bitterness from walnuts and aromatic warmth from the cumin. The orange and lemon dressing lightens and brightens the whole thing, and the optional yogurt finish makes the dish a little more substantial and indulgent. In the summer, if you can get hold of fresh baby beets, just peel and thinly slice, rather than grate them. And do experiment with other nuts – pistachios and pecans work well.

SERVES 4

¾ cup / 75g walnuts

1 teaspoon cumin seeds

About 14 ounces / 400g beets

A good handful of parsley, chopped

Juice of 1 small orange

A squeeze of lemon juice

2 tablespoons canola oil

Sea salt and freshly ground black pepper

TO FINISH (OPTIONAL)

2 tablespoons plain full-fat yogurt

A little more toasted and roughly bashed cumin

A pinch of hot smoked paprika

Heat a dry frying pan over medium heat and add the walnuts. Toast gently for a few minutes, tossing often, until they smell toasted and are coloring in a few places. Tip into a mortar. Put the cumin seeds into the frying pan and toast gently for 1 to 2 minutes, tossing a few times, just until they start to release their scent. Tip onto a plate to stop them cooking further.

Peel the beets and grate them coarsely (or cut into julienne with a mandoline) into a bowl. Add the parsley, orange juice, and a squeeze of lemon juice, 1 tablespoon of the canola oil, and some salt and pepper. Mix well, taste, and adjust the seasoning. Ideally, leave for 20 minutes or so – the dressing will lightly marinate and tenderize the beets.

Spread the beets in a dish or on a plate. Bash the walnuts with the pestle until broken into rough pieces and scatter over the beets. Tip the cumin seeds into the mortar and give them a rough bashing, too, then scatter over the salad.

Finish with the remaining 1 tablespoon of canola oil and, if you like, dot with blobs of yogurt and sprinkle with more cumin and a pinch of paprika.

Asian-inspired coleslaw

This is based on a recipe from Taste: A New Way to Cook, *by the marvelous Sybil Kapoor. It's wonderfully aromatic, quite unlike any other coleslaw I've ever tried, and I urge you to give it a go.*

SERVES 6 TO 8

1 bunch of green onions, trimmed and sliced

4 carrots, peeled

1 small green cabbage

FOR THE DRESSING

2 tablespoons white wine vinegar or rice vinegar

2 tablespoons toasted sesame oil

2 tablespoons olive oil

2 tablespoons soy sauce

1 tablespoon clear honey

1 tablespoon finely chopped ginger

1 garlic clove, finely chopped

TO FINISH

A handful of cilantro, coarsely torn

Lime juice

Put the sliced green onions into a large bowl. Cut the carrots into fine julienne with a mandoline or grate them coarsely and add to the bowl. Remove any blemished outer leaves from the cabbage, then quarter and cut away the core. Shred the leaves as finely as you can and combine with the green onions and carrots.

For the dressing, whisk together all the ingredients, making sure the honey is dissolved.

Pour the dressing over the vegetables and toss thoroughly. Leave for 10 to 20 minutes to soften and "relax."

Serve the coleslaw scattered with cilantro and sprinkled with lime juice.

Kohlrabi "carpaccio"

This elegant salad makes the most of kohlrabi's radishy, water chestnutty crunch. It takes only minutes to make. When I grow kohlrabi, I don't usually let them get any larger than a small eating apple, but they'll probably be a bit bigger than that in the store. Medium-sized ones are fine but avoid any monsters – they'll be too tough and not sweet enough to serve raw.

SERVES 4

2 medium or 3 small kohlrabi

1½ to 2 ounces / 50 to 60g hard goat cheese

A few sprigs of thyme, leaves only, bruised or coarsely chopped

½ lemon

Canola or extra-virgin olive oil

Sea salt and freshly ground black pepper

Peel the kohlrabi and slice them into paper-thin rounds with a vegetable peeler. Divide the slices among four plates or arrange on a large platter, spreading them out and overlapping them to almost cover the surface.

Shave over some goat cheese – again, using the vegetable peeler. There's no need to cover the kohlrabi with the cheese: 4 or 5 good shavings per plate is fine.

Sprinkle on the thyme, squeeze over a few drops of lemon juice, and trickle on a little oil. Season with salt and pepper and serve.

Celery, orange, and pecans ͮ

I love the bitter-sweet-sharp combination of celery and orange. Use the sweeter, less fibrous stems from the inside of the celery for this fruity salad. The rich nuts are the perfect foil to the zesty orange and crunchy celery.

SERVES 2

2 oranges

3 or 4 inner celery stalks, plus a few of the leaves

⅓ cup / 40g pecans or cashews, lightly toasted

Sea salt and freshly ground black pepper

Finely grate the zest from one of the oranges and set aside. Slice off the top and bottom from both oranges, stand the fruit upright on the board, and work your way around it with a sharp knife, cutting off the skin and all the pith. Cut out the segments from between the membranes, working over a large bowl to save the juice and letting the segments fall into the bowl. When you've finished, squeeze the juice from the remaining membrane into the bowl and add the zest.

Remove any obvious fibers from the outside of the celery stalks with a vegetable peeler and slice the stalks fairly thinly. Add to the oranges, along with the nuts and some salt and pepper.

Transfer the salad to a serving bowl. Coarsely chop the celery leaves, scatter them over the top, and serve.

Belgian endive, pears, and salty-sweet roasted almonds

Marcona almonds, if you can get them, are particularly tasty here. The nuts can be prepared well ahead and stored in an airtight container.

SERVES 4

2 heads of Belgian endive or radicchio

2 ripe pears

FOR THE SALTY-SWEET ALMONDS

½ teaspoon unsalted butter

½ teaspoon sugar

A good pinch of sea salt

½ cup / 50g blanched almonds

FOR THE DRESSING

3 tablespoons canola or olive oil

¼ teaspoon English mustard

A squeeze of lemon juice

Sea salt and freshly ground black pepper

To prepare the almonds, put the butter, sugar, salt, and almonds into a small pan and heat gently. Watch the mixture like a hawk, stirring often, as the sugar starts to caramelize. After a few minutes, the nuts will take on some color and the sugar-butter-salt mixture will be nicely caramelized. Remove from the heat and immediately tip out onto a nonstick silicone liner or a sheet of parchment paper. Leave to cool.

To make the dressing, whisk together the oil and mustard in a small cup or pitcher. Add just enough lemon juice to create a nicely sharp dressing and season with some salt and pepper.

Separate the endive leaves. Quarter and core the pears, then cut each quarter lengthwise in half again. Arrange the endive and pears on serving plates, add a scattering of salty-sweet almonds, trickle over the dressing, and serve.

Tomatoes with herbs ᵛ

This classic assembly remains one of my favorite ways to serve really good, ripe, sun-warmed tomatoes, and I like to use two or three varieties if possible. Vary the herbs as you please – chives, basil, and parsley all work well.

SERVES 4

2 pounds / 1kg ripe, full-flavored tomatoes

3 to 4 tablespoons extra-virgin olive oil

1 to 2 tablespoons balsamic vinegar (ideally apple balsamic)

A small handful of snipped chives, torn basil leaves, or chopped parsley

Sea salt and freshly ground black pepper

Thickly slice the tomatoes and arrange on a serving platter so the slices are only slightly overlapping to ensure each one will receive some of the dressing.

First trickle over the olive oil, and then the balsamic vinegar. Scatter over the herbs, season with a little salt and pepper, and serve.

VARIATION

Tomatoes and goat cheese
I sometimes scatter thinly sliced firm goat cheese over the sliced tomatoes before dressing this salad (as shown on page 7).

Tomatoes with thai dressing

This is another simple and delicious way to serve up a tomato salad. The unusual Thai-inspired dressing goes brilliantly with the mint. Again, I like to use a few different types of tomatoes.

SERVES 4

2 pounds / 1kg ripe, full-flavored tomatoes

Sea salt and freshly ground black pepper

6 to 8 mint leaves, shredded

FOR THE DRESSING

½ to 1 small fresh red chile or a good pinch of dried chile flakes

½ garlic clove, crushed with a little coarse sea salt

1 tablespoon balsamic vinegar (ideally apple balsamic)

2 teaspoons rice vinegar or cider vinegar

2 teaspoons sesame oil

1 teaspoon clear honey

For the dressing, halve, seed, and very finely chop the fresh chile, if using, until it almost forms a paste. Whisk together the garlic, balsamic vinegar, rice vinegar, sesame oil, and honey until the honey has dissolved into the mixture, adding the chile by degrees to achieve the heat you want.

Thickly slice the tomatoes and arrange them on a large platter or on individual plates. Season with salt and pepper, trickle over the dressing, and sprinkle over the mint. Serve immediately.

Avocado and ruby grapefruit with chile

A lovely, fresh zesty salad, spiked with a little chile. When available,
I like to use organic Hass avocados.

SERVES 2

1 ruby or pink grapefruit

1 small avocado

Sea salt and freshly ground black pepper

½ small or medium fresh red chile, seeded and finely chopped

A small handful of cilantro leaves

Extra-virgin olive oil

Slice off the top and bottom from the grapefruit. Stand it upright on a board and work your way around the fruit with a sharp knife, cutting off the skin and all the pith. Now hold it in your hand over a bowl to catch the juice and cut out the segments from between the membranes, letting the segments fall into the bowl. Squeeze the juice from the remaining membrane into the bowl, too.

Halve, peel, and pit the avocado, then cut lengthwise into thin slices. Arrange on a large plate with the grapefruit segments and trickle over the saved juice.

Sprinkle a little salt, pepper, and the chopped chile over the salad. Finish with the cilantro and a generous trickle of olive oil. Serve right away.

Marinated cucumber with mint

We don't always get excited about cucumber, because it isn't always served to its best advantage.
This refreshing salad takes just a few minutes to put together, but does a cucumber full justice.
Resting the salad allows the mint to infuse and takes the chilly edge off the cucumber.

SERVES 3 OR 4

1 medium-large cucumber

1 teaspoon cider vinegar

1 tablespoon olive or canola oil

A good handful of mint, finely chopped

A pinch of sugar

Sea salt and freshly ground black pepper

Peel the cucumber, halve it lengthwise, and scoop out the seeds. Slice into thick half-moons. Place in a dish with the cider vinegar, oil, and mint. Season with the sugar and a pinch each of salt and pepper, then toss together thoroughly. Leave for 15 to 30 minutes, toss again, and then serve.

Vegetable juice mixology

Once in a while it's good to get to know your veg intimately, from the inside out, as it were. That's when the juicer comes in handy. A glass of freshly juiced vegetables can be very delicious as well as feel very virtuous. I've been experimenting with lots of juices – in one session, I juiced ten different types of vegetables and tried out all sorts of blends. One of the revelations was rhubarb (which is, of course, a vegetable, not a fruit). It's too tart and astringent on its own, but is a great way to add zing to sweeter juices like carrot and beet. It can be quite tough on the juicer, though, with its fibrous stems, so don't force it.

The whole point of owning a juicer, as I see it, is to experiment, play around, and come up with your own favorite veg/fruit combinations. But, of course, I'm delighted to share some of my favorites with you. All quantities are approximate. Feel free to adjust the balance to your taste, or to use what's on hand. Vegetables juiced cold from the fridge will always make for a more refreshing drink. I prefer not to add ice, though, as it dilutes the flavors.

Beet bazaar

I've always liked the combination of cumin with root vegetables; you could also try coriander seeds or a pinch of cayenne.

Lightly toast 1/2 teaspoon of cumin seeds in a dry small frying pan for a couple of minutes until fragrant, then pulverize using a mortar and pestle. Juice 2 medium beets, 2 large carrots, and 2 celery stalks. Add the toasted cumin with a pinch of salt and a grinding of black pepper, then taste and adjust, sharpening the flavor with a few drops of lemon or orange juice if you like.

Bugs' surprise

This a great way to give a tart edge to sweet, creamy carrot juice.

Juice 3 large carrots and 1/2 to 1 medium rhubarb stalk and mix well. Serve cold, finished with a bruised sprig of mint if you like.

Cuke and tom cooler

Freshly juiced ripe tomatoes are quite different from tomato juice in a carton or bottle, which has effectively been cooked to preserve it. The cucumber is a lovely companion.

Juice 8 ounces / 250g of ripe tomatoes (any kind) and 1/2 large cucumber. Finely chop a few mint leaves and mix all well together.

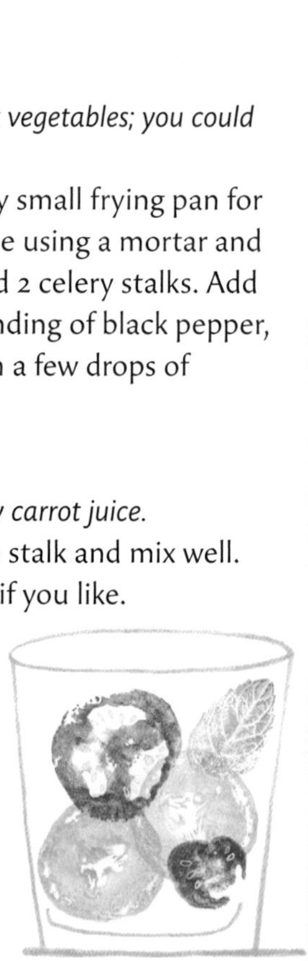

Hefty soups

I hope you're not tempted to skim over this chapter because the idea of "vegetable soup" doesn't entice you. If you are, I urge you to think again, because these soups are as varied, textured, and flavor-packed as any of the other dishes in the book. The only thing that really marks them out is that they generally need to be eaten with a spoon. Although in a couple of cases – the ribollita (see page 151) springs to mind – they're so packed with goodness and goodies that you'd probably get away with a fork.

There's certainly nothing "samey" about them. There are some broth-based soups with a whole vegetable patch of produce to be chased around the bowl, while some are smooth, thick, and creamy, and others chunky, rich, and hearty. And many hover tantalizingly between these poles. Some are almost stews: after all, the point at which a soup turns into a stew is pretty arbitrary. With many "big" soups, you're simply building up a really hearty mix of vegetables, grains, and legumes that happens to sit best in a bowl, on account of the lovely liquid in which they sit.

The purpose of almost all of these soups is to be satisfyingly substantial. A few would be perfect in small portions, as starters – the cucumber and lettuce vichyssoise (see page 134) is particularly elegant. However, for the most part, they have it in them to be main meals. They are the sort of soups I would expect you to have seconds of – not just half a ladleful, but a whole second bowl. Add some bread and you've got supper.

The lovely loose, liquid consistency of soup makes for relaxed eating but also for relaxed cooking. There are no delicate emulsions or veloutés here, just marvelous mixtures of good, tasty things. There's no need to get bogged down with precise measurements and long lists of fancy ingredients. The fact is that most of the soups I make at home – and I make soup at least once a week – are not preplanned or taken from recipe books. They are improvised from ingredients I have on hand – sometimes fresh, sometimes leftovers, sometimes from the pantry, often a combination of all three.

Only yesterday I put together a soup that bore little resemblance to one I had ever made before. In the fridge I happened to have a few leftover wedges of roasted squash (similar to the recipe on page 346). I also had a meager portion of the lovely cauliflower and chickpea curry (on page 27). I put them together in the blender with half a liter of stock from an organic vegetable stock cube and a dash of coconut milk from a can off the shelf. The result, finished with a swirl of yogurt from the fridge, was a genuinely fine soup – from a combination of ingredients that would never have been premeditated.

Even – especially – when cooking from scratch with garden-fresh ingredients, I'm still often cooking off the cuff, and many of the recipes in this chapter are the results of impromptu soup sessions. I like to knock out chunky-textured soups that showcase fresh vegetables in their greatest glory – either whole, or in bite-sized pieces for the eye to see and the mouth to savor. Often they'll feature a composite of creamy beans, leafy greens, cubed roots, and cubed fruits (generally in the savory, zucchini-ish, squashy sense of the "f" word). They tend to be put together with gay abandon after raiding the garden, and certainly don't require a session in a white lab coat and with digital scales. So please feel free to cut loose with these recipes in a similar spirit of improvisation. Add less of this, more of that, or throw in something completely different that you have a hunch about. With soups, there are so few rules and so many good outcomes.

Almost all the soups that follow are based on a light vegetable stock. Having said that, they could be equally well made with a light chicken stock if you have one on hand. When I have time, I love to make fresh vegetable stock, and the recipe on page 130 can be done and dusted in half an hour. But frankly, that's half an hour I often don't have, so I am no stranger to the stock cube – ideally an organic, yeast-free one. I'll often make a slightly weaker broth, one-half to two-thirds strength, than the package suggests, as a soup already crammed full of fresh vegetables shouldn't need much help from a stock.

I'm a great fan of the "finishing touch" for soups. I flinch from the word "garnish" – so often an addition you don't actually want to eat – but something on top, or swirled in, that adds an extra dimension of contrasting taste or texture, is usually very welcome. It also makes the lucky person who's supping on that soup feel well looked after. Don't underestimate the pleasing effect on the palate of a trickle of an herb or spice oil, a swirl of yogurt, a few gratings of cheese, a dab of pesto, or the crunch of croutons. Again, don't feel my ideas for the final flourish in these recipes are strictly prescriptive. Mix and match. Knock yourself out. It's all part of bigging up a good soup to give it the billing it deserves, a way of saying: "I love my soup. And you're going to love it, too."

Vegetable stock

A good vegetable stock, built around the deep savory notes of bay and celery and the delicate sweetness of onion and carrot, is invaluable for giving body to many soups. You'll also find it indispensable for stews, risottos, gratins, and curries. I always try to keep some in the freezer – though it can be rustled up in no time if you have the ingredients on hand.

MAKES ABOUT 1½ QUARTS / 1.5 LITERS

2 large or 3 medium onions

3 large or 4 medium carrots

3 or 4 celery stalks

1 garlic clove

1 tablespoon canola oil

1 or 2 bay leaves, coarsely torn

A sprig of thyme and/or some parsley stems, if you have them

A few black peppercorns

½ small glass dry white wine (optional)

7 cups / 1.75 liters boiling water

Coarsely grate the onions, carrots, celery, and garlic – or chop them, if you prefer, but in fairly small pieces. Heat the oil in a large saucepan over medium heat and tip in the vegetables, garlic, herbs, and peppercorns. Sauté, stirring from time to time, for about 5 minutes, or until the vegetables have softened slightly (you're largely doing this to mellow the raw onion).

Add the wine, if you are using it, then the boiling water. Bring back to a boil and simmer, uncovered. If all of the vegetables were grated, the stock will be ready in about 10 minutes. If they were in larger chunks, simmer for 20 to 30 minutes. Either way, strain the stock and use right away, or cool, then refrigerate or freeze.

VARIATION

Mushroom stock

This stock has an extra kick of 'shroomy flavor. It's ideal for a mushroom soup (see pages 152 and 154) or in a mushroom risotto. However, you can use it in almost any veg soup as a good, deep, earthy base. Make the stock as above but add about 7 ounces / 200g sliced fresh mushrooms to the other vegetables (use well-flavored mushrooms such as cremini, shiitake, or portobello). In addition, if you're including dried mushrooms in the dish the stock is to be used in, be sure to add the soaking liquid to the stock, first straining it through cheesecloth to remove any grit.

River Cottage summer garden soup

We often prepare this recipe to showcase some of our early summer produce from the River Cottage garden. You may not have access to the same range of just-picked veg, but gather some good, fresh stuff from a farm stand, farmers' market, or greengrocer, and you will get a similar result. Vary the veg according to what is available. Just chop it all into small, similar-sized pieces and "build" the soup, cooking the harder, denser vegetables for slightly longer, and you'll end up with a vibrant, fresh-tasting bowlful.

SERVES 6

2 small fennel bulbs, trimmed (any feathery fronds chopped and reserved)

2 celery stalks

A small bunch of green onions, trimmed

About 1 pound / 500g small zucchini

A bunch of ruby or rainbow Swiss chard

2 tablespoons / 30g butter

1 tablespoon canola or olive oil

1 quart / liter vegetable stock (see page 130)

Sea salt and freshly ground black pepper

3 to 5 ounces / 100 to 150g fresh shelled peas

3 to 5 ounces / 100 to 150g fresh shelled fava beans, blanched and peeled if large

2 small lettuces, such as Little Gem, shredded

2 tablespoons finely chopped mixed herbs, such as mint, lemon balm, parsley, basil, fennel fronds, and/or chives

A few fresh pea shoots (optional)

Chop the fennel, celery, green onions, and zucchini into small dice, keeping them separate. Tear the leaves from the chard stalks and shred them; cut the stalks into small pieces.

Heat a saucepan over medium heat and add the butter and oil. Add the fennel, celery, green onions, and chard stalks and cook gently for about 10 minutes, until soft but not colored. Add the stock and bring to a simmer. Season with salt and pepper.

Make sure your broth is simmering well and add the zucchini. Once returned to a simmer, cook for 1 minute, then add the peas and fava beans. Simmer for another 2 minutes. Check that the peas and beans are just tender, then add the lettuce and the shredded chard leaves. Simmer for another minute.

Add the chopped herbs along with any feathery fennel fronds and, if you have them, the pea shoots, then immediately remove from the heat. Check the seasoning, then ladle into warmed bowls and serve.

Cucumber and lettuce vichyssoise

Light, delicate, and pretty, this chilled soup – a take on the classic vichyssoise – is a great way to start a summer meal. You can also make a deep-green version with spinach instead of the lettuce.

SERVES 6

2 tablespoons / 60g butter

2 leeks, trimmed (white and pale green parts only) and sliced, or 1 large onion, sliced

1 large, starchy potato (about 8 ounces / 250g), peeled and cut into large chunks

1 quart / liter vegetable stock (see page 130)

2 cucumbers, peeled and cubed

2 Little Gem or butterhead lettuces, shredded

3 tablespoons heavy cream or crème fraîche

Sea salt and freshly ground black pepper

FOR THE CROUTONS

¼ cup / 60ml canola or olive oil

4 slices of bread, crusts removed, cut into cubes

TO FINISH

Chopped chives

Heavy cream or crème fraîche

Melt the butter in a large saucepan over medium-low heat. Add the leeks or onion, cover, and sweat gently for about 10 minutes, until soft. Add the potato and stock. Bring to a boil, then simmer for about 10 minutes, until the potato is almost cooked. Add the cubed cucumbers and shredded lettuce, return to a boil, and simmer for a further 4 minutes.

Scoop out the potato chunks and rub them through a sieve, run them through a food mill, or press them through a potato ricer into a large bowl (whizzing them in a blender would make the soup gluey). Purée the simmered mixture in a blender, add to the sieved potato, and stir well. Stir in the cream or crème fraîche and season with salt and pepper. Leave to cool completely, then chill for a couple of hours.

Meanwhile, make the croutons. Heat the oil in a frying pan over medium-high heat. Add the bread and fry, turning often, for a few minutes, until golden brown. Leave to cool.

Serve the chilled soup topped with a swirl of cream or crème fraîche, chopped chives, and croutons.

Gazpacho

This traditional chilled Spanish soup is as cooling as they come – it's the perfect thing to serve on a hot summer's day or a sultry evening. You can, if you like, press the puréed soup through a sieve to get a really smooth finish, but bear in mind you'll lose some of the volume if you do this. In any case, I like my gazpacho a little bit chunky. It goes without saying that the tomatoes need to be full of flavor or you'll be selling your soup short.

SERVES 4

2 thick slices of stale white bread (3 to 4 ounces / 100g), crusts removed

1 garlic clove, crushed

2 to 3 pounds / 1 to 1.5kg large, ripe tomatoes

½ cucumber, peeled and sliced

1 red bell pepper, seeded and chopped

½ small red onion, chopped

3½ tablespoons / 50ml extra-virgin olive oil

1 tablespoon balsamic vinegar (ideally apple balsamic)

1 teaspoon sugar

Sea salt and freshly ground black pepper

TO FINISH

Croutons (see page 134)

Shredded basil or chopped flat-leaf parsley

Tear the bread into pieces and put into a bowl with the crushed garlic. Pour in a good ¾ cup / 200ml of cold water and leave to soak while you prepare the remaining ingredients.

Cover the tomatoes with boiling water, leave for a couple of minutes, then scoop out and peel off their skins. Quarter and seed the tomatoes, putting all the seeds and clinging juicy bits into a sieve set over a bowl. Put the skinned flesh into a separate bowl. When all of the tomatoes are done, press the seedy bits in the sieve to extract as much juice as possible, then add it to the tomato flesh.

Put the soaked bread and garlic, tomatoes, cucumber, red pepper, onion, olive oil, balsamic vinegar, and sugar in a food processor (you should be able to do it in just one batch). Process to a coarse purée and season with salt and pepper to taste. You can leave the soup chunky, or whiz it a bit longer, and then press through a sieve, if you prefer.

Cover and chill for 2 to 3 hours, then taste and adjust the seasoning. Serve the gazpacho topped with croutons and shredded basil or chopped parsley.

Mexican tomato and bean soup

This fresh, piquant summer soup combines many of the ingredients you might find in a feisty salsa, but in this case they're all "souped up." Add more chiles if you like it hot, and a handful of fresh sweet corn kernels, sliced straight from the cob, is a good addition if you have them. A scattering of diced avocado can replace the sour cream, if you prefer.

SERVES 4 TO 6

2 tablespoons olive oil

2 red onions, finely chopped

3 garlic cloves, finely chopped

1 or 2 jalapeños, seeded and finely chopped

½ teaspoon ground cumin

2½ cups / 600ml vegetable stock (see page 130)

A generous ¾ cup / 200ml roasted tomato sauce (see page 366)

14 ounces / 400g ripe tomatoes, cored, seeded, and finely chopped

1 (14-ounce / 400g) can black beans or black-eyed peas, drained and rinsed

A handful of oregano, chopped

A pinch of sugar

Sea salt and freshly ground black pepper

Juice of 1 lime

A small bunch of cilantro, coarsely chopped

Sour cream, to finish (optional)

Heat the olive oil in a saucepan over medium-low heat, add most of the onions (reserving a little to finish the soup), and sauté for about 5 minutes, or until softened. Add the garlic, chile(s), and cumin and stir for a minute.

Add the stock, roasted tomato sauce, tomatoes, beans, oregano, and sugar. Season with salt and pepper, bring to a boil, and simmer gently for 10 minutes. Remove from the heat and add the lime juice and half of the cilantro. Taste and adjust the seasoning if necessary.

Serve the soup topped with dollops of sour cream, if you like, scattered with the reserved red onion and chopped cilantro, and sprinkled with freshly ground pepper.

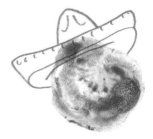

Pea and parsley soup

Using parsley instead of the more conventional mint gives this summer soup a deeper, slightly less sweet flavor. It's great hot or cold. I like it garnished with a few whole peas – especially really small and sweet raw ones. If you have some pea shoots, they look beautiful scattered over the finished soup, too.

SERVES 4

1 tablespoon olive or canola oil, plus extra to trickle

4 teaspoons / 20g butter

1 onion, finely chopped

A few sprigs of thyme, leaves only, chopped

1 quart / liter vegetable stock (see page 130)

1 pound / 500g fresh shelled peas or frozen peas

A small handful of flat-leaf parsley, chopped

Sea salt and freshly ground pepper, to taste

A few mint leaves, shredded, to finish (optional)

Heat the oil and butter in a large saucepan over medium-low heat and sweat the onion with the thyme until the onion is soft and translucent, about 10 minutes.

Add the stock, peas (reserving a handful to finish the soup if you like), and parsley. Season with salt and pepper, bring to a simmer, and cook for 5 to 10 minutes, or until the peas are very tender.

Cool slightly, then purée the soup in a food processor or blender, or with an immersion blender, until very smooth – you may need to do this in two batches if you are using a processor or free-standing blender. Return the soup to the pan, adjust the seasoning, and heat through.

Ladle the soup into warmed bowls. If you have some raw fresh peas, scatter a few on top (or you could use blanched frozen peas). Add the mint, if using, trickle over a little olive or canola oil, and serve.

Alternatively, you can let the soup cool, then chill it lightly before serving; add the scattering of peas and mint, if using, and a trickle of oil at the last minute.

Fennel and celery root soup with orange zest

This velvety, gently aniseedy soup is given warmth and definition with a touch of orange zest. The rich-but-sharp crème fraîche added at the end balances it all out nicely.

SERVES 4

2 tablespoons / 30g butter

1 tablespoon canola or olive oil

4 shallots or 1 onion, halved and sliced

3 large fennel bulbs (about 1½ pounds / 750g), trimmed and sliced (any feathery fronds reserved)

¼ large celery root (about 9 ounces / 250g, untrimmed), peeled and cubed

Finely grated zest of 1 orange

About 2 cups / 500ml vegetable stock (see page 130)

Sea salt and freshly ground black pepper

4 to 6 tablespoons crème fraîche, to finish

Heat the butter and oil in a large saucepan over medium heat. Add the shallots or onion and sweat gently for a few minutes. Add the fennel and celery root, stir well, then cover and sweat for about 10 minutes, until beginning to soften.

Add the orange zest, stock, and some salt and pepper. Bring to a boil, then simmer for about 15 minutes until all the vegetables are tender.

Purée the soup in a blender until completely smooth, adding a touch more stock or some water to loosen the consistency if necessary. (You may have to blend longer than usual to blitz out all the fibers from the fennel, but it shouldn't be necessary to pass the soup through a sieve.)

Reheat the soup if necessary, check the seasoning, and serve, with a good blob of crème fraîche on top, a few fennel fronds if you have them, and plenty of freshly ground black pepper.

Roasted beet soup with horseradish cream

Two fantastic roots take center stage here: the sharp, hot tang of horseradish is the best foil I know to beets' earthy sweetness. The resulting soup, though easy to make, is really very elegant.

SERVES 4 TO 6

2 pounds / 1kg red beets

4 garlic cloves (unpeeled), bashed

2 or 3 sprigs of thyme

1 bay leaf

3 tablespoons olive or canola oil

Sea salt and freshly ground black pepper

1 quart / liter vegetable stock (see page 130)

FOR THE HORSERADISH CREAM

1 (1½-inch / 4cm) piece of fresh horseradish, peeled and freshly grated, or 1 tablespoon creamed horseradish

¾ cup / 200g sour cream, crème fraîche, or thick, plain full-fat yogurt

TO FINISH

Dill, chopped

Preheat the oven to 400°F / 200°C. Scrub the beets well but leave them whole. Place them in a roasting pan and scatter around the garlic, thyme, and bay leaf. Trickle on the oil and season well with salt and pepper. Mix everything together with your hands so that it is well coated. Pour a wine glass of water into the pan and cover tightly with foil. Roast until the beets are tender when pierced with a knife – about an hour depending on the size of the beets.

While the beets are roasting, make the horseradish cream: in a bowl, mix the grated (or creamed) horseradish with the sour cream, crème fraîche, or yogurt.

Remove the foil from the roasting pan and leave the beets until they are cool enough to handle. Top and tail them and peel or rub off the skins – they should slip off easily. Coarsely chop the beets.

Squeeze the soft garlic from the skins and place in a blender with the beets. Process with enough of the stock to make a smooth purée, then transfer to a saucepan and thin further with stock to get the texture you like.

Heat through over medium heat until thoroughly hot but not boiling. Adjust the seasoning to taste. Serve the soup in warmed bowls with a dollop of the horseradish cream and dill scattered on top.

Porotos granados

This is my version of the traditional Chilean squash and bean stew. It's wonderfully hearty and warming and, like so many such dishes, even better if you leave it for twenty-four hours and reheat it gently before serving.

SERVES 6

2 tablespoons canola or olive oil

1 onion, chopped

2 garlic cloves, finely chopped

1 teaspoon sweet smoked paprika

A handful of oregano or marjoram, chopped

3¹/₂ ounces / 100g small dried beans, such as pinto, navy, or cannellini beans, soaked overnight in cold water, or 1 (14-ounce / 400g) can beans, drained and well rinsed

1 quart / liter vegetable stock (see page 130)

1 bay leaf

1¹/₂ pounds / 750g squash, such as butternut or red kuri, peeled, seeded, and cut into ³/₄-inch / 2cm chunks

7 ounces / 200g green beans, trimmed and cut into ³/₄-inch / 2cm pieces

Kernels cut from 2 cobs of corn

Sea salt and freshly ground black pepper

Heat the oil in a large saucepan or casserole over medium heat. Add the onion and garlic and sauté gently for about 10 minutes, until softened. Add the paprika and 1 tablespoon of the oregano. Cook for another minute.

If using dried beans, drain them after soaking and add to the pan with the stock and bay leaf. Bring to a boil, then lower the heat and simmer for about 45 minutes, or until the beans are completely tender (dried beans vary, and sometimes this may take over an hour). Add the squash, stir well, and simmer for 10 to 15 minutes, until the squash is just tender, then add the green beans and corn kernels and simmer for another 5 minutes.

If using canned beans, add the drained, rinsed beans, the squash, bay leaf, and stock at the same time, and simmer until the squash is just tender, 10 to 15 minutes. Then add the green beans and corn kernels and simmer for a further 5 minutes.

To finish, season well – I use about 1 teaspoon of salt and plenty of pepper. Stir in the remaining oregano, leave to settle for a couple of minutes, then serve.

Chickpea, chard, and porcini soup

This is a really lovely, hearty, big-flavored soup, underpinned by the earthiness of porcini mushrooms. You could use canned white beans, such as cannellini, in place of the chickpeas, and kale instead of the chard or spinach.

SERVES 4

1 ounce / 30g dried porcini mushrooms

2 tablespoons / 30g butter

3 tablespoons olive oil

1 small onion, diced

2 garlic cloves, finely chopped

1½ cups tomato sauce or 1 (14-ounce / 400g) can plum tomatoes, chopped, any stalky ends and skin removed

1 (14-ounce / 400g) can chickpeas, drained and rinsed

1 sprig of rosemary

10 ounces / 300g Swiss chard or spinach leaves, shredded

Sea salt and freshly ground black pepper

TO FINISH

Extra-virgin olive oil

Parmesan, hard goat cheese, or other well-flavored hard cheese (optional)

Soak the porcini in about 3 cups / 750ml of warm water for 30 minutes. Remove the mushrooms with a slotted spoon, reserving the soaking water. Rinse the mushrooms briefly under cold water (they can be gritty) and pat dry with paper towels. Coarsely chop them.

Strain the mushroom soaking liquid through a sieve lined with cheesecloth or paper towels into a bowl.

Heat the butter and olive oil in a saucepan over medium-low heat and sweat the onion, stirring from time to time, for about 15 minutes, until soft and translucent. Add the garlic and stir for a minute, then add the mushrooms and cook, stirring, for another couple of minutes.

Add the tomato sauce or the tomatoes with their juice, the chickpeas, rosemary, reserved mushroom soaking liquid, and a few grinds of black pepper. Bring to a boil, turn down the heat, and simmer gently for about 45 minutes. Add the chard or spinach and cook for a further 2 to 3 minutes for spinach or 8 to 10 minutes for chard.

If the soup seems too thick, thin it slightly with a little water. Discard the rosemary. Taste and add salt and pepper if needed.

Ladle into warmed bowls, trickle over some extra-virgin olive oil, and use a vegetable peeler to shave a few slivers of Parmesan or hard goat cheese over the top, if you like. Serve at once.

Ribollita ♥

Ribollita literally means "reboiled." Traditionally, this Italian soup was made in large quantities so it could be reheated on subsequent days. It proves how humble ingredients – in this case, a few vegetables and some stale bread – can yield truly delicious results. By all means, use a couple of cans of cannellini beans rather than dried beans.

SERVES 6

FOR THE BEANS

7 ounces / 200g dried cannellini beans, soaked in cold water overnight

1 onion, quartered

1 bay leaf

1 garlic clove, bashed

1 sprig of rosemary

OR

2 (14-ounce / 400g) cans cannellini beans

FOR THE SOUP

1/4 cup / 60ml olive oil

1 onion, finely chopped

1 or 2 carrots, finely chopped

1 celery stalk, finely chopped

1 leek, trimmed, washed and thinly sliced

5 or 6 tomatoes, skinned, seeded, and chopped, or 1 (14-ounce / 400g) can plum tomatoes, coarsely chopped, any stalky ends and skin removed

3 1/2 cups / 800ml vegetable stock (see page 130)

1 sprig of rosemary and 1 sprig of thyme, tied together with string

10 ounces / 300g kale or savoy cabbage, tough stems removed

Sea salt and freshly ground black pepper

TO FINISH

6 slices of slightly stale country-style or sourdough bread

1 garlic clove, halved

Extra-virgin olive oil

If you are using dried beans, drain them after soaking, rinse, and then put into a large saucepan with the onion, bay leaf, garlic clove, and rosemary. Add enough water to cover the beans by about 2 inches / 5cm, bring to a boil, lower the heat to a bare simmer, partially cover, and cook until the beans are tender, 1 to 1 1/2 hours. Drain, reserving the liquid. Pulse half of the beans with some of the cooking liquid in a blender or food processor until you have a rough purée.

If you are using canned beans, drain and rinse them well, then mash or blend half of them with a little cold water.

In a large saucepan, heat the olive oil over medium-low heat and sauté the onion for about 15 minutes, until softened. Add the carrot(s), celery, and leek and sauté for 5 minutes, stirring. Now add the tomatoes with their juice, the puréed and whole beans, the stock, rosemary, and thyme and simmer gently for about 1 hour.

Shred the kale or cabbage leaves. Add to the soup and cook for 10 minutes more, until the leaves are tender. Remove the sprigs of thyme and rosemary and add some salt and pepper.

To serve, toast the slices of bread until golden, then rub with the garlic and brush with extra-virgin olive oil. Put a slice of bread in the bottom of each bowl, ladle over the soup, and trickle some olive oil on top.

Creamy mushroom soup

There's something a little bit retro about a sherry-spiked cream of mushroom soup but, as a child of the seventies, I have no problem with that. With its beautiful dun color and rich, earthy flavor, this is a dish I'm happy to revisit regularly. To get the best flavor, I use portobello and/or cremini mushrooms.

SERVES 4 TO 6

2 tablespoons / 30g butter

2 leeks, trimmed (white and pale green part only) and thinly sliced

A sprig of thyme

1½ pounds / 750g mushrooms, coarsely chopped

Sea salt and freshly ground black pepper

1 small garlic clove, chopped

1 tablespoon all-purpose flour

5 cups / 1.2 liters hot mushroom or vegetable stock (see page 130)

A scant ½ cup / 100ml heavy cream, plus extra to finish

A few gratings of nutmeg

2 tablespoons dry sherry (optional)

A handful of chives, tarragon, or parsley, finely chopped, to finish

Melt the butter in a large saucepan over medium-low heat and sweat the leeks with the thyme, stirring from time to time, until soft, about 10 minutes.

Turn up the heat to medium-high and add the mushrooms with a pinch of salt (this will help the juices to run). Sauté for a few minutes, until the mushrooms soften and lose some of their moisture.

Add the garlic and stir for a minute, then sprinkle over the flour and stir for a couple of minutes. Pour over the hot stock. Bring to a boil and simmer gently, uncovered, for 20 minutes.

Remove the thyme. Whiz the soup in a blender until smooth (or blend three-quarters of it and leave a quarter unblended if you prefer a soup with more texture). Return it to the pan.

Add the cream to the soup, along with the nutmeg, and reheat gently, stirring. Add the sherry, if using, then taste and adjust the seasoning, adding more salt, pepper, and/or nutmeg as needed.

Spoon the soup into warmed bowls and add a swirl of cream and a sprinkling of chopped herbs before serving.

Mushroom "stoup"

Somewhere between a soup and a stew – hence the name – this dish is full of lovely earthy mushroom flavor, and can be made even more generous with the addition of some little herby dumplings. Another good way to make it a bit more substantial or suppery would be to throw in a handful of cooked pearled barley or pasta. And if you want to posh it up for a dinner party, a swirl of sour cream or thick yogurt and a sprinkling of dill is an ideal finishing touch.

SERVES 4

2 ounces / 60g dried porcini mushrooms

2 tablespoons / 30g butter

1 tablespoon canola or olive oil

2 onions, finely chopped

2 carrots, finely chopped

1 celery stalk, finely chopped

1 pound / 500g mushrooms, sliced

4 garlic cloves, finely chopped

1 quart / liter mushroom or vegetable stock (see page 130)

Sea salt and freshly ground black pepper

A bunch of flat-leaf parsley, finely chopped

A good handful of dill, finely chopped

FOR THE DUMPLINGS (OPTIONAL)

¾ cup / 100g self-rising flour, plus extra for dusting

½ teaspoon English mustard powder (optional)

¼ cup / 50g vegetable shortening

1 to 2 tablespoons finely chopped herbs (dill, thyme, parsley, chives, or chervil, or a combination)

Sea salt and freshly ground black pepper

Soak the dried porcini in 2 cups / 500ml hot water for 30 minutes.

Melt the butter with the oil in a large saucepan over medium-low heat. Add the onions and let them sweat, stirring occasionally, until they begin to turn golden, 15 to 20 minutes. Add the carrots and celery and cook, stirring occasionally, for about 5 minutes, until softened.

Meanwhile, use a slotted spoon to remove the porcini from the soaking water, rinse them briefly, and pat dry on paper towels. Strain the soaking liquid through a sieve lined with cheesecloth or paper towels (to remove any fine, sandy grit) into a bowl.

Increase the heat under the pan to medium-high and add the fresh mushrooms, stirring until they release some of their moisture. Add the porcini and garlic and sauté, stirring, for a minute. Stir in the strained soaking liquid and stock. Add some salt and pepper, then simmer, uncovered, for 15 minutes.

Meanwhile, make the dumplings. Sift the flour together with the mustard, if using, then mix in the shortening and chopped herbs using a whisk. Season well with salt and pepper. Use a knife to mix in just enough cold water – 5 to 6 tablespoons should do – to form a soft, but not too sticky, dough. The secret of light dumplings is not to work the mixture too hard. Dust your hands with flour and gently form the dough into 12 to 14 dumplings.

Check if the soup needs more salt and pepper, then add the parsley and dill. Add the dumplings and simmer, covered, for a further 12 to 15 minutes until they are fluffy and cooked through. If you are not using dumplings, continue to simmer the soup, uncovered, for a further 10 minutes. Ladle into warmed bowls and serve.

Parsnip and ginger soup

Sweet parsnips and fiery ginger are a winning and warming winter combination.

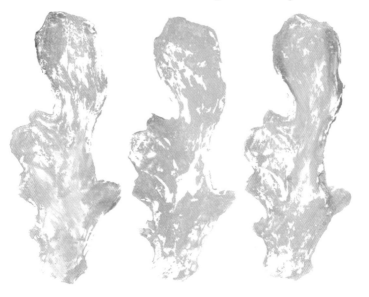

SERVES 4 TO 6

1 tablespoon olive oil

1 tablespoon / 15g butter

1 large onion, finely chopped

2 garlic cloves, finely chopped

1 (2-inch / 5cm) piece of ginger, peeled and finely chopped

1/4 teaspoon ground cardamom

1/4 teaspoon ground cumin

1/4 teaspoon cayenne pepper

1 pound / 500g parsnips, peeled and cut into 1/2-inch / 1cm cubes

3 1/2 cups / 800ml vegetable stock (see page 130)

Sea salt and freshly ground black pepper

3/4 cup / 200ml whole milk

TO FINISH

2 to 3 tablespoons sliced almonds or pumpkin seeds

1 to 2 tablespoons heavy cream or thick, plain full-fat yogurt

Heat the olive oil and butter in a saucepan over medium-low heat. Add the onion and sauté for about 10 minutes, until soft and translucent. Add the garlic, ginger, cardamom, cumin, and cayenne and stir for a couple of minutes. Tip in the parsnips and stir until well coated in the spices. Pour in the stock, season with salt and pepper, and simmer until the parsnips are very soft, about 15 minutes.

Allow the soup to cool slightly, then purée in a food processor or blender, or using an immersion blender, until smooth. Return the soup to the pan, add the milk, and adjust the seasoning. Warm through gently – if the soup is a bit thick, thin it with some hot water.

While the soup is warming, toast the almonds or pumpkin seeds in a dry frying pan until just beginning to turn golden.

Serve the soup in warmed bowls with a trickle of cream or yogurt and the toasted almonds or pumpkin seeds scattered over the top. Finish with a grinding of black pepper.

Chestnut and sage soup

This is a rich and elegant soup with a beguilingly velvety texture. A small portion makes a lovely starter, while a larger serving, with some bread and perhaps a crisp green salad, is a satisfying lunch or supper. You can use vacuum-packed precooked chestnuts for this, or fresh, whole chestnuts that have been blanched, peeled, and simmered until tender.

SERVES 4 TO 6

3 tablespoons olive oil, plus extra to trickle

1 tablespoon / 15g butter

1 onion, chopped

6 sage leaves, coarsely chopped, plus 8 to 12 whole leaves to finish

1 small garlic clove, finely chopped

1 quart / liter vegetable stock (see page 130)

14 ounces / 400g cooked, peeled chestnuts

Sea salt and freshly ground black pepper

A scant ½ cup / 100ml crème fraîche

Heat 1 tablespoon of the olive oil and the butter in a saucepan over medium-low heat. Add the onion and sweat for about 10 minutes, until soft and translucent. Add the chopped sage and garlic and sauté for a minute.

Pour in the stock and add most of the chestnuts – reserve a handful for finishing. Season with salt and pepper, increase the heat, and simmer for 15 minutes, stirring from time to time.

Remove from the heat and cool slightly, then purée until very smooth in a blender or food processor, or using an immersion blender. Return the soup to the pan, add the crème fraîche, and adjust the seasoning if necessary. Warm through gently – do not let it boil.

Meanwhile, slice the reserved chestnuts. Heat the remaining 2 tablespoons olive oil in a small frying pan over medium heat, add the sage leaves and sauté for a few seconds until crisp, then drain on paper towels.

Ladle the soup into warmed bowls, scatter on the chestnuts and sage leaves, and add a trickle of olive oil. Finish with a generous grinding of black pepper. Serve immediately.

Pearled barley broth

This is a substantial soup – serve it with a salad and some bread and you'll have a complete meal. As the barley simmers with the vegetables, it thickens the broth and gives the broth a creamy texture. You can certainly use pearled spelt in place of pearled barley.

SERVES 4 TO 6

1 tablespoon / 15g butter

2 large onions, finely chopped

1 bay leaf

A few sprigs of thyme, leaves only, chopped

1 small celery stalk, finely chopped

1 small carrot, finely chopped

1 small parsnip, finely chopped

¼ teaspoon ground coriander

A few gratings of nutmeg

A good pinch of cayenne pepper

A pinch of ground mace

½ cup / 100g pearled barley (or pearled spelt), rinsed

1½ quarts / 1.5 liters vegetable stock (see page 130)

Sea salt and freshly ground black pepper

A small handful of parsley, finely chopped

FOR THE CROUTONS (OPTIONAL)

About 7 ounces / 200g slightly stale white bread

¼ cup / 60ml olive oil

Heat the butter in a large saucepan over medium-low heat. Add the onions and gently sweat with the bay leaf and thyme for about 15 minutes, until soft and translucent. Add the celery, carrot, and parsnip and sauté for a further 5 minutes. Stir in the coriander, nutmeg, cayenne, and mace. Add the barley or spelt, pour in the stock, and add some salt and pepper. Simmer gently for 25 to 30 minutes, or until the grain is very soft. Remove the bay leaf.

You can serve the broth like this or, to make it a little thicker, scoop out a couple of ladlefuls and purée them in a blender or food processor, or with an immersion blender, until smooth, then return the puréed portion to the pan and warm through. Stir in the parsley and adjust the seasoning if necessary. Keep hot over very low heat if you are making croutons.

For the croutons, cut the bread into 1-inch / 2.5cm cubes. Heat the olive oil over medium heat in a large frying pan. Add the bread and sizzle gently until golden, turning occasionally, then drain on paper towels.

Ladle the soup into warmed bowls and scatter the hot croutons on top to serve.

ALTERNATIVE FINISHES

• Instead of serving the soup topped with croutons, sauté some sliced mushrooms in a little butter or olive oil until they give up some of their moisture and start to take on some color. Scatter the fried mushrooms over the soup just before serving.

• The soup is also very good simply served with a trickle of cream and chopped parsley scattered over the top.

Green lentil and spinach soup^ᵛ

Earthy, nutty French green lentils and a generous quantity of garlic give this simple soup a hearty and satisfying depth of flavor.

SERVES 4

2 tablespoons olive or canola oil

3 shallots or 1 onion, finely chopped

1 carrot, finely chopped

A few sprigs of thyme, leaves only, coarsely chopped

3 garlic cloves, finely chopped

3 tomatoes, cored, seeded, and diced

³/₄ cup / 150g French green lentils, rinsed

5 cups / 1.2 liters vegetable stock (see page 130)

Sea salt and freshly ground black pepper

A small bunch of parsley, finely chopped

3¹/₂ ounces / 100g baby spinach

TO FINISH

1 to 2 tablespoons extra-virgin olive or canola oil

Parmesan, hard goat cheese, or other well-flavored hard cheese (optional)

Heat the oil over medium-low heat in a large saucepan. Add the shallots or onion, carrot, and thyme and sauté gently for 5 minutes. Add the garlic and tomatoes and sauté for a further minute.

Tip in the lentils, stir, then add the stock and a little salt and pepper. Bring the soup to a boil, lower the heat, and simmer for about 25 minutes, or until the lentils are tender. Add the parsley and spinach and simmer for a further 5 minutes.

Check the seasoning, then ladle into warmed bowls, trickle over a little oil, and shave over some cheese, if you like.

Cannellini bean and leek soup with chile oil

The chile oil gives this soup a deliciously piquant finish. Once made, the oil will keep, sealed in an airtight container in the fridge, for a couple of weeks, and you can use it to add a bit of heat to marinades and salad dressings or to trickle over pizzas. However, if you don't have time to make it, you can simply trickle a little extra-virgin olive oil over the soup and finish with some shavings of Parmesan, pecorino, or hard goat cheese.

SERVES 4 TO 6

4 leeks, trimmed (white and pale green parts only)

1 tablespoon olive oil

1 tablespoon / 15g butter

A few sprigs of thyme, leaves only, coarsely chopped

1 bay leaf

3 garlic cloves, finely chopped

5 cups / 1.2 liters vegetable stock (see page 130)

2 (14-ounce / 400g) cans cannellini beans, drained and rinsed

A handful of oregano, coarsely chopped

A bunch of parsley, coarsely chopped

Sea salt and freshly ground black pepper

FOR THE CHILE OIL

4 fresh red chiles, seeded and sliced

¾ cup / 200ml olive oil

A few sprigs of thyme, leaves only

1 garlic clove (unpeeled), bashed

First, make the chile oil. Put the chiles in a small saucepan with the olive oil, thyme leaves, and unpeeled garlic clove. Heat slowly until the oil is bubbling very, very gently and cook the chiles until soft, about 20 minutes. Remove from the heat and let cool.

For the soup, halve the leeks lengthwise, wash well, and slice thinly. Heat the olive oil and butter in a saucepan over medium-low heat. Add the leeks with the thyme and bay leaf, and sweat gently, stirring from time to time, for about 15 minutes, until very soft. Add the garlic and stir for a minute.

Add the stock and cannellini beans, the oregano, and half of the parsley. Season with salt and plenty of pepper, increase the heat, and bring to a simmer. Cook gently for 20 minutes.

Remove the bay leaf, taste the soup, and adjust the seasoning if necessary. Stir in the rest of the parsley. Serve in warmed bowls with a trickle of chile oil over the top.

Curried sweet potato soup ♥

This is a warming soup for a cold evening. The heat of the spices is softened by the sweetness of the coconut milk and lime.

SERVES 4 TO 6

2 tablespoons olive or canola oil

2 onions, chopped

4 garlic cloves, finely chopped

1 (2-inch / 5cm) piece of ginger, peeled and grated

1 or 2 fresh red chiles, to taste, seeded and finely chopped

1 tablespoon garam masala

2 teaspoons curry powder

3 sweet potatoes (about 1½ pounds / 700g), peeled and cut into ¾-inch / 2cm dice

Sea salt and freshly ground black pepper

1 quart / liter vegetable stock (see page 130)

1 (14-ounce / 400ml) can coconut milk

A small handful of cilantro, coarsely chopped

Juice of 1 or 2 limes (a good tablespoonful)

TO FINISH

A few tablespoons plain full-fat yogurt (optional)

A small handful of cilantro, coarsely torn

Freshly ground black pepper

Heat the oil in a saucepan over medium-low heat. Add the onions and sauté for about 10 minutes, until soft and translucent. Add the garlic, ginger, chiles, garam masala, and curry powder and stir for a minute.

Tip in the sweet potatoes and stir until they're well coated with the spices. Add some salt and pepper and pour in the stock. Increase the heat and bring to a simmer. Cook gently until the sweet potatoes are very tender, about 15 minutes.

Remove from the heat, let cool slightly, and then purée the soup in a blender or food processor, or with an immersion blender, until very smooth. Return to the pan, stir in the coconut milk, and warm through gently.

Remove from the heat and add the cilantro and lime juice. Taste and adjust the seasoning if necessary. Serve the soup topped with a good dollop of yogurt, if you like, and scatter over some torn cilantro. Finish with a little black pepper.

VARIATION

Curried red lentil soup ♥

Sweat the onions as above, but add some chopped carrot and celery, and a couple of bay leaves. Add the aromatics and spices, along with 1 cup / 180g red lentils (in place of the sweet potatoes). Pour in about 5 cups / 1.2 liters vegetable stock and simmer for 25 to 30 minutes until the lentils are very soft. Remove the bay leaves, then purée until very smooth. Return to the pan, add the juice of ½ lemon, season with salt and pepper, and warm through gently. If the soup is a little thick, thin with some hot water. Serve, as above, topped with yogurt, if you like, and cilantro. A sprinkle of cumin seeds, lightly toasted in a dry frying pan, is a lovely finishing touch.

Bready things

For the versatile cook, bread is not just there to mop up the juice on the plate, although of course it will always be welcome to perform that role. It's a useful and adaptable ingredient in its own right. And when you concentrate more on vegetables in your cooking, and less on meat, the importance of bread is greater still, as is its potential.

Bread has always been a good friend to the vegetable eater. Take a look at cultures that rely primarily on vegetarian food and you'll often find that they have developed an exciting range of breads to complement it. I'm thinking particularly of the Indian subcontinent, where so many regions are largely meat-free, and where you will find puris, parathas, rotis, naans, and chapatis. From here on you, too, should feel entitled to ask a bit more of your bread – and as long as it's good bread, it won't let you down.

For many of us, bread-based meals were the first we learned how to make, and are the ones we return to time and again when we need good, comforting food, fast – we know a slice of hot buttered toast or a cheese and pickle sandwich will always fill the gap. We may have a few marginally more complex bready recipes up our sleeves, too – cheese on toast, mushrooms on toast, garlic bread, maybe bruschetta – but these hardly scratch the surface. It's time to find out how bread, so often the sidekick, will happily carry the show if given the chance.

This is an ingredient that generally requires little preparation – beyond removing the loaf from the bread box and sawing off a slice. The problem is, when it comes to using bread, we're too bound by convention and habit. As the toast with your pâté, the roll with your soup, even the bit of baguette you nibble at in a restaurant while waiting for the real meal to arrive, bread is part of our culinary vernacular. We take it for granted. We are all guilty of having low expectations of bread: we make do with the mediocre stuff, and we get by without asking too much of it. But, actually, if you change your tactics and challenge your loaf a little more often, it will reward you by bringing many delicious new things to your table.

Think of bread less as a journeyman accompaniment, more as a blank canvas waiting to be turned into something fine, and you will soon discover some simple, delicious new dishes. I would say that half a good loaf on the breadboard puts you as close to a satisfying meat-free meal as a package of pasta simmering in a pan.

Start with what you know and work upward and outward from there. If you like cheese on toast, try adding a few leftover vegetables, or some gently sautéed fresh ones, and before long you'll be rolling out all kinds of toothsome toasties and rarefied rarebits. If you love pizza, put aside your default toppings – the mozzarella and even the tomato sauce – and explore the delightfully creative alternatives the vegetable garden can provide. New potatoes and blue cheese, anyone? If a filled wrap is a familiar lunch, think how much better you can do with fresh ingredients at home, experimenting with veggie foldovers, maybe even using homemade flat breads (see page 176). And I'm certainly not sniffy about sandwiches: try a couple of my favorites (on page 195); or turn to page 402 for a list of the recipes from the book that can be turned into fantastic fillings.

None of these adventures will be fulfilling, of course, if the quality of the bread itself is not top-notch. It doesn't matter how good your rarebit topping is – if you put it on some pappy white-sliced-from-a-package, you won't get pleasing results. So take the time to look for bread with character and substance. Sourdough is a real favorite of mine, not just for its flavor but for its robust, open texture: it responds so well to being toasted then generously topped. But there are other good-quality breads to be had: a proper pullman loaf or rye bread from the bakery, as well as the baguettes, ciabatta, focaccia, and fougasses that have come our way from the bread-loving continent of Europe. Don't forget flat breads, naans, and pitas either – different sizes, shapes, and densities point to different culinary possibilities.

Of course, exploring meat-free meals could even be the spur you need to turn to baking your own bread, if you haven't already. I can't recommend it highly enough. In *River Cottage Every Day*, I explained how my own baking odyssey unfolded as I went from a bread novice, rather wary of the whole mixing, kneading, rising, and baking palaver, to someone who now eats homemade bread – usually homemade sourdough – almost every day of the week. I'll concede that sourdough does require a certain amount of commitment, but it's by no means the only sort of bread worth making at home. In fact, if you want one recipe that's very simple, very versatile, and almost immediately rewarding (taking you from dry ingredients to hot, oil-trickled flat breads in little more than an hour), my magic bread dough will do the trick. Which is why it's the first recipe in this chapter.

Magic bread dough🍃

I call this "magic" because it can grant you so many wishes. It is one of those recipes that can be turned to any manner of different endings – all of them delicious. The tender bread dough, made with half bread flour and half all-purpose flour, is perfect for the pizza recipes on the following pages. In addition, it makes the most irresistible flat breads, pita breads, breadsticks, and even, if you have any left, soft bread rolls or a simple white loaf. You can also freeze it, either raw or baked, which is why I suggest never making it in less than the following quantity. It's also very easy, and very worthwhile, to simply double the measurements.

MAKES 3 PIZZAS, 8 FLAT BREADS, 12 PITAS, OR UMPTEEN BREADSTICKS

2 cups / 250g all-purpose flour

2 cups / 250g bread flour

1¹/₂ teaspoons fine sea salt

1 teaspoon instant dried yeast

1 tablespoon canola or olive oil, plus a little extra for oiling

1¹/₃ cups / 325ml warm water

Put the two flours into a large bowl with the salt and yeast. Mix well. Add the oil and warm water and mix to a rough dough. Flour your hands a little. Tip out the dough onto a work surface and knead rhythmically for 5 to 10 minutes, until smooth. This is quite a loose and sticky dough, which is just as it should be – you get better-textured bread this way – so try not to add too much flour if you can help it. It will become less sticky as you knead.

Trickle a little oil into a clean bowl, add the kneaded dough, and turn it in the oil so it is covered with a light film. Cover with a kitchen towel and leave in a warm place to rise until doubled in size – at least an hour, probably closer to two. You can also proof it in a floured, cloth-lined proofing basket or banneton, like the one in the picture.

When the dough is well risen and puffy, tip it out and "punch it down" by poking it with your outstretched fingers until it collapses to its former size. It's now ready to be shaped to your will.

CONTINUED

Pizzas

The dough makes 3 pizzas, each large enough to serve 2 or 3 people. Follow the instructions in the individual pizza recipes (on pages 180–86).

Flat breads ♥

The dough makes about 8 flat breads. Follow the recipe on page 176, omitting the garlicky oil for plain flat breads, or if you are using them for wraps or foldovers.

Pita breads ♥

Take egg-sized balls of punched-down dough and roll them out on a floured surface into oval shapes no more than ¼ inch / 5mm thick. Transfer to a greased baking sheet and leave to rise for 10 to 15 minutes, then bake at 425°F / 220°C for about 8 minutes, until puffed up and just starting to brown. Remove from the oven and immediately wrap the pita breads in a clean kitchen towel. Leave to cool completely before unwrapping (the trapped steam keeps the pitas soft).

Breadsticks ♥

After punching down, take walnut-sized pieces of dough and roll them out into long, thin rods. Place on a lightly greased baking sheet. Leave to rise for 10 to 15 minutes, then bake at 400°F / 200°C for about 10 minutes. Cool on a rack.

Rolls ♥

Take roughly lemon-sized chunks of punched-down dough (about 4 ounces / 125g each) and shape into neat rounds. Place these on a baking sheet and leave until doubled in size – an hour or so. Bake at 425°F / 220°C for 15 minutes, until risen and golden.

River Cottage garlicky flat breads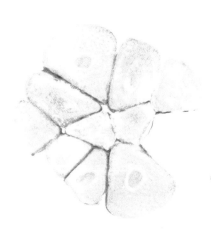

This is perhaps the easiest way to use my magic bread dough. Once you've got the dough risen and punched down, you're just minutes away from these smoky, hot, oily, salty, garlicky rounds. Serve them with any kind of dip or hummus, or alongside soup, or with saucy dishes like chachouka (see page 20) or caponata (see page 307). I bet you won't be able to resist snaffling one or two bits before you've even got them to the table, though . . .

This is also the recipe to follow for making plain flat breads – perfect for the foldovers and wraps on pages 188–93, and surprisingly good used as the base of a toasted sandwich. Just leave out the garlicky oil bit.

MAKES 8 FLAT BREADS

1 recipe magic bread dough (see page 172)

A little flaky sea salt

FOR THE GARLIC OIL

About ½ cup / 120ml olive oil

1 fat garlic clove, very finely chopped

First make the garlic oil: combine the olive oil and garlic in a frying pan and place over medium heat. You're not going to fry the garlic, just warm it through to take off the raw edge. So as soon as you see the first signs of a sizzle, pour the oil and garlic out of the pan into a small bowl and leave to cool and infuse for a few minutes.

After punching down the risen dough, take lemon-sized balls (around 4 ounces / 125g each) and roll them out into rough circles, ⅛ inch / 2 to 3mm thick. Leave to rest for 5 minutes. Meanwhile, heat a heavy-bottomed, nonstick frying pan over very high heat until smoking hot (I always find it's worth opening the windows or switching on the hood vent at this point).

Lay one flat bread in the pan and cook for about 2 minutes, until bubbly on top and patched with brown spots (even a touch black) on the bottom. Flip it over and cook for 1 to 2 minutes more until patchily browned on the other side, too. Remove immediately to a warmed plate and trickle with some of the garlicky oil. Scatter with a little sea salt, too, if you like. Repeat with all the dough. Cut the oiled flat breads into wedges to serve.

It's worth using the whole quantity of dough, even if it makes more flat breads than you need right away. Extras can be wrapped in a clean kitchen towel and left until cool. The trapped steam will keep the flat breads soft, and they will make great wraps or bases for various toppings. Either way, eat them within 24 hours, or freeze.

Crostini [V]

Crostini are a fantastic way to use up good bread that's heading toward staleness. I make them most often with sourdough or a good-quality baguette, but any decent, fairly open-textured bread will work. Thinly cut and lightly baked, the bread becomes crunchy, crisp, and delicious, and is the perfect vehicle for all manner of toppings. I prefer to stick to fairly finely chopped or puréed toppings – pâtés and dips, pestos or tapenades, or chunky pastes such as fava bean purée (see below for specific suggestions). You could also serve crostini plain, simply for preprandial munching, or alongside soup, or break them into rough shards for use as a kind of crouton in salads.

Slightly stale, good-quality, robust bread

Olive or canola oil

Sea salt

Preheat the oven to 400°F / 200°C. Slice the bread very thinly – to a ¼-inch / 5mm maximum thickness. Depending on what kind of loaf you are slicing from, you may want to cut larger slices into halves or quarters. If you want small crostini – perhaps to present with various toppings as party food – then cut the slices to the size you want before you bake then. Once baked, they'll be too crisp to cut and will shatter if you try.

Arrange the slices on a baking sheet (or two), as close together as possible. Brush or trickle each slice with oil and sprinkle with a little salt. Bake for 5 to 8 minutes. The slices should be golden and crisp, with still a little bit of give in the center; they will crisp up further as they cool. Leave to cool, then add your chosen topping(s). I like to place my toppings over one half of the crostini, leaving the other half uncovered for a final, topping-free, palate-cleansing crunch.

The crostini will keep at room temperature in an airtight container for a couple of days.

TOPPINGS

Refried beans (page 190) • Garlicky fava bean purée (page 196)
Crushed garlicky zucchini (page 200) • Pesto (page 256) • Mint pesto (page 266)
Carrot hummus (page 296) • Lemony guacamole (page 296)
Cambodian wedding day dip (page 299) • Beet and walnut hummus (page 300)
Cannellini bean hummus (page 300) • Artichoke and white bean dip (page 303)
Baba ganoush (page 303) • Caponata (page 307) • Herbed goat cheese (page 316)
Romesco (page 336) • Garlicky, minty mushy peas (page 387)

Beet pizza with cheddar

I like this smoky-sweet pizza with a slick of tomato sauce on the base. You can use any one of the sauces on page 58, 362, or 366; a good bought tomato sauce; or even a tablespoon or two of good-quality concentrated tomato paste. Then again, it really wouldn't be the end of the world if you left off the tomato altogether. The beets need to be cooked before you start: just scrub a root or two; enfold in a loose foil parcel with some garlic, thyme, and a slosh of oil; and roast at 400°F / 200°C for about an hour.

MAKES 3 PIZZAS, EACH SERVING 2 OR 3

1 recipe magic bread dough (see page 172)

FOR THE TOPPING

3 tablespoons olive oil, plus a little extra to trickle

2 onions, halved and thinly sliced

Sea salt and freshly ground black pepper

5 to 6 tablespoons tomato sauce or a bit less tomato paste (see above)

About 5 ounces / 150g cooked, skinned beets (not pickled), thickly sliced

2½ ounces / 75g medium-sharp cheddar, grated

1 ball of buffalo mozzarella (about 4 ounces / 125g)

Prepare the dough, leave it to rise, and then punch it down according to the instructions on page 172.

While the dough is rising, heat the olive oil in a frying pan over medium heat and add the onions. Once sizzling, decrease the heat to low and cook gently, stirring from time to time, until the onions are soft and golden, about 15 minutes. Season with salt and pepper.

Preheat the oven to 500°F / 250°C, if it goes that high, or to at least 425°F / 220°C. Put in a baking sheet to heat up.

After punching down the risen dough, leave it to rest for a few minutes, then cut it into three. Roll out one piece as thinly as you can.

Scatter a baking peel (if you have one) or another baking sheet with a little flour and place the rolled-out dough on it. Spread one-third of the tomato sauce very thinly over the dough, then spread over one-third of the onions. Distribute one-third of the beet pieces over the onions, then one-third of the grated cheese. Scatter over one-third of the mozzarella, tearing it into small pieces, then season with salt and pepper. Trickle with a little olive oil.

Slide the pizza onto the hot baking sheet in the oven if formed on a peel, or if formed on a baking sheet, simply lay the baking sheet on the hot one in the oven. Bake for 10 to 12 minutes, until the crust is crisp and the top bubbling and golden. Repeat with the remaining dough and topping. Serve hot, cut into wedges.

Pizza with new potatoes, rosemary, and blue cheese

This pizza really packs a punch and is a lovely way to use up leftover new potatoes. It definitely wants some salad standing by – I love it served with a big, tangled pile of arugula. As ever, for those who are not wild about blue cheese, a crumbly goat cheese or a combination of ricotta and Parmesan makes a good alternative.

**MAKES 3 PIZZAS,
EACH SERVING 2 OR 3**

1 recipe magic bread dough
(see page 172)

FOR THE TOPPING

3 tablespoons canola or olive oil, plus a little extra to trickle

2 onions, halved and thinly sliced

2 garlic cloves, finely chopped

2 tablespoons finely chopped rosemary

Sea salt and freshly ground black pepper

About 7 ounces / 200g cold, cooked new potatoes, cut into ⅛-inch / 3mm thick slices

5 ounces / 150g blue cheese, crumbled or coarsely sliced

Prepare the dough, leave it to rise, and then punch it down according to the instructions on page 172.

Preheat the oven to 500°F / 250°C, if it goes that high, or to at least 425°F / 220°C. Put in a baking sheet to heat up.

While the dough is rising, heat the oil in a frying pan over medium heat and add the onions. Once sizzling, lower the heat and cook gently, stirring from time to time, until they are soft and golden, about 15 minutes. Turn off the heat and stir in the garlic, rosemary, and some salt and pepper.

After punching down the risen dough, leave it to rest for a few minutes, then cut it into three. Roll out one piece as thinly as you can.

Scatter a baking peel (if you have one) or another baking sheet with a little flour and place the rolled-out dough on it. Spread one-third of the onion mixture evenly over the dough, then one-third of the potato slices, then one-third of the cheese. Sprinkle with salt and pepper and trickle with a little oil.

Slide the pizza on to the hot baking sheet in the oven if formed on a peel, or, if formed on a baking sheet, simply lay the baking sheet on the hot one in the oven. Bake for 10 to 12 minutes until the crust is crisp and the top bubbling. Repeat with the remaining dough and topping. Serve at once, in generous slices, with lots of arugula or green salad.

Asparagus pizza

Roasting asparagus on top of a pizza in a super-hot oven makes it deliciously tender and a bit caramelized. Use slender spears that will cook through quickly – or, if you only have thick spears, halve them lengthwise.

**MAKES 3 PIZZAS,
EACH SERVING 2 OR 3**

1 recipe magic bread dough
(see page 172)

FOR THE TOPPING

3 tablespoons olive oil, plus a little extra to trickle

2 onions, halved and thinly sliced

Sea salt and freshly ground black pepper

About 12 ounces / 350g slender asparagus spears, trimmed

2 balls of buffalo mozzarella (about 4 ounces / 125g each)

A little grated Parmesan, hard goat cheese, or other well-flavored hard cheese

Prepare the dough, leave it to rise, and then punch it down according to the instructions on page 172.

Preheat the oven to 500°F / 250°C, if it goes that high, or to at least 425°F / 220°C. Put in a baking sheet to heat up.

While the dough is rising, heat the olive oil in a frying pan over medium heat and add the onions. Once sizzling, decrease the heat to low and cook gently, stirring from time to time, until the onions are soft and golden, about 15 minutes. Season with salt and pepper.

After punching down the risen dough, leave it to rest for a few minutes, then cut it into three. Roll out one piece as thinly as you can.

Scatter a baking peel (if you have one) or another baking sheet with a little flour and place the rolled-out dough on it. Spread one-third of the onions over the dough, then arrange one-third of the asparagus over the top. Tear up the mozzarella and distribute one-third of it over the asparagus. Scatter over a little grated cheese, some salt and pepper, and add a generous trickle of oil.

Slide the pizza onto the hot baking sheet in the oven if formed on a a peel, or, if formed on a baking sheet, simply lay the baking sheet on the hot one in the oven. Bake for 10 to 12 minutes, until the crust is crisp, the edges browned, and the asparagus tender. Repeat with the remaining dough and topping. Serve hot, cut into slices or wedges.

Kale and onion pizza

There's no tomato here because I like to emphasize the more unusual flavor of the kale. In the heat of the oven, the kale becomes crisp and dark, and takes on a flavor not dissimilar to that delicious deep-fried "seaweed" you can get in Chinese restaurants in the UK. I sometimes add a few sautéed sliced mushrooms to the pizza before it goes into the oven.

**MAKES 3 PIZZAS,
EACH SERVING 2 OR 3**

1 recipe magic bread dough
(see page 172)

FOR THE TOPPING

A 10-ounce / 300g bunch of
curly or Lacinato kale, stems
removed

3 tablespoons canola or olive
oil, plus a little extra to trickle

2 onions, halved and thinly
sliced

2 garlic cloves, finely slivered

Sea salt and freshly ground
black pepper

About 3½ ounces / 100g mature
cheddar, grated

Prepare the dough, leave it to rise, and then punch it down according to the instructions on page 172.

Preheat the oven to 500°F / 250°C, if it goes that high, or to at least 425°F / 220°C. Put in a baking sheet to heat up.

While the dough is rising, shred the kale leaves into ¼ to ⅓-inch / ½ to 1cm wide ribbons. Heat the oil in a frying pan over medium heat and add the onions. Once sizzling, decrease the heat to low and cook gently, stirring from time to time, until the onions are soft and golden, 10 to 15 minutes, adding the garlic halfway through. Stir the shredded kale into the onions and cook for a further 5 minutes, stirring often, until the leaves have wilted. Season with salt and pepper.

After punching down the risen dough, leave it to rest for a few minutes, then cut it into three pieces. Roll out one piece as thinly as you can.

Scatter a baking peel (if you have one) or another baking sheet with a little flour and place the rolled-out dough on it. Spread one-third of the kale and one-third of the onions on the dough, then top with one-third of the grated cheddar. Trickle with a little oil.

Slide the pizza onto the hot baking sheet in the oven if formed on a peel, or, if formed on a baking sheet, simply lay the baking sheet on the hot one in the oven. Bake for 10 to 12 minutes, until the crust is crisp and golden. Repeat with the remaining dough and topping. Serve hot, cut into wedges.

Hot squash fold over

Foldovers are a great way to use freshly made flat breads (though you can stuff any foldover filling into a warm pita bread with very pleasing results).

Roasting a small pan of squash is so easy, and can be done while the bread dough is rising so, although I couldn't honestly call this a quick meal, it's certainly a very straightforward one. The onion, salad greens, chile, and cheese allow you to "dress" this as though it were a kebab – feel free to customize it further, to your taste. Dukka, the spicy seed mix on page 294, is a great addition.

SERVES 4

1 pound / 500g squash or pumpkin, peeled, seeded, and cut into bite-sized chunks

3 garlic cloves (unpeeled), bashed

1 sprig of thyme, leaves only

2 tablespoons canola or olive oil

Sea salt and freshly ground black pepper

4 freshly cooked, soft flat breads (see page 176)

A handful of arugula or other salad greens

1 small red onion, finely chopped (optional)

1 fresh red chile, seeded and finely chopped, or a dash of chile sauce

2 ounces / 60g hard goat cheese or cheddar, grated

Extra-virgin olive oil, to trickle

Preheat the oven to 375°F / 190°C. Put the squash in a roasting pan with the garlic, thyme leaves, oil, and plenty of salt and pepper. Toss together well and roast for 50 to 60 minutes, stirring once, until the sqush is soft and caramelized.

Lay one flat bread on a board. Place a few salad greens in the center, then spoon on one-quarter of the hot squash. Sprinkle over one-quarter each of the onion, if using, chile, and cheese. Season with salt and pepper and finish with a trickle of extra-virgin olive oil. Fold or roll the flat bread tightly, enclosing the filling. Repeat with the remaining flat breads and filling.

Leave the foldovers for a minute or two before eating, so the cheese starts to melt.

VARIATIONS

You can do the same thing with all sorts of other roasted vegetables, including roasted potatoes or eggplant – or potatoes *and* eggplant (see page 351). A hot roasted beet foldover, with some sour cream or plain yogurt instead of the cheese, is also quite delicious.

Refried beans foldover

This Mexican-inspired foldover – a kind of burrito, really – is deliciously savory and satisfying. It's particularly good with some avocado inside or alongside – or you could make a quick guacamole. There are various other optional extras, listed below, that you can stuff in with the beans to make the foldover even more tempting.

SERVES 3

2 tablespoons canola or olive oil

1 small onion, finely chopped

1 garlic clove, chopped

½ fresh red chile, seeded and chopped

A pinch of dried oregano (optional)

1 large or 2 medium tomatoes

1 (14-ounce / 400g) can cannellini or borlotti beans, drained and rinsed

Sea salt and freshly ground black pepper

Cayenne pepper or hot smoked paprika (optional)

3 freshly cooked, soft flat breads (see page 176)

2 to 3 tablespoons sour cream

OPTIONAL EXTRAS

Grated cheddar or hard goat cheese

Thinly sliced red onion

Sliced pickled chiles

Sliced or diced avocado, or lemony guacamole (see page 296)

Cayenne pepper or hot smoked paprika

Heat the oil in a small frying pan over medium heat. Add the onion and sauté for about 10 minutes, until soft, adding the garlic and chile a few minutes before the end, along with the oregano, if using.

Halve the tomato(es) and grate the flesh directly into the pan (discard the skin), then let the mixture bubble and reduce for a few minutes. Add the beans and cook gently, crushing them down with a fork to make a coarse purée. Season well with salt and pepper and add a pinch of cayenne or hot smoked paprika if you like things spicy.

Lay out the flat breads on a board and put a spoonful of the bean mixture in the center of each. Top with a dollop or two of sour cream and any optional extras that you fancy. Fold and eat.

VARIATION
Nachos with refried beans
Instead of flat bread, by all means open a bag of tortilla chips and use them to scoop the beans. The sour cream and optional extras all still apply.

Spicy carrot and chickpea pita pocket

This is one of those recipes that transforms everyday fridge and pantry staples into something special. The chickpeas don't dominate: they provide a nutty, creamy counterpoint to the spiced, buttery carrots that are the stars of the show. You can also serve the mixture on bruschetta or in a foldover – or indeed bread-free as part of a vegetable meze-style feast.

SERVES 4

2 tablespoons / 60g butter

1 tablespoon canola or olive oil

1 heaped teaspoon cumin seeds

4 large carrots (about 1 pound / 500g), peeled and cut into ⅛-inch / 3mm thick slices

1 large garlic clove, thinly sliced

Finely grated zest of 1 orange, plus a good squeeze of juice

1 teaspoon hot smoked paprika

1 (14-ounce / 400g) can chickpeas, drained and rinsed

Sea salt and freshly ground black pepper

4 pita breads, cut in half and split open

4 heaping tablespoons plain full-fat yogurt or sour cream

Heat the butter and oil in a frying pan over medium heat. Add the cumin seeds and let them fry for a minute or two. Add the carrots and fry for 8 to 10 minutes, stirring often, until tender and starting to brown, but still with some bite.

Add the garlic, orange zest, paprika, and chickpeas and cook until the chickpeas are heated through. Remove from the heat, season with salt and pepper, and add the orange juice. Taste and add more salt, pepper, and/or orange juice as needed.

Spoon some of the carrot mixture into the pocket of each warmed pita half and top with a spoonful of yogurt or sour cream. Serve right away.

Two veggie sandwiches

Do I really need to tell you how to make a sandwich? Of course I don't – but I can certainly give you a few ideas for some great veg-based fillings. On page 402, you'll find a list of the many recipes in this book that can be put to good use in a sandwich. But here are two of my other favorite bespoke veggie fillings.

Mushroom, watercress, and blue cheese

Hot, garlicky fried mushrooms make a substantial sandwich filling, especially when coupled with a tangy, creamy blue cheese, such as Roquefort.

SERVES 1

2 portobello mushrooms, trimmed

A little softened butter

A dash of olive or canola oil

½ garlic clove, chopped

Sea salt and freshly ground black pepper

About 2 ounces / 60g blue cheese

A little yogurt or crème fraîche

A good handful of watercress

2 slices of whole-grain bread

Thickly slice the mushrooms. Heat a small knob of the butter with the oil in a frying pan over medium heat. Add the mushrooms, garlic, and some salt and pepper, and fry until tender and nicely browned.

Meanwhile, crumble the blue cheese and combine with a little yogurt or crème fraîche. Remove any tough stems from the watercress. Butter one side of both slices of bread.

Put the cheese mixture on the buttered side of one piece of bread, top with the hot mushrooms, and finish with the watercress. Add the second slice of bread, buttered side down, cut the sandwich in half, and serve.

Curried egg, lentils, and flat-leaf parsley

Lentils in a sandwich? Why not? The curried mayonnaise and egg hold them nicely, giving you a lovely textured mouthful. Include the raisins for a little fruity sweetness.

SERVES 1

1 large hard-boiled egg, peeled

½ to 1 tablespoon mayonnaise

½ to 1 teaspoon curry powder

1 to 2 tablespoons cooked, cold French green lentils

A few raisins (optional)

Sea salt and freshly ground black pepper

2 slices of bread

A little softened butter

A handful of flat-leaf parsley, or lettuce or baby spinach leaves

Coarsely chop the hard-boiled egg and mix with the mayonnaise and curry powder, then stir in the lentils, and raisins, if using. Season with salt and pepper to taste – and mix in a little more mayo if you want to loosen the mixture a bit.

Lightly butter one side of each slice of bread. Spread the eggy mixture on the buttered side of one slice, then top with the parsley leaves, lettuce, or spinach. Add the second slice of bread, buttered side down, and close the sandwich. Slice in half and serve.

Bruschetta with fava beans and asparagus

This is a fantastic celebration of the crossover between the last of the asparagus and the first baby fava beans. Later, in the summer, you can use a few green beans, just blanched and still crunchy, instead of the asparagus.

SERVES 4

12 to 15 asparagus spears, trimmed

7 ounces / 200g shelled baby fava beans

A bunch of green onions

2 tablespoons olive oil

Sea salt and freshly ground black pepper

4 large slices of sourdough or other robust bread

1 garlic clove, halved (optional)

Extra-virgin olive oil, to trickle

About 2 ounces / 60g mild, crumbly goat cheese

Bring a pan of salted water to a boil, add the asparagus spears, and blanch for 2 minutes. Scoop them out and drain. Let the water come back to a boil. Now add the baby fava beans and blanch for just 30 to 60 seconds until tender, then drain.

Trim the green onions, leaving just a little of the green ends attached. Slice on the diagonal into ½-inch / 1cm pieces. Heat the olive oil in a frying pan over medium heat, add the onions, and fry fairly gently for 2 to 3 minutes, until just starting to soften.

Cut the asparagus spears into 1-inch / 2 to 3cm pieces and add them, along with the fava beans, to the onions in the pan. Add salt and pepper and toss the whole lot together for just a minute, then remove from the heat.

Meanwhile, toast the bread. Rub very lightly with the garlic, if you like. Trickle the toast with a little olive oil. Crumble the goat cheese over the veg in the pan and stir very lightly again. Pile the mixture onto the toast, trickle with a touch more olive oil, and serve.

VARIATION
Bruschetta with garlicky fava bean purée, ricotta, and mint
This works with larger, more starchy fava beans or frozen ones. Cook 1⅓ pounds / 600g shelled fava beans in boiling water until tender. Drain and, as soon as they are cool enough to handle, pop the beans out of their skins. Melt 2 tablespoons / 30g unsalted butter with 2 tablespoons canola or olive oil over very low heat, add 2 finely chopped garlic cloves, and warm gently for a minute or two. Add the beans to the garlicky butter and then blitz to a coarse purée in a food processor. Add a little more butter if needed. Pile the warm purée onto the hot toasted bread, prepared as above, then scatter over 2 ounces / 60g crumbled ricotta salata, a trickle of extra-virgin oil, and some chopped mint.

Tomato bruschetta 🌱

This is one of the best ways to enjoy really ripe, flavorsome tomatoes – any kind from tiny cherries to big, beefy slicers. You can add cheese if you want to – shaved hard goat cheese, perhaps, or torn buffalo mozzarella – but it's very good just as it is.

SERVES 2

8 ounces / 250g ripe, sweet tomatoes

2 tablespoons extra-virgin olive oil, plus extra to trickle

A pinch of sugar

Sea salt and freshly ground black pepper

2 large slices of sourdough or other robust bread

1 garlic clove, halved

A handful of basil, coarsely torn, or chives, chopped

Cut the tomatoes into small chunks. For cherry tomatoes, this generally means quarters – or eighths if they are on the larger side. Big tomatoes should be cut into similarly small pieces – slice them thickly, then cut the slices into 6 to 8 pieces. Put the tomatoes in a bowl with the olive oil, a pinch of sugar, and plenty of salt and pepper. Toss together well.

Toast the bread and, while still hot, rub lightly with the halved garlic clove. Trickle the toast with a little oil. Pile the tomatoes onto the toast, scatter over the basil or chives, trickle over a little more oil, then serve right away.

Celery and blue cheese bruschetta

Much as I love celery in a supporting role, I like to see it as the star ingredient from time to time. Avoid using the outer stalks, which may be a bit coarse and fibrous – save those for stocks. If you don't fancy blue cheese, use goat cheese or Parmesan.

SERVES 2

3 or 4 celery stalks

2 slices of sourdough or other robust bread

1 garlic clove, halved

Canola or extra-virgin olive oil, to trickle

About 2 ounces / 60g blue cheese, crumbled

Sea salt and freshly ground black pepper

1 to 2 teaspoons clear honey

Check out the celery by snapping a stalk in half. If it's a bit too fibrous, use a potato peeler to strip the tougher fibers from the outside of the stalks. Thinly slice the celery on the diagonal.

Toast the bread. While still hot, rub lightly with the halved garlic clove. Trickle over a little oil, then pile the celery onto the toast. Scatter on the crumbled cheese, then some salt and pepper, and finish with a fine trickle of honey. Serve right away.

Bruschetta with lacinato kale

Cabbage on toast? Try it. This is a simple way to appreciate the earthy taste of lovely, dark Lacinato kale. If you can't get that particular leaf, any good kale will work – or chard leaves or the greener outer leaves of a savoy cabbage.

SERVES 2

About 5 ounces / 150g Lacinato kale

1 large garlic clove

Sea salt and freshly ground black pepper

2 slices of sourdough or other robust bread

1 to 2 tablespoons extra-virgin canola or olive oil

Parmesan, hard goat cheese, or other well-flavored hard cheese shavings

Strip the kale leaves from their stems and put the leaves into a saucepan. Cut off a third of the garlic clove and set aside; coarsely chop the rest and add to the pan. Cover with water, add salt, and bring to a boil. Lower the heat and simmer for 4 to 5 minutes – a little longer if need be – until the kale is tender. Drain well in a colander.

Tip the kale and garlic onto a board and chop together coarsely. Return to the hot pan, season well with salt and pepper, and toss in a tablespoon or so of oil.

Toast the bread under the broiler and, while still hot, rub lightly with the reserved bit of garlic clove. Trickle with a little more oil. Pile the kale and cheese shavings onto the bread and serve.

Zucchini bruschetta

This old favorite appears in the original River Cottage Cookbook. *Garlicky, slightly bashed-up zucchini remains one of my all-time favorite toppings for bruschetta.*

SERVES 2

2 tablespoons olive or canola oil

9 ounces / 250g small zucchini, sliced

1 small garlic clove, crushed, plus another, halved, for the bread

Sea salt and freshly ground black pepper

A squeeze of lemon juice

2 thick slices of robust bread, such as sourdough

Extra-virgin canola or olive oil, to trickle

1 or 2 sprigs of thyme, leaves only

1 to 2 ounces / 30 to 60g mild, crumbly goat cheese

Heat the oil in a large frying pan over medium heat, then add the zucchini, the crushed garlic, and a pinch of salt. Once sizzling, turn down the heat a little and cook, stirring often, for at least 15 minutes, until the zucchini are very soft. You want to drive off their moisture without letting them brown. As they start to soften, you can bash them up a bit with a spatula or spoon. When you have a concentrated, tender, zucchini-ish mess, remove from the heat.

Season with a little more salt if necessary, plus some black pepper and a squeeze of lemon juice. Leave the zucchini to cool slightly while you prepare the bread.

Toast the bread and, while still hot, rub lightly with the halved garlic clove. Trickle with some extra-virgin olive oil, then pile the zucchini on top. Sprinkle over the thyme leaves and crumble over the goat cheese. Add a final trickle of oil and serve.

Leek and cheese toastie

Over the years, I've experimented with and improvised all kinds of leek-based, cheesy toast toppings. Most of them have been a delight, if I may say so myself, but this is perhaps the simplest and most midweek-friendly.

SERVES 2

1 tablespoon / 15g butter

2 medium leeks, trimmed (white and pale green parts only) and sliced

A couple of sprigs of thyme, leaves only, coarsely chopped (optional)

3 tablespoons heavy cream

About 2 ounces / 60g strong cheddar, grated

Sea salt and freshly ground black pepper

2 thick slices of sourdough or other robust bread

Melt the butter in a small frying pan over medium heat and add the leeks. As soon as they are sizzling, turn down the heat and sweat gently, stirring often, for about 10 minutes, until tender. Stir in the thyme, if using, and the cream and cook for a minute or two longer, until the cream is bubbling. Remove from the heat and stir in two-thirds of the cheese. Add salt and pepper to taste.

Preheat the broiler and broil the bread until lightly toasted. Spread the leek mixture thickly over the bread and top with the remaining grated cheese. Broil until bubbling and golden, and serve right away.

Squash and walnut toastie

If you're roasting squash or pumpkin, do a little extra and have this quick lunch the day after. You could use other leftover roasted veg, too, such as celery root, beets, or carrots, and different nuts, such as hazelnuts, cashews, or pine nuts. No nuts is fine, too . . .

SERVES 2

A handful of walnuts

1 tablespoon canola or olive oil

1 tablespoon butter

About 8 ounces / 200 to 250g leftover roasted squash or pumpkin

A couple of sprigs of thyme, leaves only (optional)

About 2 ounces / 60g blue cheese (or cheddar or goat cheese), crumbled

Sea salt and freshly ground black pepper

2 slices of sourdough or other robust bread

A trickle of clear honey

Heat a nonstick frying pan over medium heat. Add the walnuts and toast gently, tossing the pan, for a few minutes, until they start to smell toasty and take on a little color. Tip out of the pan; set aside.

Return the pan to the heat and add the oil and butter. When foaming, add the squash and cook for 3 to 4 minutes, crushing it down a bit, until heated through. Stir in the thyme, if using, then remove from the heat. Add the nuts and the crumbled cheese and stir into the squash. Taste and add a little salt and some pepper if you think it needs it.

Preheat the broiler and lightly toast the bread. Pile the squash mixture on to the bread, packing it down a little and making sure some chunks of cheese are on top. Trickle over a little honey and broil until golden brown and bubbling. Serve right away, with some salad greens if you like.

Apple and blue cheese toastie

This simple blend of tart apple and salty, savory cheese is immensely satisfying, and makes a great quick lunch. A spoonful of mayonnaise helps to bind the mix but isn't essential. And if blue cheese isn't your thing, try a good, tangy cheddar.

SERVES 2

1 medium or 2 small tart eating apples

3½ ounces / 100g crumbly blue cheese

Sea salt and freshly ground black pepper

1 tablespoon mayonnaise (optional)

2 slices of sourdough or other robust bread

1 garlic clove, halved

Grate the apple(s), skin and all, into a bowl. Grate or finely crumble the cheese and add this too, along with a little salt (the blue cheese will already be quite salty) and some pepper. Add the mayonnaise if you like, and mix well.

Preheat the broiler and lightly toast the bread. Rub the cut garlic clove lightly over the toasted bread, for just a hint of garlic. Spread the apple and cheese mixture in a thick, even layer on the toast. Return to the broiler, not too close to the heat, and let the mixture heat up gently so the apple gets a chance to soften. After 5 minutes or so, when the apple is softened and the cheese is melted, bring the toast closer to the heat and broil until golden brown and bubbling. Serve at once.

"Vegiflette" toastie

My very easy tartiflette toastie, which appears in River Cottage Every Day, was inspired by the classic rich and greedy Swiss mountain dish of cheese, ham, cream, and spuds. This is an equally irresistible, meat-free version. The classic cheese for a tartiflette is Reblochon, but Camembert, Stinking Bishop, and other well-flavored "washed rind" cheeses all work well. And, frankly, so do most goat cheeses, and even cheddar.

Indulgent, creamy, cheesy combinations like this are well-complemented by a few bitter salad leaves, and here I've actually made them an integral part of the toastie topping.

SERVES 2

2 tablespoons canola or olive oil

2 smallish, cold, cooked potatoes, thickly sliced

8 to 10 leaves of Belgian endive, radicchio, or other bitter salad greens, coarsely sliced

2 to 3 tablespoons heavy cream or crème fraîche

Sea salt and freshly ground black pepper

2 slices of sourdough or other robust bread

About 2 ounces / 60g cheese (see above)

Heat the oil in a nonstick frying pan over medium heat. Add the potatoes and cook for a few minutes, turning every now and then, until starting to turn golden. Add the sliced endive or other salad greens and cook for a minute or so, until they are starting to wilt. Add the cream and let it bubble and reduce for a minute or two, then season with salt and pepper to taste.

Preheat the broiler and toast the bread lightly. Heap the mixture from the pan onto the toast. Lay the cheese slices on top, sprinkle with more pepper, and broil until bubbling. Serve right away.

Various rarebits

Welsh rarebit is so much more than cheese on toast. My version is based on a simple béchamel sauce with cheese added. Other recipes include beer, and you might like to replace some or all of the milk with warmed good ale. Rarebit can be customized with various veggies, too (see below). It's also worth trying it on a homemade flat bread instead of toast. The result – somewhere between cheese on toast and an indulgent pizza – is fantastic. While Worcestershire sauce contains anchovies, vegetarian brands are available.

SERVES 4

1¼ cups / 300ml whole milk

1 bay leaf (optional)

½ onion (optional)

Sea salt and freshly ground black pepper

3½ tablespoons / 50g unsalted butter

7 tablespoons / 55g all-purpose flour

5 ounces / 150g fairly strong cheddar, grated

½ teaspoon English mustard, or to taste

A dash of Worcestershire sauce (optional)

4 slices of good bread or 4 small flat breads (see page 176)

Put the milk in a saucepan, with the bay leaf and onion if you have them on hand, along with a grinding of black pepper. Bring the milk to just below a simmer, then turn off the heat.

Melt the butter in another saucepan over medium-low heat. Stir in the flour to make a smooth roux and let it bubble and seethe for a couple of minutes. Remove from the heat. If you've infused the milk with bay and onion, strain them out. Add the milk to the roux in three or four batches, beating well after each addition to create a smooth sauce.

Return the thick sauce to low heat and cook for another 2 minutes. Turn off the heat and stir in the cheese until melted, then add the mustard and season with salt and pepper to taste, adding a dash of Worcestershire sauce if you like (not for vegetarians, unless you have a vegetarian brand).

Preheat the broiler and toast the bread. If you're serving your rarebit just as it comes, then spread the cheese sauce thickly on the toast. Alternatively, add your veggie extras (see below) before spreading on the toast. Either way, broil the rarebit reasonably slowly, not too close to the heat, so the thick sauce is bubbling hot all the way through before the top gets too brown. Serve right away.

ALTERNATIVE TOPPINGS

Tomato rarebit (shown left)
Top the cheese sauce with a few thick slices of tomato and sprinkle with pepper before placing under the broiler.

Celery rarebit
Thinly slice 4 celery stalks and sauté them in a tablespoon of butter for 5 minutes, until tender but still a bit crunchy. Season and stir into the rarebit mixture before spreading on toast and broiling.

Broccolini or kale rarebit
Lay some lightly cooked broccolini or curly kale across your toast before smothering with the sauce and broiling.

Poached egg on toast

You may have your own preferred method for poaching an egg – in which case, stick to it. This is mine. I concede that there are no actual vegetables involved in this recipe: I'm including it not just because it makes such a very fine, quick meal in its own right, but because a perfectly poached egg is an excellent finishing touch or accompaniment to a great many of the dishes in this book. Frankly, there's barely a recipe in this chapter that I would want to discourage you from serving with a poached egg on top. Indeed, if on reading any of the recipes in this book, you find yourself thinking, "I wonder what that would be like with a poached egg?" . . . well, there's only one way to find out.

The absolute most important thing is to make sure the egg you use is fresh. Old eggs almost invariably produce raggedy poached whites.

SERVES 1

1 large egg, at room temperature

1 slice of bread

Butter

Sea salt and freshly ground black pepper

Pour a 2-inch / 5cm depth of water into a saucepan and bring to a boil. Meanwhile, break the egg carefully into a mug or small jug, taking care not to damage the yolk.

When the water is at a rolling boil, stir it fast in one direction with a wooden spoon to create a vortex or whirlpool in the center. When you have a distinct vortex, remove the spoon and immediately tip the egg straight into the center. Turn off the heat, put a lid on the pan, and leave it for exactly 2½ minutes. Meanwhile, lightly toast your bread and butter it.

Remove the lid. Use a slotted spoon to carefully scoop up the egg. Check that the white is set, with no jellyish clear bits left – if there are, return it to the water for 30 seconds. Give the egg half a minute in the spoon for the water to drip and steam away. You can dab carefully with a piece of paper towel to help get rid of any remaining water.

Slide the egg carefully onto the hot toast, sprinkle with a little salt and pepper, and serve.

Pantry suppers

There will always be occasions when you're really pushed for time, or tired and hungry, and you crave something filling and satisfying but simple and quick. When you are in that frame of mind, the temptation can be strong to reach for the sausages or bacon. But really, you don't have to default to meat just because you're in a hurry.

With a well-stocked pantry and the fridge in a supporting role, you can pretty much throw together meat-free meals from things readily on hand, even when there are no actual fresh vegetables in the house. On pages 400–401, you'll find a list of some key pantry ingredients that I always like to have waiting in the wings. But I think it's worth going into a bit of detail here about the ones that are particularly steadfast friends to the weary and the time-poor.

First of all, my shelves always harbor a few cans of beans, chickpeas, and/or lentils. You'll find legumes popping up in various recipes throughout the book, but in this chapter they are the focus of some very fast and tasty meals. They are such great standbys – instantly ready, and offering a substantial dose of both protein and starch. It's just a matter of building a dish around them with a few well-chosen, contrasting flavors and textures.

My second crucial ingredient is eggs. I try to make sure there are always half a dozen in the house. If the tally falls below this, I become panicky, and I'll threaten the hens with early retirement into the stockpot, even as I head down to the village shop. It goes (almost) without saying that an egg offers a nutritious little package – one that boiled, poached, or fried can top off not just a plate of toast fingers, but also a hearty salad or even a tray of roasted vegetables, so that where you might have had a snack or a side dish, you find you've got yourself a meal. And when it comes to midweek quickies, eggs can be more than the last-minute meal-maker. They can be the central "planned" ingredient too, as the upcoming frittata recipes testify.

Then there's instant noodles. These can be the base of meals so effortless that you don't even need to get out a saucepan. I've discovered that it's amazingly easy to create a fast, hot meal based around noodles and your kettle. Okay, it wasn't my discovery. But I have had fun reworking the concept of the instant noodle meal to exclude nasties such as MSG and embrace some genuinely virtuous ingredients. These are particularly great one-dish, one-person meals – the sort you might find yourself eating in the kitchen, standing up, perhaps before you've even got your coat off. And they can be taken to work, as a just-add-boiling-water instant lunch box.

Puff pastry, tucked away in the freezer, is an ingredient I turn to more and more these days. It's now possible to buy very good all-butter, and even organic, puff pastry that is a world away from the usual margarine-based ones, which so often have a rather stale flavor. What's more, puff pastry is often sold in ready-rolled sheets. They defrost in minutes and then offer you a blank canvas – ready and waiting for the tastes and textures of a few well-chosen vegetables, a pinch of herbs, and perhaps a scattering of cheese and a trickle of good extra-virgin olive or canola oil. A little bit indulgent, but, once in a while, why not?

The good old potato is, of course, a slightly more ordinary starchy standby. Spuds are a midweek mainstay for many of us, and I hope to do them justice in this chapter. They can be cooked from scratch, which may not be exactly quick, but is certainly straightforward – you'll find my current favorite twists on fries and baked potatoes on pages 225 and 226. But in my house, more often than not, potatoes appear midweek as leftovers.

I rarely cook spuds without deliberately adding a few more than are needed immediately, so they can go into the fridge and stand by for supper duty. Rehashed (quite literally sometimes) in the frying pan, they never fail to please. Although cooked potatoes may be the most versatile of leftover veg, they are by no means the only ones. Almost any leftover roots, along with leftover greens, beans, and peas, can be improvised into a frittata, or hash, or some variation on the theme.

There are other incredibly useful things – onions, frozen peas, well-flavored cheese (you can't beat a good cheddar), dried lentils, couscous, pasta, and rice, of course – which extend my arsenal of ever-ready ingredients. The list may sound mundane, but the uses to which they are put are anything but. Your pantry should be a rich source of delicious goodies that, even in the absence of lovely fresh vegetables, can feed you warmly, generously, and without recourse to meat. So keep it well stocked but – and this bit is vital – make sure there's as much coming out of it as there is going in. The larder is not an emergency bomb shelter; don't be afraid to use it, even in peacetime.

Tomato, thyme, and goat cheese tart

*This is a very simple tart to make, using good-quality ready-made puff pastry.
I've suggested various cheese and herb options below, but the basic principle
is the same: crisp pastry, soft caramelized tomato, tangy cheese.*

SERVES 4 TO 6

A little sunflower oil

½ teaspoon fine cornmeal or polenta (optional)

13 ounces / 375g all-butter, ready-made puff pastry

1 large egg, beaten, for brushing

About 12 ounces / 350g tomatoes

Sea salt and freshly ground black pepper

1 garlic clove, finely chopped

A little extra-virgin olive or canola oil

3½ ounces / 100g rinded goat cheese

A handful of thyme sprigs, leaves only

Preheat the oven to 375°F / 190°C. Lightly oil a baking sheet and scatter over a little fine cornmeal or polenta, if you have some – this helps to keep the pastry really crisp.

Roll out the pastry fairly thinly and trim to a rectangle measuring about 10 by 12 inches / 30 by 25cm. Put it on the baking sheet. Cut a ½-inch / 1cm strip from each edge. Brush these strips with a little beaten egg, then stick them onto the edges of the rectangle to form a slightly raised border. Brush the edges with a little more egg.

Thinly slice the tomatoes crosswise into ⅛-inch / 3mm slices; discard the stalky top and skinny bottom slices. Scatter the garlic over the pastry, then arrange the tomato slices on top, overlapping them only slightly. Season with salt and pepper and trickle with a little oil. Bake for about 15 minutes, until the tomatoes are tender and lightly browned.

Take the tart out of the oven, scatter over the cheese and thyme, add another twist of pepper and a trickle of oil, and return to the oven. Bake for another 10 minutes or so, until the cheese is melty and bubbly and the pastry golden brown. You can serve the tart hot, but I think it's better half an hour or so after it comes out of the oven, with a green salad.

VARIATIONS

Tomato, basil, and mozzarella tart
Replace the goat cheese with 1 ball of buffalo mozzarella (about 4 ounces / 125g), torn into small pieces. Replace the thyme with a couple of tablespoons of shredded basil – but add this after the tart is cooked, not before.

Tomato, rosemary, and pecorino tart
Replace the goat cheese with a generous grating of pecorino or Parmesan, and the thyme leaves with 1 tablespoon of chopped rosemary.

Tomato, blue cheese, and chive tart
Replace the goat cheese with crumbled blue cheese. Omit the thyme. Scatter a handful of chopped chives over the tart once it is baked.

Upside-down onion tart

This is now a favorite "cupboard's-bare" recipe, shown to me by my friend Sarah Raven. With just two main ingredients – onions and puff pastry – you can produce, in a short space of time, something rather stylish and very tasty. It's another tarte tatin variation, of course.

SERVES 4

About 7 ounces / 200g all-butter, ready-made puff pastry

3 or 4 onions (about 12 ounces / 350g)

1 tablespoon / 15g butter

1 tablespoon canola or olive oil

Sea salt and freshly ground black pepper

1 tablespoon balsamic vinegar

Preheat the oven to 375°F / 190°C. Roll out the pastry on a lightly floured surface to a ⅛-inch / 3mm thickness and cut out an 8-inch / 20cm circle. Wrap the pastry disk and place it in the fridge.

Peel the onions and slice each one into 6 or 8 wedges, keeping the root end attached. Heat the butter and oil in an 8-inch / 20cm tarte tatin pan or ovenproof frying pan over medium heat. Add the onions, arranging them roughly in a pinwheel pattern. Sprinkle with salt and pepper and cook for 15 to 20 minutes, turning once or twice, until they are fairly tender and starting to caramelize around the edges.

Trickle the balsamic vinegar over the onions and cook for a couple of minutes more, so the vinegar reduces a little. Remove from the heat and make sure the onions are fairly evenly spread around the pan.

Lay the pastry disk over the onions and put the pan into the oven. Bake for 20 minutes, until the pastry is fully puffed up and golden.

Invert the tart onto a plate so the sticky caramelized onions are facing up, on top of the crispy pastry. Serve right away, ideally with a green leafy salad. You could also crumble or grate over a favorite cheese.

Woodbourne
Library Closing
for Renovations
December 31st, 2016.

Woodbourne @ Cross Pointe
Grand Opening 10 AM,
January 3rd.

Centerville Library
111 W. Spring Valley Rd
Centerville, OH 45458
Business Hours:
Mon-Fri 10AM - 9PM
Sat 10AM - 5PM
OPEN Sun 1-5 PM

Woodbourne @ Cross Pointe
101 E. Alex Bell Rd, Suite 118,
Centerville, OH 45459
Business Hours:
Mon-Thu 10AM - 9PM
Fri 10AM - 6PM
Sat 10AM - 5PM
CLOSED Sun

washington**centerville**
PUBLIC LIBRARY
www.wclibrary.info

Green onion galette

This is a really tasty, quick supper. The green onions should be just charred in places and slightly chewy on the outside, yet steamed-tender in the middle.

SERVES 4

13 ounces / 375g all-butter, ready-made puff pastry, ready-rolled if you like

About 1 pound / 500g green onions (3 large bunches)

3 tablespoons olive oil

About 2 ounces / 60g Parmesan, mature cheddar, or hard goat cheese, grated

Sea salt and freshly ground black pepper

Preheat the oven to 400°F / 200°C. Roll out the puff pastry, if it isn't ready-rolled, to a rectangle ¼-inch / 5mm thick. Lay the pastry on a lightly oiled baking sheet.

Trim off the root ends and the green ends of the onions, leaving about 2 inches / 5cm of the tender green part attached. Strip off the outer layer, too, if it looks a bit tired. Rinse briefly and pat dry. If the onions are slender, use them whole; halve thicker ones lengthwise. Put the onions in a bowl, add the olive oil, cheese, and some salt and pepper and toss together thoroughly.

Lay the green onions on the pastry in a single layer, leaving a 1-inch / 2.5cm clear margin around the edges. Dot any cheese and oil left in the bowl over the onions and bake for 25 minutes. Serve hot or warm.

Cheesy peasy puff turnover

An ideal way to use pastry left over from another recipe. Choose a well-flavored (not too strong) cheese and don't be afraid to use up odds and ends – a little Parmesan never goes amiss.

SERVES 2 OR 3

A little sunflower oil (optional)

About 7 ounces / 200g all-butter, ready-made puff pastry

About 2½ ounces / 75g frozen peas or petite peas

Sea salt and freshly ground black pepper

About 2½ ounces / 75g mature cheddar, hard goat cheese, or other well-flavored hard cheese, grated

1 large egg, beaten

Preheat the oven to 400°F / 200°C. Lightly oil a baking sheet or line with a nonstick liner.

If your puff pastry isn't ready-rolled, roll it out and trim to a rough 8-inch / 20cm square. Place it on the baking sheet. Carefully place the frozen peas in the center and scatter over a little salt and pepper. Scatter the grated cheese evenly over the peas.

Brush the edges of the pastry with beaten egg. Trickle most of the rest of the egg over the cheese and peas, reserving a teaspoonful or so. Fold the pastry over to form a large triangle and pinch the edges together firmly to seal. Brush the pastry with the remaining egg and bake for 20 minutes, or until golden brown. Serve hot.

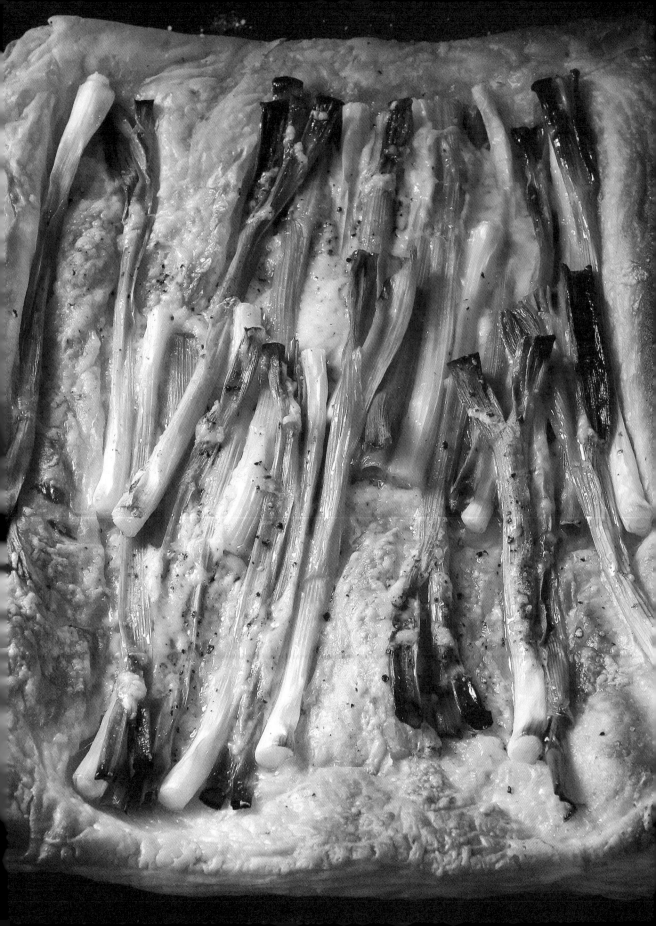

Green beans, new potatoes, and olives🌱

Straightforward it may be, but this is one of my favorite recipes in this chapter. It's such a simple combination: just two vegetables mixed with a few aromatic ingredients, which form a sort of deconstructed tapenade. It's very easy to throw together, looks glossy and gorgeous, and always seems to hit the spot. A perfect summer supper.

SERVES 2 OR 3

1 pound / 500g small new potatoes

Sea salt and freshly ground black pepper

7 ounces / 200g green beans, trimmed and cut into 1½-inch / 4cm lengths

2 tablespoons olive oil

2 garlic cloves, thinly slivered

2 ounces / 60g pitted black olives, very coarsely chopped

A good handful of basil, shredded

A generous squeeze of lemon juice

Cut the potatoes into 2 or 3 pieces each. Put them in a saucepan, cover with water, add salt, and bring to a boil, then lower the heat. Simmer for about 8 minutes, until tender, adding the beans for the last 2 or 3 minutes. Drain well and return to the hot pan.

Meanwhile, heat the olive oil in a small frying pan over low heat. Add the garlic and cook very gently for a couple of minutes, without letting it color. Add the chopped olives and cook for a minute more. Remove from the heat.

Tip the oil, garlic, and olives into the pan with the potatoes and beans. Add the basil, a generous squeeze or two of lemon juice, and some salt and pepper. Toss together and serve warm.

VARIATION

Potatoes and "deconstructed pesto"
Omit the beans. Heat the garlic in the oil, as above, then toss with the drained potatoes and loads of shredded basil (a good bunch), some lemon juice, and plenty of slivered or finely grated Parmesan, hard goat cheese, or other well-flavored hard cheese.

Spicy merguez oven fries with yogurt dip

It's impossible to resist these spicy fries. You can use starchy or waxy potatoes – either will be good – but starchy ones will give you more crumbly, crispy bits.

SERVES 4

About 2 pounds / 1kg potatoes

1/3 cup / 80ml canola or olive oil

FOR THE MERGUEZ SPICE MIX

1 teaspoon cumin seeds

1 teaspoon fennel seeds

1 teaspoon coriander seeds

1 teaspoon caraway seeds (optional)

10 to 12 black peppercorns

1 teaspoon sweet smoked paprika

A pinch of cayenne pepper

1/4 teaspoon fine sea salt

FOR THE DIP

6 heaping tablespoons plain full-fat yogurt

A scrap of garlic (about 1/4 clove), crushed with a little salt

A pinch of cayenne pepper, to sprinkle

Preheat the oven to 400°F / 200°C. Give the potatoes a good scrub (you don't need to peel them), then cut into thick batons. Put them into a saucepan and cover with cold water. Bring to a rolling boil and boil for 1 minute, then immediately drain well.

Meanwhile, for the spice mix, crush the cumin, fennel, coriander, and caraway seeds, if using, with the black peppercorns to a powder, using a mortar and pestle. Combine with the paprika, cayenne, and salt.

Pour the oil in a large, shallow roasting pan and put into the oven for 5 minutes to heat up.

Set aside about 1 heaped teaspoon of the spice mix. Add the rest to the drained potatoes and toss together. Take the hot roasting pan from the oven, add the spiced potatoes, and turn to coat in the oil. Roast for 35 to 45 minutes, giving a stir halfway through, until golden and crisp.

Meanwhile, for the dip, stir the remaining spice mix into the yogurt along with the crushed garlic. Transfer to a serving bowl and sprinkle with a pinch of cayenne.

Taste one of the fries and sprinkle with a little more salt if needed, then serve them hot, with the cool yogurt dip.

VARIATION

Roasted new potatoes with harissa

Cut 1 1/2 pounds / 750g new potatoes into even-sized chunks and spread out in a large roasting pan. Add 3 tablespoons canola or olive oil and some salt and pepper and toss the potatoes to coat well. Roast at 375°F / 190°C for 30 to 40 minutes, until the potatoes are starting to turn golden brown and crisp. Give them a good stir, then add 1 tablespoon harissa and toss to coat. Return to the oven for about 10 minutes until the harissa just starts to caramelize. Serve hot, scattered with chopped parsley. You can just eat these as they are or add some crumbled ricotta salata, French green lentils (see page 237), or a poached egg (see page 210).

Twice-baked potatoes

The baked potato remains one of the best stand-by options when you find yourself tired, hungry, and lacking the will to try something new. This way of preparing them is still simple but turns them from a predictable supper to a rich and indulgent one. There are lots of different ways to jazz them up, as you'll see from my suggestions below.

SERVES 4

4 large baking potatoes

3 tablespoons / 45g butter

¾ cup / 190g sour cream or crème fraîche

4 ounces / 120g mature cheddar, grated

2 or 3 green onions, trimmed and thinly sliced

Sea salt and freshly ground black pepper

Preheat the oven to 400°F / 200°C. Place the potatoes on a baking sheet and bake for about an hour, until tender when pierced with a knife. Remove from the oven but leave the oven on.

When the potatoes are just cool enough to handle, carefully halve them lengthwise – you might want to hold them with a kitchen towel when you do this – and scoop most of the insides into a bowl, leaving a shell about ¼ inch / 5mm thick. Return these shells to the oven to crisp up while you make the filling (don't let them bake for more than 10 minutes).

Mash the scooped-out potato flesh with the butter, then stir in the sour cream or crème fraîche, cheddar, and green onions. Season generously with salt and pepper. Spoon the mixture back into the shells and bake until heated through, 10 to 15 minutes. Cool slightly before serving.

VARIATIONS

• Instead of cheddar, mash a little crumbled blue cheese, such as Stilton, and the leaves from a few thyme sprigs, to the potato flesh.

• Cook, drain, squeeze, and chop some spinach. Add to the potato flesh with a handful of grated Gruyère instead of cheddar and a grating or two of nutmeg.

• Sauté some chopped onion until soft and golden, add 1 or 2 finely chopped garlic cloves, 1 teaspoon curry powder, and a handful of peas and cook until the peas are heated through. Mix into the mashed potato flesh, adding, if you like, some cubes of paneer, cottage cheese, or cream cheese instead of the cheddar.

Curried bubble and squeak^v

Bubble and squeak, a fried mixture of potatoes and cabbage, is surely one of the finest leftovers dishes known to man. This is just a mildly spicy riff on the theme – but a great one, nonetheless. Some recipes bind everything together, perhaps with an egg, to form a fryable cake, but I prefer a more rough-and-tumble approach, like a hash. This is good as it is, but absolutely excellent with a poached egg.

SERVES 3 OR 4

2 tablespoons canola or sunflower oil, plus extra if needed

1 onion, halved and thinly sliced

1 garlic clove, crushed

1 heaping teaspoon curry powder

About 14 ounces / 400g cold cooked potatoes (boiled, baked, roasted, or mashed), in rough chunks

About 7 ounces / 200g cold cooked cabbage, greens, kale, or brussels sprouts, coarsely shredded or chopped

Sea salt and freshly ground black pepper

Heat the oil in a large, nonstick frying pan over medium heat. Add the onion and fry for 6 or 7 minutes, until soft and just starting to color. Add the garlic and curry powder and cook for another 2 minutes.

Add the potato chunks and cook for a few minutes, stirring often, until they start to color. You may want to add a little more oil at this stage, and you'll probably need to use the edge of a spatula to scrape up some of the lovely crusty bits from the bottom of the pan. Add the cabbage or greens and cook, stirring, for a further 2 to 3 minutes, until the mixture is heated through.

Season with salt and pepper and serve right away, topping each portion with a poached egg (see page 210) if you like.

Quick couscous salad with peppers and feta

Although you can cook the couscous especially for this salad, this is the sort of thing I often throw together with what's left over from the day before. In fact, I nearly always cook more couscous than I need to be sure that I have leftovers for a dish like this. Do vary the flavorings: try basil, cilantro, or mint with – or in place of – the parsley, and spice it up with a pinch or two of dried chile flakes if you like. It pays to be generous with the herbs: some Middle-Eastern couscous dishes are almost green with the amount of herbs used, and that's the way I like them.

SERVES 4

9 ounces / 250g couscous

2 tablespoons olive oil

Juice of ½ lemon

Sea salt and freshly ground black pepper

1 (9½-ounce / 280g) jar roasted red peppers, drained and cut into ½-inch / 1cm dice

1 small cucumber, cut into ½-inch / 1cm dice

1 small red onion, finely chopped

7 ounces / 200g feta cheese, cut into ½-inch / 1cm cubes

A large handful of flat-leaf parsley, finely chopped

Cook the couscous according to the instructions on the package. As soon as it's cooked, trickle over the olive oil and lemon juice, season with salt and pepper, and fork the couscous gently to separate the grains. Leave to cool a little, and fork again.

While the dressed couscous is warm (but not hot) or cool, add the red peppers, cucumber, onion, feta, and parsley and toss gently until thoroughly combined. Taste and add more salt and pepper if needed, and trickle over a little more olive oil if the salad tastes at all dry. Serve still slightly warm, or at room temperature.

VARIATIONS

Tomato and olive couscous ♥

Prepare the couscous as above, tossing it with the olive oil, lemon juice, salt, and pepper. While still warm, toss with 10 ounces / 300g cored, seeded, and diced tomatoes or halved cherry tomatoes; 4 ounces / 125g coarsely chopped pitted black olives; 6 finely chopped trimmed green onions; 3½ ounces / 100g of toasted pine nuts; and a finely chopped small handful each of parsley and basil. Check the seasoning and add a little more olive oil if needed.

Moroccan-spiced couscous ♥

Prepare the couscous as above, adding ½ teaspoon each ground cumin and coriander and ¼ teaspoon ground cinnamon to the cooking water. Toss with the olive oil, lemon juice, salt, and pepper. While still warm, toss with a drained, rinsed 14-ounce / 400g can of chickpeas, 1½ ounces / 40g chopped dried apricots, 1½ ounces / 40g golden raisins, 1½ ounces / 40g toasted chopped almonds or pistachios, and a finely chopped handful each of parsley and cilantro. You can also add leftover roasted vegetables, such as carrots or squash, cut into cubes. Taste and add more salt and pepper and a little more olive oil if needed.

Frittata with summer veg and goat cheese

A traditional frittata is a lovely way to celebrate the arrival of early summer vegetables. If you have some cooked new potatoes on hand, or indeed any other leftover vegetables, you can use them here – but cooking them from scratch doesn't take long. I like to use two or three different green veggies.

SERVES 4 TO 6

14 ounces / 400g new potatoes

Sea salt and freshly ground black pepper

About 10 ounces / 300g mixed vegetables, such as asparagus, green beans, shelled young fava beans, shelled fresh peas or frozen peas (defrosted), and broccoli

2 tablespoons canola or olive oil

2 bunches of green onions, trimmed and coarsely chopped

A good handful of chives and/ or flat-leaf parsley, chopped

7 large or 8 medium eggs

About 2½ ounces / 75g medium-strong goat cheese (hard or soft, it doesn't matter)

Preheat the oven to 350°F / 180°C, or preheat the broiler.

Cut the new potatoes into ¼-inch / 6mm slices. Put them into a large saucepan, cover with plenty of water, add salt, and bring to a boil. Meanwhile, if using green beans and asparagus, cut them into 1½-inch / 4cm lengths; if using broccoli, cut it into small florets.

When the potatoes come to a boil, add the green vegetables. Once the water has returned to a boil, lower the heat and simmer for 3 or 4 minutes, by which time all the vegetables should be just tender. Drain well.

Heat the oil in a large nonstick ovenproof frying pan (about 11 inches / 28cm) over medium heat. Add the green onions and sweat for about 5 minutes, until soft. Add the drained vegetables and herbs and toss with the onions. Turn the heat to medium-low.

Beat the eggs together with plenty of salt and pepper and pour over the veg in the pan. Cook gently, without stirring, until the egg is about two-thirds set, with a layer of wet egg still on top. Crumble or coarsely chop the cheese and scatter over the surface of the frittata, then transfer the pan to the oven or broiler and cook for a further 4 to 5 minutes, until the egg is all set and the top is starting to color.

Leave to cool slightly, then slide the frittata out onto a plate or board. Serve warm or cold, cut into wedges.

Oven-roasted roots frittata

This is a great way to use up odds and ends of fresh veg, and leftovers, too. You can use more or less whatever you fancy from the list, though I do think some kind of onion is essential. As the egg is poured straight into the roasting dish full of hot vegetables, you don't need to fry this frittata at all, but it helps to have a heavy ceramic or cast-iron dish, which retains heat well. And the eggs should be at room temperature, not cold from the fridge.

SERVES 4 TO 6

About 1⅓ pounds / 600g mixed winter vegetables, such as shallots or onions, carrots, squash or pumpkin, parsnips, celery root, beets, and potatoes

1 large garlic clove, finely chopped

3 tablespoons canola or olive oil

Sea salt and freshly ground black pepper

7 large or 8 medium eggs, at room temperature

A handful of mixed herbs, such as curly parsley, chives, and thyme, finely chopped

¾ ounce / 20g Parmesan, hard goat cheese, or other well-flavored hard cheese, grated

Preheat the oven to 375°F / 190°C. Prepare your chosen veg: peel shallots or onions and quarter or thickly slice; peel carrots and cut into ¼-inch / 6mm slices; peel squash or pumpkin, seed, and cut into 1-inch / 2.5cm cubes; peel parsnips, celery root, and beets and cut into ½-inch / 1cm cubes; cut potatoes into ½-inch / 1cm cubes.

Put all the vegetables into an ovenproof dish, about 9 inches / 23cm square. Add the garlic, oil, and plenty of salt and pepper and toss well. Roast for about 40 minutes, stirring halfway through, until the vegetables are all tender and starting to caramelize in places.

Beat the eggs together with the chopped herbs and some salt and pepper. Remove the dish from the oven, pour the egg evenly over the vegetables and scatter over the grated cheese. Return to the oven for 10 to 15 minutes, until the egg is all set and the top is starting to color. If your oven has a broiler, you can use that to accelerate the browning of the top once the eggs have set.

Leave to cool slightly, then slide the frittata out onto a plate or board. Serve warm or cold. Perfect lunch box fare . . .

Dressed green lentils ♥

These lovely, speckled green lentils are an absolute mainstay of my cooking. They get their distinctive earthy flavor from the volcanic soils around Puy in the Auvergne region of France. Their firm, nutty texture makes them great for adding to salads or jumbling up with all manner of tasty companions.

SERVES 4 TO 6

1¹/₃ cups / 250g French green lentils

Vegetable stock (see page 130) or water

1 bay leaf

2 garlic cloves, bashed

A few parsley stems (optional)

2 tablespoons olive oil

A squeeze of lemon juice

Salt and freshly ground black pepper

Put the lentils in a saucepan and add plenty of water. Bring to a boil and simmer for a minute only, then drain. Return the lentils to the pan and pour in just enough stock or water to cover them. Add the bay leaf, garlic, and parsley stems, if using. Bring back to a very gentle simmer, and cook slowly for about half an hour, until the lentils are tender but not mushy.

Drain the lentils and discard the herbs and garlic. Dress with the olive oil and lemon juice, and season with salt and pepper to taste. Serve warm or cold.

FOUR WAYS WITH LENTILS

Lentil and parsley salad ♥ (shown left)
For the dressing, make a mustardy vinaigrette: shake 3 tablespoons olive oil, 1 tablespoon cider vinegar, 1 teaspoon mustard, a pinch each of salt and sugar, and a few twists of black pepper together in a screw-top jar. Toss the warm or cooled lentils with the leaves from a good bunch of flat-leaf parsley; 3 trimmed green onions, cut into short lengths; and the vinaigrette.

Summer garden lentils niçoise
Toss the warm lentils in a mustardy vinaigrette (see above) and mix in some crisp cooked green beans, finely diced shallot or red onion, chopped black olives, and quartered cherry tomatoes. Serve warm with poached eggs on top, or cold with quartered hard-boiled eggs.

Lentil and tomato salad
Toss the warm or cold lentils with honey-roasted cherry tomatoes (see page 343) and a handful of arugula. You could finish with some shavings of Parmesan or hard goat cheese, too, if you like.

Lentils with beets and feta
Dress the warm lentils with olive oil and some balsamic vinegar and toss with wedges of roasted beets and cubes of feta or goat cheese.

Dal ^v

A simple red lentil dal is such a great complement to so many vegetable dishes – not just curries or biryanis, pakoras or bhajis, but even simple fare such as shredded, stir-fried greens and a scoop of rice. It's a delicious way to add protein to a vegetable-based meal, too. This easy but authentic example is based on a recipe from the wonderful Indian chef Udit Sarkhel.

SERVES 4

1$\frac{1}{3}$ cups / 250g red lentils

1 teaspoon ground turmeric

$\frac{3}{4}$ teaspoon fine sea salt

2 tablespoons sunflower oil

1 teaspoon cumin seeds

1 onion, halved and thinly sliced

A small bunch of parsley or cilantro, or a couple of sprigs of mint, coarsely chopped, to finish (optional)

Put the lentils in a saucepan with 3$\frac{1}{2}$ cups / 800ml of water and bring to a boil. Skim off any scum, then stir in the turmeric and salt. Lower the heat and simmer, uncovered, for about 15 minutes, stirring or whisking vigorously every now and then, until the lentils have broken down completely and you have a purée with the consistency of a thick soup or thin porridge. You can whisk in a little boiling water if you need to thin it a bit. Keep warm in the pan.

When the dal is just about done, heat the oil in a frying pan over medium heat. Add the cumin seeds and fry for a couple of minutes until browned and fragrant. Add the onion and fry fairly briskly for 5 to 10 minutes until golden brown, even just a smidge burnt.

Tip the onion mixture onto the hot lentils in the pan, cover, and leave for 5 minutes, then stir it into the dal. Taste and adjust the seasoning. This is very good finished with parsley, cilantro, or mint sprinkled on top, but that's not essential.

White beans with artichokes ♥

Decent oil-preserved grilled or roasted artichoke hearts, available from delis and some supermarkets, are a great pantry standby. They're full of flavor and their oil is useful, too.

SERVES 2

5 ounces / 150g grilled or roasted artichoke hearts in oil, cut into wedges, 1 tablespoon of the oil reserved

1 garlic clove, slivered

1 (14-ounce / 400g) can cannellini or other white beans, drained and rinsed

Juice of ½ lemon

Sea salt and freshly ground black pepper

A good handful of salad greens

A little crumbled or shaved goat cheese or Parmesan, to finish (optional)

Heat the oil reserved from the artichokes in a small frying pan over medium-low heat. Add the garlic and fry gently for a minute or two. Add the artichokes and heat for a minute or so, then stir in the beans. Cook, stirring, for 2 to 3 minutes, until everything is hot. Remove from the heat, add the lemon juice, and season with salt and pepper to taste (the artichokes may already have contributed some salt).

Arrange the salad greens on two plates and top with the hot beans and artichokes. Finish with goat cheese or Parmesan, if you like, and serve warm.

VARIATION

White bean salad with tomatoes and red onion ♥

Here's another very quick but really quite substantial beany supper. To make a creamy dressing, whisk 3 tablespoons canola or olive oil, 1 tablespoon lemon juice, ½ teaspoon English mustard, a pinch of sugar, and some salt and pepper together in a large bowl. Thinly slice ½ small red onion and add to the dressing along with a drained and rinsed 14-ounce / 400g can of white beans. Add about 5 ounces / 150g ripe, sweet tomatoes (any kind, but cherry tomatoes are good), cut into smallish pieces (or halved, if cherry type) and toss well. Serve with parsley sprinkled on top, or salad greens underneath – or both – and some bread on the side.

Raid-the-larder
bean and spelt broth 🌱

*This is a quick but sustaining broth. Stock, spelt,
and beans form the heart of it, and the fresh
vegetables you then add pretty much depends on
you – or what's in your fridge/freezer/garden.*

SERVES 2

3 cups / 750ml vegetable stock
(from a cube or bouillon
powder is fine)

¼ cup / 50g pearled spelt (or
pearled barley)

A few leaves of cabbage, kale, or
other cooking greens, or a
couple of handfuls of spinach

1 carrot, peeled and diced

3½ ounces / 100g frozen peas
or petite peas

1 (14-ounce / 400g) can
cannellini or other white beans,
drained and rinsed

Sea salt and freshly ground
black pepper

Extra-virgin olive oil, to finish

Bring the stock to a boil in a saucepan. Add the spelt (or barley), lower
the heat, and simmer until almost tender, about 15 minutes (or a bit
longer for barley).

Meanwhile, remove any tough stalks or stems from the greens or
spinach and shred the leaves coarsely.

Add the carrot, peas, and canned beans to the broth. Once it returns
to a simmer, add the greens or spinach and cook for a further 2 to
3 minutes, until the leaves are just tender. Season with salt and pepper
to taste, then ladle into bowls. Finish with a generous trickle of olive oil
and serve.

VARIATIONS

Try diced parsnip instead of carrot, or sliced green beans instead of peas.
Almost any shredded greens will work, even brussels sprouts or lettuce.

Chickpea ketchup curry[v]

I have no problem with using "cheaty" ingredients when a quick meal is called for – as long as they are good-quality cheats. I cadged the idea of basing a curry on a ketchup from a Martha Stewart recipe. The condiment lends bags of spice and a delicate, mango chutney-like sweetness to the dish. The logical variation – a ketchup and bean chili – is also a winner.

SERVES 2

2 tablespoons sunflower oil

1 small onion, thinly sliced

1 (1-inch / 2cm) piece of ginger, peeled and finely grated

A pinch of dried chile flakes

1 garlic clove, crushed

2 teaspoons curry powder

1 (14 ounce / 400g) can chickpeas, drained and rinsed

5 tablespoons ketchup

Juice of ½ lemon

Sea salt and freshly ground black pepper

A handful of cilantro, to finish

Heat the oil in a frying pan over medium-low heat. Add the onion and sweat for about 8 minutes, until soft and golden, then stir in the ginger, chile flakes, garlic, and curry powder. Fry, stirring, for 1 to 2 minutes more.

Add the chickpeas, ketchup, and enough water to just loosen the mixture to a thick sauce consistency. Simmer gently for about 5 minutes, then stir in the lemon juice. Taste and add salt and pepper if needed.

Serve in warmed bowls scattered with cilantro leaves. Plain rice, instant noodles, naan, or flat breads are all good accompaniments.

VARIATION

Ketchup chili

This spiced-up bean chili is unbelievably simple and really good. Use a 14-ounce / 400g can of kidney (or other) beans instead of the chickpeas and 2 teaspoons sweet paprika (or 1 teaspoon each of sweet and hot paprika) instead of the curry powder. The chili is great served on rice, baked potatoes, or toast, or with tortillas or tostadas, and with toppings such as sour cream, grated cheese, guacamole . . .

Quick chickpea pasta

Wholesome, hearty, and quick, this is a lovely pantry supper just as it is.
Or, you could jazz it up a little if you like, perhaps adding some frozen petite
peas along with the chickpeas, or some chopped fresh herbs at the end.

SERVES 2

Sea salt and freshly ground
black pepper

4 ounces / 125g small pasta
shapes, such as orecchiette or
conchigliette

1 (14-ounce / 400g) can
chickpeas, drained and rinsed

3 tablespoons olive oil

1 garlic clove, slivered

1 fresh red chile, seeded and
finely chopped

A good squeeze of lemon juice

Parmesan, hard goat cheese,
or other well-flavored hard
cheese, grated, to serve

Bring a saucepan of water to a boil, salt it well, then add the pasta and cook according to the package instructions. About 2 minutes before the pasta is done, add the chickpeas to the pan, to heat them through.

Meanwhile, heat the olive oil in a large frying pan over low heat. Add the garlic and chile and cook very gently for 2 to 3 minutes, without letting the garlic color. Remove from the heat.

Drain the pasta and chickpeas well and add to the pan containing the garlic, chile, and oil. Stir well, then add salt and pepper and a good squeeze of lemon juice, to taste. Serve topped with plenty of grated cheese.

Chickpeas with cumin and spinach❧

This delicately spiced quickie is very good with some warm pita or flat breads.

SERVES 2

2 tablespoons sunflower or
canola oil

1 small onion, sliced

1 garlic clove, chopped

$\frac{1}{2}$ fresh red chile, seeded and
finely chopped, or a pinch
of dried chile flakes

1 teaspoon ground cumin

Grated zest of 1 lemon

4 to 6 large fresh plum
tomatoes or 1 (14-ounce / 400g)
can plum tomatoes

About 5 ounces / 150g spinach

1 (14-ounce / 400g) can
chickpeas, drained and rinsed

Sea salt and freshly ground
black pepper

Heat the oil in a saucepan over medium-low heat. Add the onion and sweat gently for about 8 minutes, stirring occasionally, until tender and golden. Add the garlic, chile, cumin, and lemon zest and cook for another 1 to 2 minutes.

Halve the fresh tomatoes and grate their flesh directly into the pan, discarding the skins. Alternatively, finely chop canned tomatoes, discarding any skin and stalky ends, then add to the pan. Stir well and bring the mixture to a simmer, then simmer gently for a few minutes, until saucy.

Meanwhile, remove any tough stems from the spinach and coarsely shred the larger leaves. Add to the pan and stir until wilted, then add the chickpeas and some salt and pepper. Cook for a few minutes, just to heat the chickpeas through, then taste and adjust the seasoning if needed. Serve with warm flat breads or pita.

DIY pot noodles

I first experimented with these when I was looking at ways to improve workday lunches. However, the concept works equally well as a fast and very satisfying supper. It's important to find the right kind of noodle – one that will soften nicely in boiling water from the kettle without the need for pan-cooking. I find flat, thin, quick-cooking egg noodles fit the bill very well. The "pot" should be covered once the water is added . . . with this in mind, a sealable heatproof jar, such as a canning jar, is ideal.

SERVES 1

1 nest of thin, quick-cooking egg noodles

1 teaspoon vegetable bouillon powder or ¼ vegetable stock cube

A good pinch of brown sugar

1 small carrot, peeled and very thinly sliced or cut into fine julienne

3 or 4 green onions, trimmed and finely sliced

6 sugar snap peas, shredded, or a few frozen petite peas

1 leaf of green cabbage or a couple of leaves of bok choy, stalks removed, finely shredded

½ teaspoon freshly grated ginger

½ garlic clove, grated

¼ fresh red or green chile, seeded and finely chopped

2 teaspoons soy sauce

Juice of ½ lime

Put all of the ingredients, except the soy sauce and lime juice, in a pint-sized glass jar. Pour over boiling water to just cover everything, pressing the ingredients down. Cover and leave for 8 to 10 minutes, stirring once or twice, then add soy sauce and lime juice to taste, and eat.

VARIATION

Curried mushroom pot noodles
This works "instantly" with raw mushrooms and defrosted frozen peas; you can, of course, add other finely sliced or shredded cooked vegetables, too. Mix ½ teaspoon cornstarch with 1 teaspoon curry powder, and put into a pint-sized glass jar along with a nest of thin, quick-cooking egg noodles, 3 or 4 thinly sliced mushrooms, 1 tablespoon defrosted frozen peas, 1 finely grated small garlic clove, and a finely grated ½-inch / 1 to 2cm piece of ginger, along with about 1 ounce / 25g of paneer (Indian cheese), if you can get hold of some. Season with salt and pepper. Pour over boiling water to just cover everything, pressing the ingredients down. Cover and leave for 8 to 10 minutes, stirring once or twice, then eat.

Pasta & rice

When tummies are rumbling and time is tight, pasta, rice, and what I think of as their sister ingredients – grains such as spelt, barley, and quinoa – are ideal. You don't really need to cook them – you can just ask a helpful pan of simmering water to do it for you. Even a risotto, which requires a bit of hands-on cooking, needn't be more than half an hour in the making. So while not all the recipes here are as quick as those in the Pantry Suppers chapter, they're certainly pretty undemanding.

Pasta is an easy fallback – too easy, maybe – in danger of losing its charm and selling itself short. Personally, if forced to choose, I would rather eat rice than pasta every day. That's because I accept rice as a kind of neutral ballast and flavor carrier, whereas pasta is, or should be, a little more than that. Served up with the right sauce, something that fits its shape and coats its curves, it's a proper treat. In the interest of eating it a little less but enjoying it a lot more, it's worth thinking about how to get the very best out of pasta.

In most of the pasta recipes in this chapter, I've suggested a particular pasta shape that I think would go well with the other ingredients. I do believe the form of the pasta makes a difference to the eating experience – but I would never want to become a pasta pedant. For myself, I'm perfectly happy to replace linguine with spaghetti, or macaroni with penne, or conchiglie with farfalle. I certainly wouldn't avoid a pasta recipe simply because I didn't have the right shape in the cupboard.

When it comes to cooking pasta, be generous with the salt you add to the water. Most of that salt will remain in the water, of course, but the pasta will absorb and be seasoned by some of it in a way that cannot be replicated by adding salt later. Some Italian cooks swear by the 1000:100:10 formula, which means 1000 grams (about 1 quart) of water per 100 grams (3^1/$_2$ ounces) of pasta and 10 grams (2 teaspoons) of salt. I think that's a bit too much, but I'd certainly put a good tablespoon of salt in roughly 4 to 5 quarts / liters of boiling water, in which I'll usually cook 12 ounces / 350g or so of pasta to feed four or five of us.

Cooking time is the other crucial variable. Perfect pasta should be, as I'm sure you know, al dente – or "to the tooth." I recommend that you start testing it a good minute or two before the cooking time suggested on the package is up. You aren't looking for any kind of chalky uncooked-ness in the pasta, just a little bit of resistance. Pasta cooked to this degree really is much nicer to eat than when it is softened to the point of collapse – and it holds sauces and dressings better as well.

I want to say a bit more about rice, too. It's a grain I'm turning to more frequently. I find it, paradoxically, a light way to fill up – satisfying but somehow never heavy. An increasing number of people have problems digesting wheat and opt for rice instead – you can even buy rice pasta, though it's not as good as wheat pasta. Whether or not you have specific issues with wheat, I think it's a good idea to vary the starches you eat. Making sure rice appears on your table as often as bread or pasta is one way to do that.

Cooking rice for many seems to be freighted with anxieties, but it needn't be. You might consider investing in a proper rice cooker. They are surprisingly inexpensive, and I've been impressed with the results from these machines – the grains emerge tender and well separated. (I'm skeptical of the word "fluffy" being applied to rice. Surely that's for kittens?) When cooking rice in a saucepan, I still rely on the simple kitchen-towel-under-the-lid absorption method used in the "vegeree" on page 276. I don't claim to understand why that kitchen towel makes a difference, but it works for me. However you cook "plain" rice, such as long-grain or basmati, thoroughly rinsing the rice *before* cooking, to remove all excess starch, is important – as is simmering the rice gently, rather than boiling.

Risotto rice is a different proposition, of course, because here you want to keep all the starch that clings to the grains, to thicken it into a lovely soupy texture. Cooking risotto is not difficult, but you do need to get a bit of a feel for it, to catch the rice at the right point of doneness. That's a matter of personal taste, of course, but I like just the faintest hint of chalkiness in the middle of the grain. It's something that simply comes with practice. I hope the comforting risotto recipes in this chapter will keep you keen.

The other grains you'll find here include quinoa – a fantastically proteinaceous little Latin American seed, which I heartily recommend. It might take you two or three tries to be won over – it did me – but I bet you'll end up a fan. Then there's spelt – the whole, pearled grains of which have almost completely sidelined pearled barley in my cooking (though of course you can use barley instead). I use a locally produced, organic spelt grain that cooks very easily to a nutty, nubbly finish. It also soaks up a flavorful stock to great effect: the "speltotto" (see pages 280 and 283) is now a pillar of my kitchen and I urge you to give it a try.

I have found that forgoing meat more often, and excluding it deliberately from dishes that are built around pasta, rice, and other grains, has heightened my enjoyment of these brilliant ingredients. I hope it'll do the same for you.

Pasta with raw tomatoes[v]

This wonderfully simple raw tomato sauce can be tweaked and flavored to your taste: sometimes I use mint instead of basil, or add a little finely chopped raw red onion or fennel, or replace the capers with sliced olives. Feel free to have fun with it and use several different varieties of tomato if you like.

SERVES 4

1½ pounds / 750g large, ripe tomatoes

1 garlic clove, finely chopped

1 tablespoon capers, rinsed

½ small fresh red chile, seeded and finely chopped, or a pinch of dried chile flakes

About 10 large basil leaves, shredded

½ cup / 100ml extra-virgin canola or olive oil

Sea salt and freshly ground black pepper

12 ounces / 350g pasta, such as conchigliette, small penne, or orecchiette

Parmesan or hard goat cheese, to serve (optional)

Put the tomatoes into a bowl, cover with boiling water, and leave for just 1 minute, then remove and peel off their skins. Quarter and seed the tomatoes, putting all the seeds and clinging juicy bits into a sieve set over a bowl.

Coarsely chop the seeded tomato flesh and put into another bowl. Press the juice from the seeds in the sieve, adding it to the chopped tomatoes. Add the garlic, capers, and chile, half of the shredded basil, and the oil and toss to mix. Add a little salt and pepper (the capers may be quite salty). Set aside somewhere fairly cool, but not the fridge, for about an hour to allow the flavors to mingle.

Put a large pot of well-salted water on to boil. Add the pasta to the boiling water and cook until al dente, then drain well. Combine the pasta with the raw tomato sauce, then taste and adjust the seasoning.

Serve scattered with the remaining shredded basil and a grinding of black pepper. You can add a few shavings of Parmesan or hard goat cheese, but I prefer it without.

Pasta with new potatoes, green beans, and pesto

This is a traditional Ligurian pasta dish: substantial but not as heavy as you might think. The green olives are authentic, but you can easily leave them out; I often do. A decent ready-made pesto would work here, but the dish is taken to a whole new level if you make your own. I've used a combination of basil and parsley for the pesto, but you can use all basil or all parsley if you prefer.

SERVES 4

10 ounces / 300g new potatoes

10 ounces / 300g pasta, such as penne, trofie, or orecchiette

7 ounces / 200g green beans

FOR THE PESTO

⅓ cup / 50g pine nuts or walnuts, lightly toasted

A large bunch of basil (about 1 ounce / 30g), leaves only

A large bunch of parsley (about 1 ounce / 30g), leaves only

A few mint leaves (optional)

1 garlic clove, chopped

About 1¾ ounces / 50g Parmesan, hard goat cheese, or other well-flavored hard cheese, finely grated

Finely grated zest of ½ lemon

½ to ⅔ cup / 100 to 150ml extra-virgin olive oil

Sea salt and freshly ground black pepper

A good squeeze of lemon juice

TO SERVE

2 ounces / 60g pitted green olives, coarsely sliced or chopped (optional)

Extra cheese (as above)

Extra-virgin olive oil (optional)

First make the pesto: put the toasted nuts into a food processor along with the herbs, garlic, grated cheese, and lemon zest. Blitz to a paste, then, with the motor running, slowly pour in the olive oil until you have a thick, sloppy purée. Scrape the pesto into a bowl and season with salt, pepper, and a good squeeze of lemon juice. It will keep in the fridge for a few days.

Put a very large pot of well-salted water on to boil. Meanwhile, cut the potatoes into thick matchsticks. Add the potatoes and pasta to the boiling water and cook until the pasta is al dente – probably 10 to 12 minutes, which should be the right amount of time for the potatoes, too. If the pasta is a type that cooks very quickly, put the potatoes in a few minutes before. (If using very freshly dug new spuds, they'll cook quicker, 6 to 7 minutes, so add them about halfway through the pasta cooking). In the meantime, cut the beans into lengths that roughly match the size of the pasta. Add them to the pot about 4 minutes before the pasta and potatoes are done cooking.

Drain the pasta and vegetables, and let them steam off for a minute or two, then add the pesto and mix thoroughly but gently. Check the seasoning (it will probably benefit from a generous grinding of black pepper).

Divide between warmed serving bowls and scatter over the green olives, if using. Grate over some cheese and trickle over a little extra-virgin olive oil if you like. Have extra cheese for grating on the table.

Mushroom "risoniotto"

Risoni (or orzo) is a tiny rice-shaped pasta with a unique charm. There's something deeply satisfying about its texture, and it's quicker and easier to cook than rice. Here, it's combined with a rich mushroom ragout for a warming autumn or winter dish. Use a dark and flavorsome variety of mushroom, such as cremini, portobello, or shiitake, and include a few wild mushrooms if you have some on hand.

SERVES 2

2 tablespoons canola or olive oil

1 tablespoon / 15g butter

1 pound / 500g mushrooms (see above), cleaned, trimmed, and thickly sliced

5 ounces / 150g risoni or orzo pasta

2 garlic cloves, chopped

A few sprigs of thyme, leaves only

1 teaspoon balsamic vinegar

About ⅓ cup / 75ml dry white wine

About 3½ tablespoons / 50ml heavy cream or crème fraîche

Sea salt and freshly ground black pepper

A good handful of flat-leaf parsley, chopped, to serve

Put a large saucepan of well-salted water on to boil so that you're ready to cook the pasta while the sauce is coming together.

Heat 1 tablespoon of the oil and half of the butter in a large frying pan over medium-high heat. Add half of the mushrooms and cook briskly, stirring often, until all the liquid released has evaporated and the mushrooms are starting to caramelize. Transfer to a dish and repeat with the rest of the oil, butter, and mushrooms. (Cooking in two batches like this avoids overcrowding the pan and ensures the mushrooms do not stew.)

When the second batch of mushrooms is nearly cooked, add the pasta to the pan of boiling water and cook until al dente.

Return the first lot of mushrooms to the frying pan. Add the garlic, thyme, and balsamic vinegar and cook, stirring, for a minute or two. Add the wine and cook until there is almost no liquid left. Add the cream or crème fraîche, lower the heat a little, and stir until the sauce is just about simmering. Season with salt and pepper to taste.

Drain the pasta as soon as it is al dente, add to the mushroom mixture, and toss well. Serve scattered with lots of chopped parsley.

Pasta with greens, garlic, and chile

*Wilted greens combined with a hearty portion of pasta and spiked with garlic
and chile make a satisfying supper. The following variations on that theme
are equally delicious, sustaining, and easy to put together.*

SERVES 4

2 or 3 bunches of Swiss chard
or kale or 1 savoy cabbage

6 tablespoons / 80ml olive oil

1 onion, halved and thinly sliced

½ to 1 fresh red chile, seeded
and finely chopped, or 2 good
pinches of dried chile flakes

2 garlic cloves, finely slivered

Sea salt and freshly ground
black pepper

10 ounces / 300g pasta, such
as penne, fusilli, trofie, or
strozzapreti

TO SERVE

Extra-virgin olive oil

Parmesan, pecorino, hard goat
cheese, or other well-flavored
hard cheese

Put a large pot of well-salted water on to boil so that you're ready to
cook the pasta while the sauce is coming together. Remove the thick
stems from the kale or the core from the cabbage and shred the leaves.

Heat the olive oil in a large frying pan over low heat. Add the onion
and cook gently for 10 minutes, or until soft. Add the chile and garlic
and some salt and pepper, and continue to cook for about 3 minutes,
until the garlic is no longer raw.

When the onion is almost cooked, add the pasta to the pan of boiling
water and cook until al dente, adding the greens to the pan about
3 minutes before the pasta is done cooking.

Drain the pasta and greens thoroughly and toss with the onion
mixture in the frying pan. Check the seasoning, then serve with
extra-virgin olive oil for trickling and lots of grated cheese.

VARIATIONS

Pasta with broccoli

Use a head of broccoli, cut into small florets, instead of the greens, and
give it a good 5 minutes' cooking with the pasta – it should be well
done so that it starts to break down and cling to the pasta. Omit the
onion, and just warm the oil with the chile and garlic for a few minutes.

Orecchiette with chickpeas and lacinato kale

Adding chickpeas makes this a more substantial main course dish. Use
8 ounces / 250g orecchiette (little ear-shaped orecchiette are great
with chickpeas, which get stuck in the "earholes"). You can use any
greens, but the dish is particularly good with Lacinato or curly kale;
prepare the kale and cook with the pasta as above. Gently fry the
onion, chile, and garlic, as above, then add a drained and rinsed
14-ounce / 400g can of chickpeas with a pinch of ground cumin and
heat through before tossing together with the pasta and greens. Serve
trickled with extra-virgin oil, but omit the cheese.

Pasta with fennel, arugula, and lemon

This is such a lovely combination of flavors. Use ribbon pasta, linguine, spaghetti, or whatever pasta shape you have on hand, and you'll end up with a fantastic summery pasta dish.

SERVES 2

1 large fennel bulb

1 tablespoon canola or olive oil

1 garlic clove, slivered

5 ounces / 150g tagliatelle, pappardelle, or other pasta

2 or 3 good handfuls of arugula

Finely grated zest of 1 lemon

3 tablespoons crème fraîche

Sea salt and freshly ground black pepper

Parmesan, hard goat cheese, or other well-flavored hard cheese, to serve

Put a large saucepan of well-salted water on to boil so that you're ready to cook the pasta while the sauce is coming together.

Trim the fennel, removing the tougher outer layer or two, then slice thinly. Heat the oil in a large frying pan over medium heat. Add the garlic and fennel and sauté gently for about 10 minutes, until the fennel is tender.

When the fennel is almost cooked, add the pasta to the pan of boiling water and cook until al dente.

Add the arugula to the fennel and stir until wilted, then add the lemon zest and crème fraîche. Stir well until the crème fraîche coats all the vegetables, then add salt and pepper to taste.

Drain the pasta well, toss with the fennel mixture, and serve right away, with grated cheese.

Macaroni peas

Peas and pasta with bacon or ham is a classic combination. In this dish (inspired by a lovely Nigella Lawson risotto recipe), Parmesan gives the desired salty-savory note. Some of the peas remain whole, to give a pleasing, pop-in-the-mouth texture; the rest are blitzed to form a creamy pea sauce.

SERVES 4

1 pound / 500g shelled peas (fresh or frozen) or petite peas

10 ounces / 300g small macaroni or smallish pasta shapes, such as orecchiette, fusilli, or orzo

3 tablespoons / 45g butter

1 garlic clove, chopped

1 ounce / 30g Parmesan, hard goat cheese, or other well-flavored hard cheese, coarsely grated, plus extra to serve

Sea salt and freshly ground black pepper

Shredded basil or flat-leaf parsley, to serve (optional)

Put a large pot of well-salted water on to boil so that you're ready to cook the pasta while the sauce is coming together.

Put the peas in a saucepan, cover with water, bring to a boil and simmer until tender – just a couple of minutes for frozen or very tender, fresh peas, longer for older fresh peas.

When the peas are almost cooked, add the pasta to the pot of boiling water and cook until al dente.

Meanwhile, melt the butter in a small frying pan over low heat and add the garlic. Let it cook gently for just a couple of minutes, without coloring, then remove from the heat.

Drain the peas, reserving the cooking water. Put about half of them in a blender with 6 tablespoons of the cooking water, the butter and garlic, and the grated cheese. Blitz to a smooth, loose purée, adding a little more water if needed. Combine with the whole peas and season with salt and pepper to taste.

Drain the pasta as soon as it is ready and toss immediately with the hot pea sauce. Serve topped with plenty of ground black pepper and more grated cheese. Shredded basil or chopped flat-leaf parsley is a good, but by no means essential, finishing touch.

Linguine with mint and almond pesto and tomatoes ᵛ

This light, zesty pesto is perfect for summer. I've always preferred linguine to spaghetti – something about the flat shape makes it more pleasing in the mouth – but of course spaghetti would work here. I make the pesto without cheese, as I often serve the pasta topped with Parmesan or hard goat cheese. The quirky pesto is versatile: thin it with a little oil and it makes a great salad dressing – try it with crisp Little Gem lettuces and quartered hard-boiled eggs.

SERVES 4

10 ounces / 300g linguine or spaghetti

14 ounces / 400g tomatoes, cut into wedges

FOR THE MINT PESTO

⅓ cup / 50g blanched almonds, lightly toasted

A large bunch of mint (about 2 ounces / 60g), leaves only

1 garlic clove, chopped

Finely grated zest of 1 lemon, plus a squeeze of juice

½ teaspoon Dijon mustard

A pinch of sugar

About ⅓ cup / 75ml canola or olive oil

Sea salt and freshly ground black pepper

TO SERVE (OPTIONAL)

Parmesan, hard goat cheese, or other well-flavored hard cheese

First make the pesto: put the toasted almonds into a food processor along with the mint, garlic, and lemon zest. Blitz until very finely chopped. Add the mustard and sugar, then, with the motor running, slowly pour in the oil until you have a thick, sloppy purée. Season with salt, pepper, and a good squeeze of lemon juice. This will keep in the fridge for a few days.

Put a large pot of well-salted water on to boil. Add the pasta to the boiling water and cook until al dente. Drain well, then toss with the mint pesto and about half of the tomatoes.

Divide between warmed serving bowls or plates and top with the remaining tomatoes. Serve right away, scattered with cheese shavings if you like.

VARIATIONS
In place of the tomatoes, you could use lightly cooked asparagus, peas, or fava beans, or a mixture of summer vegetables.

Baby carrot and fava bean risotto

This is a perfect summer supper dish: tender baby carrots and bittersweet
fava beans wrapped in a creamy, delicate risotto.

SERVES 4

1 tablespoon canola or olive oil

3 tablespoons / 45g butter

1 large onion, finely chopped

About 3½ cups / 800ml vegetable stock

1 cup / 200g risotto rice

A scant ½ cup / 100ml dry white wine

8 to 10 ounces / 250 to 300g baby carrots, scrubbed and halved or quartered lengthwise

⅔ cup / 150g baby fava beans

About ¾ ounce / 20g Parmesan, hard goat cheese, or other well-flavored hard cheese, finely grated

A handful of flat-leaf parsley, chopped

Sea salt and freshly ground black pepper

Canola or extra-virgin olive oil, to serve

Heat the oil and 2 tablespoons / 30g of the butter in a large saucepan over medium heat. Add the onion and fry gently for 8 to 10 minutes, until softened. Meanwhile, bring the stock to a simmer in a small saucepan, then keep warm over very low heat.

Stir the rice in to the onion, cook for a minute or two without stirring, then stir again. Add the wine and bring to a simmer. Cook for a few minutes, stirring from time to time, until the wine is absorbed.

Now add the hot stock, about one-quarter at a time, making sure each addition has been absorbed before you add the next. Keep the risotto simmering and stir frequently. It should take 20 to 25 minutes for the stock to be absorbed and for the rice to be cooked but still al dente. Add the carrots after the rice has been cooked for about 12 minutes; put the fava beans in just a couple of minutes before the rice is done.

When the rice and vegetables are cooked, turn off the heat. Scatter the cheese and dot the remaining 1 tablespoon butter over the risotto, then cover and leave for a couple of minutes. Now stir the melted cheese and butter in to the risotto with most of the parsley and salt and pepper to taste.

Divide the risotto among warmed bowls. Scatter over the remaining parsley, trickle over a little oil, and add a grinding of pepper to serve.

Leek risotto with chestnuts

This creamiest and palest of risottos tastes fantastic with the contrasting chestnuts. Vacuum-packed, precooked chestnuts are easy to use but if you can roast and peel your own, you'll get that sublime chargrilled flavor, too. If you have any risotto left over, use it to make arancini (see below).

SERVES 4

4$\frac{1}{2}$ tablespoons / 75g butter, plus extra to serve

A little canola or olive oil

3 large leeks (about 1 pound / 500g), trimmed and thinly sliced

About 3$\frac{1}{2}$ cups / 800ml vegetable stock

1$\frac{1}{4}$ cups / 250g risotto rice

$\frac{2}{3}$ cup / 150ml dry white wine

7 ounces / 200g cooked, peeled chestnuts, crumbled

Sea salt and freshly ground black pepper

Thyme leaves, to finish

Heat 3 tablespoons / 45g of the butter and a little oil in a large saucepan over medium heat. As soon as the mixture begins foaming, add the leeks, lower the heat, and sweat gently, covered, for about 20 minutes, until silky, stirring occasionally. Bring the stock to a low simmer in a saucepan; keep warm over very low heat.

Add the rice to the leeks and stir well, then add the wine. Increase the heat a little and let bubble until the liquid has evaporated. Now start adding the hot stock, about one-quarter at a time. Stir often, adding more hot stock as it is absorbed. After about 25 minutes, the rice should be cooked, with just a hint of bite to it, and all the stock should be used.

While the risotto is cooking, heat the remaining 1$\frac{1}{2}$ tablespoons / 25g of butter and a little oil in a frying pan over medium heat. Add the chestnuts with a pinch of salt. Turn the heat up a bit and fry, stirring often, for 2 minutes, until the chestnuts and butter are browned (don't let either burn). Remove from the heat.

When the risotto is cooked, turn off the heat, season with salt and pepper to taste, then dot a little more butter over the surface. Cover the pan and leave for a couple of minutes, then stir in the butter. Serve scattered with the chestnuts and thyme.

VARIATION/LEFTOVERS
Arancini
Cool the risotto quickly (if it's quite sloppy, drain in a sieve), then refrigerate until cold and firm. Take a tablespoonful of the rice and squash it into a thick patty. Put a couple of cubes of cheese (mozzarella or blue, or other nice melting cheese) in the center and a little dollop of pesto, then add a little more rice on top and mold the rice around the cheese to enclose it. Repeat until you've used up all the rice. Dust each rice patty with flour, dip in beaten egg, then roll in fine bread crumbs. Fry fairly gently in a little oil until golden brown all over and hot right through.

Tomato and mozzarella risotto

As long as you have some roasted tomato sauce on hand, this is one of the easiest risottos you'll ever make. It's soothing and rich, just as risotto should be, and carries a faint evocation of childhood canned tomato soup – in a good way. You could omit the mozzarella for a cheese-free version.

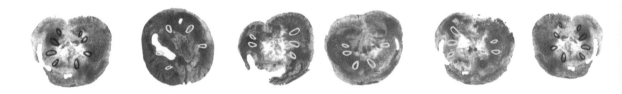

SERVES 4

3 cups / 750ml vegetable stock

1 generous tablespoon / 20g butter

1 onion, finely chopped

1¼ cups / 250g risotto rice

¾ to 1 cup / 200ml roasted tomato sauce (see page 366)

Sea salt and freshly ground black pepper

1 ball of buffalo mozzarella (about 4 ounces / 125g), torn or cut into chunks

TO SERVE

Extra-virgin olive oil

A couple of large handfuls of arugula (optional)

Bring the stock to a low simmer in a small saucepan. Keep warm over very low heat.

Heat the butter in a large saucepan over medium-low heat. Add the onion and sweat for 8 to 10 minutes, until soft. Add the rice and cook, stirring, for a couple of minutes.

Now start adding the hot stock, about one-quarter at a time. Let the risotto cook, stirring often, adding more hot stock as it is absorbed. After 20 to 25 minutes, the rice should be cooked, with just a hint of chalkiness in the middle, and you should have used up the stock.

Add the tomato sauce and cook for another couple of minutes, until piping hot, then remove from the heat. Stir in some salt and pepper, then add the mozzarella. Leave the risotto covered for a minute, then stir through the melting mozzarella, but not too thoroughly – you want to encounter stretchy, melty bits as you eat.

Serve topped with a generous trickle of extra-virgin olive oil and a tangle of arugula on the side, if you like.

Vegetable biryani᷾

For a biryani, the rice and curry are first cooked separately, then together, for a final mingling of textures and flavors. You can cheat by using a medium-hot curry powder instead of the individual spices and fresh chile, but you'll get a more exciting final flavor if you follow this route.

SERVES 6

5 tablespoons sunflower oil

1 bay leaf

3 cardamom pods, bashed

1 teaspoon cumin seeds

5 large onions, halved and thinly sliced

2 garlic cloves, crushed

2 teaspoons finely grated ginger

1 large fresh red chile, finely chopped (seeded for a milder curry)

1 teaspoon ground cumin

1 teaspoon ground coriander

1/2 teaspoon ground cinnamon

About 9 ounces / 250g carrots, peeled and sliced into thin discs

About 10 ounces / 300g waxy potatoes, cut into 1/2-inch / 1cm cubes

7 ounces / 200g peas (fresh or frozen and defrosted)

Sea salt and freshly ground black pepper

A generous squeeze of lemon juice

1/3 cup / 50g golden raisins

1 3/4 cups / 350g basmati rice

A large pinch of saffron strands

TO SERVE

2 ounces / 60g slivered almonds, lightly toasted

Chopped cilantro or mint

Heat 2 tablespoons of the oil in a large casserole over medium-high heat. Add the bay leaf, cardamom pods, and cumin seeds and fry for a few minutes. Add 1 sliced onion and fry over medium heat, stirring often, for about 15 minutes, until golden and soft. Lower the heat and add the garlic, ginger, chile, and ground spices. Cook, stirring, for 2 minutes.

Add the carrots, potatoes, and peas and enough water to almost cover the vegetables. Bring to a boil, then lower to a simmer. Cover and cook, stirring from time to time, for 10 to 15 minutes, or until the vegetables are al dente. Season with salt and pepper to taste and add a squeeze of lemon juice. Sprinkle the golden raisins on top. Preheat the oven to 325°F / 160°C.

Meanwhile, rinse the rice thoroughly in several changes of water. Put into a saucepan with the saffron and a large pinch of salt. Add enough water to cover the rice by 1 inch / 2.5cm. Bring to a boil, stir once, then simmer very gently until the water is nearly all absorbed (indicated by deep steam holes on the surface).

Cover the rice pan with a damp kitchen towel and a tight-fitting lid and turn the heat as low as possible. Cook for 5 minutes. Remove the lid and use a fork to separate the rice grains.

Spoon the rice in a thick layer over the curry in the casserole. Cover the pot with the damp kitchen towel and put on the lid tightly. Place over high heat for a few minutes to get the curry bubbling again, then transfer to the oven for 20 minutes. Remove and leave to stand for 10 minutes.

While the biryani is cooking, heat the remaining 3 tablespoons of oil in a large frying pan over medium-high heat and add the remaining sliced onions. Cook briskly, stirring often, for about 20 minutes, until well browned and reduced down. Season with salt.

Uncover the biryani and scatter over the browned onions, almonds, and cilantro or mint. Serve with a cooling, yogurty raita (the tamarind raita on page 318 is particularly good), and/or a spicy chutney.

Vegeree

I love a good kedgeree: that incredibly warming, comforting combination of rice, curry spices, and smoked fish. I wondered if it would be possible to create a similarly satisfying dish without fish – and, it turns out, it is. Roasted eggplant is the key – smoky and sweet, it certainly hits the spot when combined with all that spicy, ricey goodness. Onions and a few "soft, hard-boiled" eggs on top round out the dish nicely. You can make this with just eggplant and onions, but I like the addition of a few zucchini, too.

SERVES 4

3 onions

1 large eggplant (about 12 ounces / 350g)

2 medium zucchini (about 9 ounces / 250g), halved lengthwise

3 tablespoons sunflower oil

1 tablespoon good curry powder

Sea salt and freshly ground black pepper

1¹/₂ cups / 300g basmati rice

4 large eggs, at room temperature

Preheat the oven to 375°F / 190°C. Slice the onions from root to tip into eighths, keeping them together at the root end. Quarter the eggplant lengthwise, then cut each quarter into ¹/₂-inch / 1cm thick slices. Cut the zucchini into ¹/₂-inch / 1cm thick slices.

Toss together all the vegetables in a large roasting pan. Pour over the sunflower oil, sprinkle with the curry powder, and add some salt and pepper. Toss together again. Roast for 40 minutes, stirring 2 or 3 times.

Meanwhile, cook the rice. Rinse the grains well in several changes of water, then put into a saucepan, add salt and pour on enough water to cover by 1 inch / 2.5cm. Bring to a boil, stir once, then simmer until the water is nearly all absorbed (there should be deep steam holes in the surface). Cover the pan with a damp kitchen towel and a tight-fitting lid and turn the heat as low as possible. Cook for 10 minutes. Turn off the heat and leave the rice for a further 5 minutes. Remove the lid and use a fork to separate the rice grains.

To cook the eggs, bring a saucepan of water to a boil, add the eggs, and boil for 7 minutes. Remove the eggs from the pan, run them under cold water to stop the cooking, and leave until cool. Shell, peel, and halve the eggs.

Toss the cooked rice with the roasted spiced vegetables. Taste and add more salt and pepper if needed. Serve topped with the halved boiled eggs and a grinding of black pepper.

Quinoa with zucchini and onions

Quinoa is a highly nutritious little seed that makes a nice alternative to rice or couscous (in fact, you can substitute it for those ingredients in all manner of recipes). I love it with tender zucchini, sweet onions, and crunchy pine nuts in this simple supper dish. The more wintry leek and squash version below is a real favorite, too.

SERVES 4

1³⁄₄ pounds / 800g zucchini

1 tablespoon / 15g butter

2 tablespoons canola or olive oil

3 onions, halved and thinly sliced

A few sprigs of thyme, leaves only

Sea salt and freshly ground black pepper

3 garlic cloves, finely chopped

1¹⁄₄ cups / 200g quinoa

A good handful of flat-leaf parsley, coarsely chopped

A squeeze of lemon juice

2 ounces / 60g pine nuts, lightly toasted

Cut the zucchini on the diagonal into ¹⁄₄-inch / 6mm thick slices. Melt the butter with the oil in a large frying pan over medium heat. Add the onions, zucchini, thyme, and some salt and pepper. Cook for 20 to 25 minutes, stirring from time to time, until the zucchini is tender and starting to turn golden. Add the garlic and fry for another couple of minutes.

Meanwhile, rinse the quinoa well in several changes of cold water. Put into a saucepan with a pinch of salt and cover with plenty of cold water. Bring to a boil, lower the heat, and simmer for about 12 minutes, until the quinoa is tender with just a bit of bite. Tip into a sieve and leave to drain and steam a little to drive off excess moisture.

Add the drained quinoa to the zucchini, along with the chopped parsley and lemon juice. Stir well, then taste and add more salt and pepper if needed. Serve topped with the toasted pine nuts.

VARIATION

Quinoa with leeks and squash
Replace the zucchini and onions with 1 to 1¹⁄₄ pounds / 500 to 600g squash or pumpkin and 3 trimmed medium leeks (white and pale green parts only). Peel and seed the squash and cut into ¹⁄₂-inch / 1cm dice. Cut the leeks into roughly ¹⁄₂-inch / 1cm slices. Heat the butter and oil in a large frying pan and add the squash, leeks, thyme, and some salt and pepper. Cover the pan and sweat for 20 to 25 minutes, stirring from time to time, until the leeks and squash are tender. Cook the quinoa as above. Add the drained quinoa to the squash and leeks. Stir well and check the seasoning. Serve topped with the pine nuts.

Kale "speltotto" with goat cheese

This is very similar to a risotto, but based on nutty grains of pearled spelt, rather than rice. We enrich this lovely wintry dish with Quickes hard goat cheese – but any tasty, hard goat cheese would be good, or Parmesan. If you prefer, you can finish the dish with some slices of soft, rinded goat cheese, as shown.

SERVES 4

1 quart / liter vegetable stock (see page 130)

3½ tablespoons / 50g butter

2 tablespoons olive or canola oil, plus a trickle to finish

1 onion, finely chopped

1 garlic clove, finely chopped

A few sprigs of thyme, leaves only, chopped

2 or 3 medium leeks, trimmed (white and pale green parts only)

About 5 ounces / 150g kale

10 ounces / 300g pearled spelt (or pearled barley)

½ cup / 125ml dry white wine

2 ounces / 60g hard goat cheese, Parmesan, or other well-flavored hard cheese, grated, plus extra to serve

Sea salt and freshly ground black pepper

Bring the stock to a low simmer in a saucepan and keep warm over very low heat.

Heat about half of the butter and 1 tablespoon of the oil in a large saucepan over medium heat. Add the onion, garlic, and thyme and sweat gently for about 10 minutes, until the onion is soft.

In the meantime, cut the leeks on the diagonal into 1-inch / 2cm thick slices. Remove the tough stems from the kale and shred the leaves.

Stir the spelt (or barley) through the softened onion mixture and cook gently for a minute or two. Add the wine and let it bubble until all the liquid is absorbed.

Now start adding the hot stock, about one-quarter at a time, as you would for a risotto, stirring often and letting each addition be absorbed before you add the next. It should take about 25 minutes for the spelt (or a bit longer for barley) to cook to a tender texture with a hint of bite still in the grains.

While the spelt (or barley) is cooking, sweat the leeks in the remaining butter and oil in a small frying pan over medium heat, stirring occasionally, until tender but still with a slight bite. In a covered saucepan over medium heat, wilt the kale with a little water for 3 to 4 minutes, until just tender. Drain if necessary.

Remove the "speltotto" from the heat and stir in the leeks, kale, and grated cheese. Add salt and pepper to taste. Serve topped with extra cheese, a grinding of black pepper, and a final trickle of oil.

VARIATION
Nettle "speltotto"
Instead of kale, use tender, young stinging nettles. Wash the leaves thoroughly (wear rubber gloves for this!) and then wilt in a pan of salted water for 5 to 6 minutes, until tender. Drain in a sieve, pressing out the water, then chop fairly finely. Stir through the "speltotto" with the leeks and cheese, then serve.

Rutabaga "speltotto"

Spelt has a nutty flavor that goes very well with earthy root vegetables. Roasted wedges of pumpkin or beets work brilliantly in place of the rutabaga, but instead of adding them at the beginning, stir in the diced flesh of the roasted vegetables just a minute or two before the "speltotto" is finished.

SERVES 4

1 quart / liter vegetable stock (see page 130)

1½ tablespoons / 20g butter

2 tablespoons canola or olive oil

2 onions, chopped

1 garlic clove, finely chopped

12 ounces / 350g rutabaga, peeled and cut into ½-inch / 1cm dice

10 ounces / 300g pearled spelt (or pearled barley)

A good handful of parsley, finely chopped

2 ounces / 60g Parmesan, hard goat cheese, or other well-flavored hard cheese, grated, plus extra to serve

Sea salt and freshly ground black pepper

A few gratings of nutmeg

Bring the stock to a low simmer in a small saucepan and keep warm over very low heat.

Heat the butter and oil in a large saucepan over medium-low heat. Add the onions and sweat gently, stirring, for about 10 minutes, until soft. Add the garlic and rutabaga and stir for a couple of minutes.

Add the spelt (or barley) to the pan and stir for a couple of minutes, making sure all the grains are well coated with fat.

Now start adding the stock, about one-quarter at a time, as you would for a risotto, stirring often and letting each addition be absorbed before you add the next. It should take about 25 minutes for spelt (or a bit longer for barley) to cook to a tender texture with a hint of bite still in the grains. By this time, the rutabaga will be completely tender, too.

Stir in the chopped parsley and grated cheese. Add salt, plenty of black pepper, and a few gratings of nutmeg. Serve, topped with more grated cheese. A crisp green salad is the ideal accompaniment.

New potato gnocchi

Gnocchi – little savory potato dumplings that beg to be smothered in a rich sauce, pesto, or just lots of butter and cheese – may be the ultimate comfort food. And these may well be the easiest gnocchi you'll ever make.

SERVES 4

1 pound / 500g new potatoes

Sea salt and freshly ground black pepper

3½ ounces / 100g soft goat cheese, crumbled

1½ cups / 200g all-purpose flour

1 large egg, lightly beaten

TO SERVE

Roasted tomato sauce (see page 366), pesto (see page 256), butter, or olive oil

A handful of parsley and/ or chives, finely chopped (optional)

Parmesan, hard goat cheese, or other well-flavored hard cheese (optional)

Scrape or scrub all the skin from the potatoes, removing any blemishes, bruises or "eyes," then cut the potatoes into similar-sized chunks. Put them in a saucepan, cover with water, salt well, and bring to a boil. Lower the heat and simmer for 8 to 12 minutes, until tender, then drain well.

Mash the potatoes but not too thoroughly – the gnocchi should have a little texture to them. Transfer to a bowl and let cool until tepid, then add the goat cheese, flour, egg, and some salt and pepper. Using a wooden spoon or your hands, mix thoroughly and bring together to form a firm dough. Knead gently for a few minutes, then roll the dough into sausages about ¾ inch / 2cm in diameter. Cut each one into 1-inch / 2.5cm lengths.

Bring a large saucepan of water to a gentle simmer. Cook the gnocchi in batches for a minute or two. As they rise to the surface, scoop them out with a slotted spoon and transfer to a lightly buttered warmed dish.

Serve with roasted tomato sauce, pesto, or just butter or olive oil and plenty of black pepper. Finish with a scattering of chopped herbs and/ or grated or finely shaved cheese, if you like.

Summer stir-fry with fried rice

It's best to prepare all the ingredients for this lovely green dish before you start cooking. Once the wok is on the go, it's all ready in a matter of minutes. You don't have to serve the stir-fry with the fried rice – plain steamed rice or a couple of nests of softened instant noodles will do.

SERVES 2

1 medium zucchini
(about 4 ounces / 125g)

A few green onions, trimmed

A good handful of baby spinach, arugula, mizuna, bok choy, or any other tender green leaf (about 2 ounces / 60g)

About 3 ounces / 75g snow peas

About 3 ounces / 75g small fresh shelled peas or defrosted petite peas

1 tablespoon canola or sunflower oil

1 (1-inch / 2.5cm) piece of ginger, peeled and finely grated

1 garlic clove, crushed

1 green chile, seeded and chopped

A dash of soy sauce

A dash of toasted sesame oil

A handful of mint, finely shredded

1 tablespoon lightly toasted sesame seeds

FOR THE FRIED RICE

1 tablespoon canola or sunflower oil

A generous ³/₄ cup / 150g freshly cooked basmati or jasmine rice

1 teaspoon soy sauce

1 large egg, beaten

TO SERVE

Soy sauce

Toasted sesame oil

Prepare the vegetables first: halve the zucchini lengthwise, then slice thinly on the diagonal. Slice the green onions on the diagonal. Trim the spinach or other greens of any tough stems and coarsely shred the leaves. Set the vegetables aside, keeping them separate.

Heat a large wok over medium-high heat and add the canola oil. When it's hot, add the snow peas and stir-fry for about 2 minutes, until starting to soften. One at a time, add the zucchini, peas, green onions, and greens, giving each vegetable a minute or so of stir-frying before you add the next. Keep the heat fairly high so the moisture is driven off and the mixture doesn't start to simmer, and keep everything moving so nothing starts to stick and burn.

After you've added the greens and they've wilted down, throw in the ginger, garlic, and chile. Stir-fry for another 2 minutes, then remove from the heat. Transfer to a hot serving dish and trickle with the soy sauce and sesame oil. Finally, add the mint and sesame seeds.

Now, quickly cook the fried rice: wipe out the wok with a wad of paper towels. Add the canola oil and place over medium-high heat. When the oil is hot, add the rice and stir-fry over fairly high heat until the grains are coated in oil and the rice is piping hot. Create a bit of space in the base of the pan. Mix the soy sauce into the beaten egg and pour into the space. As the egg starts to cook, scrape it up and stir it into the rice. Keep going until the egg is completely cooked and distributed throughout the rice.

Serve the fried rice immediately alongside the stir-fry. Have some more soy sauce and sesame oil on the table.

Winter stir-fry
with
chinese five-spice

The warming hint of star anise in Chinese five-spice powder gives this dish character. You can chop and change the vegetables a little depending on what you have on hand – celery root instead of parsnip, for instance, or shredded cabbage rather than sprouts – but I do think this is a particularly fun way of using brussels sprouts.

SERVES 2

1 large carrot, peeled

1 small parsnip, peeled

About 3½ ounces / 100g shiitake, cremini, or firm button mushrooms, trimmed

About 3½ ounces / 100g brussels sprouts, trimmed

2 nests of fine egg noodles (about 2 ounces / 60g)

2 tablespoons sunflower oil

3 shallots or 1 onion, thinly sliced

½ to 1 medium-hot fresh red chile, seeded and finely chopped

1 garlic clove, finely chopped

A good pinch of sugar

Sea salt and freshly ground black pepper

2 tablespoons soy sauce

2 tablespoons rice wine

½ teaspoon Chinese five-spice powder

A good squeeze of lime juice

Prepare the vegetables first: cut the carrot into thin batons and the parsnip into thin disks; thinly slice the mushrooms; and finely shred the brussels sprouts.

Prepare the egg noodles according to the package instructions.

Meanwhile, heat the sunflower oil in a wok over high heat. Add the shallots or onion and chile and stir-fry for 1 minute. Add the carrot and parsnip and cook for 2 minutes, then add the mushrooms and garlic and stir-fry for a couple more minutes. Finally, add the brussels sprouts and cook for another couple of minutes until wilted. Season well with salt, pepper, and a good pinch of sugar and scoop out of the wok to a bowl.

Drain the noodles. Lower the heat under the wok and add the soy sauce, rice wine, five-spice powder, and the noodles. Cook, stirring for a couple of minutes, then return the vegetables and toss the lot together over the heat.

Heap the stir-fry into warmed serving bowls and finish with a good squeeze of lime juice.

Meze & tapas

This is as much a plea for a way of eating as it is an introduction to a batch of recipes. It's important to me, personally, as over the last couple of years, it has become increasingly the style in which my family chooses to eat together. It's also how we like to feed our extended family and friends. Of course, it isn't always a meat-free table. But it often is.

It's all about sharing. We're sitting down at the table to a kind of indoor picnic – a range of dishes in bowls and on platters that are passed around, put down, grazed, picked up, and passed around again. It's the kind of cooking and eating that makes me rub my hands with glee – not just because of the way it shows off the fantastic ingredients that have gone into it, but also because it heightens the anticipation of sharing a really wonderful table of food with people I love.

I've said before, there is a wonderful democracy to cooking without meat, because so often you are putting a range of dishes on the table of roughly equal weight and importance. These are all, in a sense, "little" dishes – but I don't mean this in a derogatory sense. They might not, alone, have quite enough substance for a meal, but they support and enhance each other, so that just a few of them together will give you and your fellow diners the feeling that you're sitting down to a feast.

There are not many dishes in this book that do not lend themselves to this "indoor picnic" approach. But the recipes corralled in this chapter are particularly designed for it – some of them by me, others by the cultures the dishes have evolved in over generations. They represent what I see as the very exciting end of mixed-spread eating. There are some real favorites of mine here, from the delicious roasted carrot hummus (see page 296) and vibrant beet and walnut hummus (see page 300) to the lovely stuffed zucchini flowers (see page 313) and spicy cauliflower pakoras (see page 318). So many of these can be rustled together without a great deal of effort, then placed on the table, maybe just two or three together, with some salad and bread, to produce a really generous spread.

If you choose to embrace this way of eating, then I hope you will go beyond this chapter and pick and mix from all over the book – and indeed from other books and from all over your culinary repertoire. But the chapters perhaps most complementary to this one are Roast, Grill, and Broil (pages 330–67) and Side Dishes (pages 370–99). I'm sure you can see how a tray of roasted pumpkin wedges or a few big, juicy baked mushrooms might fit delightfully into this scheme.

Presenting a patchwork of dishes in this way is something that other cultures do much better than we do in the UK. Middle Eastern meze, Spanish tapas, Italian antipasti, the Scandinavian smorgasbord – all are perfect examples of the relaxed relish to be had in a collection of "little" dishes. It's such a civilized, and civilizing, way of eating – particularly shared eating. I think we have much to gain by exploring it ourselves, using the beautiful, seasonal, fresh ingredients that our climate and countryside bestow on us. We will be international meze magpies, for sure, thieving recipes from here and there and mixing them up and reworking them in ways that might distress a purist. But frankly, that's what British cooks do best – it's *our* national culinary characteristic, and we may as well flaunt it.

If the thought of a meal based around several dishes fills you with a fear of overwork, then take a second look. It's true that preparing ten or so of these recipes from scratch for a big celebration meal would take some time (spectacular though the result would be). But you really don't need that many for a family meal, and in any case a simple hunk of good bread and a salad of ripe cherry tomatoes, say, or a pile of scrubbed raw carrots will be just as much appreciated as a dish that requires chopping, cooking, and mixing. Preparing a bowl of simply dressed lentils takes mere minutes. The vast majority of these things can be made ahead and left to marinate happily in the fridge or larder.

In my house, food like this tends to be prepared and consumed in a sort of rolling relay from meal to meal. I might make a fresh salad for supper, then eat it with the leftovers of caponata, or a frittata, or a dish that doesn't even end in "ata," that I made over the weekend. Some leftover roasted beets might get hummussed in the blender, a can of chickpeas might get the merguez spice treatment, and some green beans fresh from the garden, lightly steamed, might get tossed with a few chopped olives. None of these preparations need be arduous.

This should be a genuinely relaxing way of cooking and eating. In fact, in my experience, the resulting spread always looks like far more work than it actually was. And that's a good way to make any cook feel relaxed.

Pistachio dukka

This traditional Egyptian combination of nuts, seeds, and spices is usually served in a small dish, alongside a bowl of olive oil. You dip a piece of bread in the oil, then into the dukka, capturing every last delicious crumb. I sometimes use canola oil for a change. Dukka has other uses, too – try scattering it over grilled vegetables or over a simple salad of lettuce and "soft, hard-boiled" eggs.

If you can only find roasted, salted pistachios, skip the roasting bit and perhaps rub off some of the salt before chopping them. And you can use other nuts – almonds and cashews are particularly good.

MAKES ABOUT 4 OUNCES / 125G

1 cup / 120g shelled, unsalted pistachios

1 tablespoon cumin seeds

1 tablespoon coriander seeds

3 tablespoons sesame seeds

A good sprig of mint, leaves only, chopped (optional)

1 teaspoon dried chile flakes

1 teaspoon flaky sea salt

Preheat the oven to 400°F / 200°C. Scatter the pistachios on a baking sheet and roast in the oven for about 5 minutes, until just starting to turn golden. Cool, then chop them coarsely.

In a dry small frying pan over medium heat, warm the cumin and coriander seeds until they begin to release their aroma. Transfer to a mortar and bash with the pestle until broken up, but not too fine. In the same pan, lightly toast the sesame seeds

Add the coarsely chopped nuts to the mortar and bash until they are broken up into smallish pieces. Stir in the sesame seeds, mint if using, chile flakes, and salt and transfer to a serving bowl.

The dukka will keep for a couple of weeks at room temperature in a screw-top jar.

Lemony guacamole ᵛ

A good guacamole is creamy and comforting, and peppy and invigorating at the same time. This one is great with triangles of hot garlicky flat bread (see page 176), or stuffed into a sandwich or wrap.

SERVES 4

½ to 1 small fresh red chile, seeded and finely chopped

2 tablespoons finely chopped cilantro

Juice of 1 lemon, or ½ lemon and 1 lime

2 large, ripe avocados

1 tablespoon canola oil

Sea salt and freshly ground black pepper

½ to 1 tablespoon plain full-fat yogurt (optional)

Put the chile, cilantro, and lemon (or lemon and lime) juice into a bowl. Halve, pit, and peel the avocados, then cut into chunks and drop into the bowl. Add the oil and plenty of salt and pepper.

Now mash the lot together – you can keep it a bit rough and lumpy if you like, or keep mashing until smooth. And you can make it even smoother and saucier (ideal for dressing wraps, kebabs, and foldovers) by whisking in a little yogurt. Check the seasoning and serve.

Carrot hummus

Another delicious member of the ever-expanding family of River Cottage hummi. It's lovely with crudités, warm garlicky flat breads (see page 176), or pita and salad greens, and I often serve it as part of a meze-style spread, as shown on pages 6–7.

SERVES 4

1 teaspoon cumin seeds

1 teaspoon coriander seeds

6 tablespoons olive or canola oil

1 teaspoon clear honey

1 pound / 500g carrots, peeled

3 large garlic cloves, bashed

Flaky sea salt and freshly ground black pepper

Juice of ½ lemon

Juice of 1 orange

3 tablespoons tahini (or smooth peanut butter)

Preheat the oven to 400°F / 200°C. In a dry frying pan, toast the cumin and coriander seeds for about a minute until just fragrant. Grind to a fine-ish powder using a mortar and pestle. In a large bowl, whisk 4 tablespoons of the oil with the honey and toasted spices.

Cut the carrots into ¼-inch / 6mm chunks and add to the spiced oil with the garlic. Toss to coat and season with salt and pepper. Tip into a small roasting pan and roast, turning once, until the carrots are tender and just starting to char slightly around the edges, about 35 minutes.

Allow to cool slightly, then scrape everything into a food processor, slipping the garlic cloves out of their skins as you do so. Add the lemon and orange juices, tahini (or peanut butter), and remaining 2 tablespoons oil and pulse to a purée. Adjust the seasoning if necessary and serve.

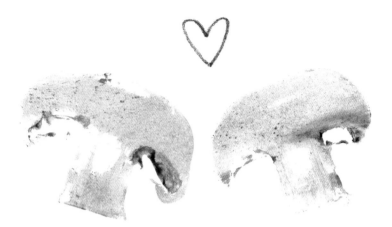

Cambodian wedding day dip ♥

*This is my version of a delicious, easy dish shown to me by David Bailey,
formerly head chef of the lovely vegetarian restaurant Saf, and now
running his own catering company. As well as presenting it as part of
a spread, you can make a meal of it by serving it hot with rice and maybe
some garlicky steamed veggies (see page 372). A good teaspoon of chile
and garlic paste from a jar can be used instead of the fresh garlic and chile.*

SERVES 8

1 pound / 500g cremini
mushrooms

1 tablespoon sunflower oil

1/2 small, hot fresh chile, such as
bird eye (with seeds), finely
chopped

3 garlic cloves, crushed

1 tablespoon curry powder

2 tablespoons crunchy peanut
butter

1 (14-ounce / 400ml) can
coconut milk

Juice of 1/2 lime

A dash of soy sauce

Finely chopped cilantro,
to finish (optional)

Finely dice the mushrooms into 1/4-inch / 6mm pieces. Alternatively,
chop them in a food processor – but don't blitz them too fine.

Heat the sunflower oil in a wok or large frying pan over high heat.
Add the mushrooms and cook briskly, stirring often, until all the
liquid they release has evaporated. Add the chile and garlic and fry
for another 1 minute.

Add the curry powder and peanut butter, stir in thoroughly, and then
stir in the coconut milk. Let it all bubble rapidly, stirring occasionally
to make sure it doesn't burn, until thick and reduced,
up to half an hour. Add the lime juice and soy sauce to taste.

Scoop the dip into a bowl. Scatter, if you like, with chopped cilantro,
and serve warm or at room temperature. Flat breads - or any good
bread – as well as fresh vegetable crudités are ideal accompaniments.

Beet and walnut hummus[♥]

I make no apology for including this recipe – tweaked from its River Cottage
Every Day *incarnation. It's such a great way to use beets, and superb as a starter,
dip, or lunch box treat. I love it with hot, garlicky flat breads (see page 176).*

SERVES 4

½ cup / 50g walnuts

1 tablespoon cumin seeds

½ ounce / 15g stale bread,
crusts removed and torn into
chunks

7 ounces / 200g cooked beets
(not pickled), cut into cubes

1 tablespoon tahini
(or smooth peanut butter)

1 large garlic clove, crushed

Juice of 1 lemon

A little canola or olive oil

Sea salt and freshly ground
black pepper

Preheat the oven to 350°F / 180°C. Toast the walnuts on a baking
sheet in the oven for 5 to 7 minutes, until fragrant. Leave to cool.

Warm a small frying pan over medium heat and toast the cumin
seeds, shaking the pan, until they start to darken and release their
aroma – this should take less than a minute; don't burn them. Crush
the still-warm seeds with a mortar and pestle or spice grinder.

Put the bread and toasted nuts into a food processor or blender and
blitz to fine crumbs. Add the beets, tahini (or peanut butter), most of
the garlic and cumin, the juice of ½ lemon, 1½ teaspoons of oil, a little
salt, and a grinding of pepper. Blend to a thick paste. Taste and adjust
by adding a little more cumin, garlic, lemon, salt and/or pepper and
blending again. Loosen with a dash more oil if needed. Refrigerate
until required (it'll keep for a few days). Serve at room temperature.

Cannellini bean hummus[♥]

*Perfect with warm pita or garlicky flat breads (page 176), this is also
delicious with roasted leeks (see page 336).*

SERVES 4

1 (14-ounce / 400g) can
cannellini or other white beans,
drained and rinsed

½ garlic clove

1 tablespoon tahini

2 tablespoons extra-virgin
olive oil

A good squeeze of lemon juice

A sprig of thyme, leaves only

Sea salt and freshly ground black
pepper

FOR THE PAPRIKA OIL

1 tablespoon canola or olive oil

½ teaspoon paprika (smoked
or sweet)

Put the beans in a food processor. Crush the garlic with a little salt
and add about half of it to the processor, along with the tahini,
extra-virgin olive oil, lemon juice, thyme leaves, 1 tablespoon water,
and some salt and pepper. Process to a purée. Taste and adjust the
flavor by adding more garlic, lemon juice, salt and/or pepper, if you
like. Transfer to a serving dish.

For the paprika oil, in a small saucepan, warm the oil and paprika very
gently for a couple of minutes to infuse; let cool. Trickle over the
hummus to serve.

Baba ganoush ♥

Serve this classic, smoky purée as a dip, or cram it into pita bread or soft tortillas, along with some chopped tomatoes, cucumber, green onion, and/or peppery salad greens.

SERVES 4

4 medium eggplants
(about 2 pounds / 1kg)

1 large garlic clove, crushed

2 tablespoons tahini (or smooth peanut or cashew nut butter)

A good squeeze of lemon juice

Sea salt and freshly ground black pepper

TO FINISH

A handful of parsley, chopped

Extra-virgin olive oil

1 to 2 teaspoons ground cumin

Preheat your broiler to high. Prick the eggplants once or twice with a fork. Lay them on a foil-lined baking sheet and broil, turning often, for at least 10 minutes, until the skin is blackened all over and the flesh beneath is tender. Leave until cool enough to handle, then peel off the skin. Put the eggplant flesh into a colander and coarsely chop it, using a small, sharp knife. Leave to drain until completely cool.

Tip the eggplant into a food processor and add the garlic, tahini (or nut butter), lemon juice, and plenty of salt and pepper. Process to a purée. Taste for seasoning and add more lemon juice if you like.

Serve scattered with chopped parsley, trickled with oil, and dusted generously with cumin. To use as a sandwich filling, stir the oil, cumin, and parsley into the purée.

Artichoke and white bean dip

This rich, creamy, deeply savory dip is wonderful with crudités or dolloped onto warm flat bread. It also works well served on some crisp lettuce, as a salad.

SERVES 4 TO 6

2 tablespoons olive oil

1 small onion, chopped

7 ounces / 200g artichoke hearts in olive oil, drained, oil reserved

3 garlic cloves, finely chopped

A few sprigs of oregano, leaves only, finely chopped

1 (14-ounce / 400g) can cannellini beans, drained and rinsed

Juice of ½ lemon

½ teaspoon dried chile flakes

2 tablespoons thick, plain full-fat yogurt

Sea salt and freshly ground black pepper

1 ounce / 30g walnuts, toasted (optional)

Heat 1 tablespoon of olive oil in a frying pan over medium-low heat and sauté the onion for about 10 minutes, until soft and translucent. Meanwhile, coarsely chop the artichoke hearts.

Add the garlic to the pan and stir for another couple of minutes. Tip in the oregano, cannellini beans, and artichokes and cook, stirring, for a couple of minutes, until everything is heated through.

Tip the mixture into a food processor and add the lemon juice, chile flakes, and yogurt. Blend to a coarse purée. Add salt and pepper to taste and thin with a couple of tablespoons or so of the olive oil from the artichokes, until you have the texture you like.

Serve the dip warm or cold, trickled with the remaining olive oil, and scattered with toasted walnuts if you like.

Oven-dried tomatoes ⱽ

I find commercially produced "sun-dried" tomatoes are often lip-pursingly intense, sharp, and sometimes a little leathery. Home-dried ones are altogether different. The beauty of drying your own is that you can control their plumpness, sweetness, and chewiness. Here I'm aiming for a semidried state – intense but still a touch juicy.

This is also, I must concede, a good way to use out-of-season or less-full-flavored tomatoes, as the seasoning and drying will bring out the best in them. Dried tomatoes are delicious stirred into salads, pasta, or couscous, or just served as a piquant nibble with a selection of other dishes. Try them also in a sandwich with goat cheese, in a frittata with potatoes and onions, or even stirred into scrambled eggs.

SERVES 4 TO 6

2 pounds / 1kg tomatoes

½ teaspoon sugar

Fine sea salt and freshly ground black pepper

A few sprigs of thyme, broken up

3 bay leaves, each snipped into 2 or 3 pieces

2 to 3 tablespoons olive oil, plus extra for storage

Halve the tomatoes, or quarter particularly large ones. Scoop out and discard the seeds, if you prefer. Set a wire rack over a doubled sheet of newspaper.

Combine the sugar with ½ teaspoon of fine salt in a small bowl. Sprinkle a tiny pinch of this mixture over the inside of each tomato half, then put the tomatoes upside down on the rack. Leave for 1 hour for the juices to drip.

Preheat the oven to very low, about 225°F / 100°C. Transfer the tomatoes, turning them cut side up, to a large rimmed baking sheet. Scatter with the thyme, bay, some black pepper, and the olive oil and place in the oven. Check after an hour or two – just in case your oven is hotter than it says! It should take 4 to 5 hours to get the tomatoes "semi-dried" – that is, considerably reduced but still quite tender and plump. This is how I like them. However, you can leave them in the oven for 7 to 8 hours – to become much more like commercial "sun-dried" tomatoes.

Tossed in a generous amount of olive oil, these oven-dried tomatoes will keep for a few days in the fridge. You'll find endless uses for them.

Caponata

As well as being a lovely element in a spread of vegetable dishes, this classic, sweet-sour eggplant stew makes a fabulous crostini topping (see page 178). It's also a very good accompaniment to grilled foods.

SERVES 4

2 medium eggplants (about 1 pound / 500g), cut into ½-inch / 1cm cubes

Sea salt and freshly ground black pepper

2 tablespoons olive oil

1 onion, finely chopped

2 inner celery stalks, thinly sliced

1 garlic clove, chopped

6 large plum or other ripe tomatoes, peeled, seeded, and chopped or a 14-ounce / 400g can plum tomatoes, chopped, any stalky ends and skin removed

2 tablespoons balsamic vinegar

1 tablespoon brown sugar

1 tablespoon finely grated dark chocolate (optional)

⅓ cup / 50g golden raisins

2 tablespoons capers, rinsed

2 ounces / 60g pitted green olives, sliced

A good handful of flat-leaf parsley or mint, chopped, to finish

Put the eggplant cubes into a large colander and sprinkle with 2 teaspoons of salt. Toss together and then leave to draw out the juices for about half an hour. Rinse the eggplant and pat/squeeze dry with a kitchen towel.

While the eggplant is salting, heat 1 tablespoon of the olive oil in a large saucepan over fairly low heat. Add the onion, celery, and garlic and fry for about 10 minutes until tender and golden. Add the tomatoes with their juice and simmer for 5 minutes to reduce a little.

Now add the balsamic vinegar; sugar; chocolate, if using; golden raisins; capers; and olives to the pan. Simmer for another 5 to 10 minutes, stirring often, then turn off the heat.

In a large frying pan, heat the remaining 1 tablespoon of oil over medium-high heat. When hot, fry the eggplant cubes for about 5 minutes, stirring occasionally, until golden and tender. Tip them into the tomato mixture.

Return to a simmer and cook for another 10 minutes, then remove from the heat, cover, and leave until completely cooled. Taste and adjust the seasoning.

You can serve the caponata right away or leave it in the fridge or a very cool place for a day or two to allow the flavors to deepen even further; bring it to room temperature before serving. Sprinkle with plenty of chopped parsley or mint just before serving.

Vegetable tempura with chile dipping sauce ^v

All kinds of vegetables are excellent deep-fried within a crisp, light coating of tempura batter. But I'm not averse to doing this with one type of veg only, as in the picture. It may sound extravagant, but it's actually a brilliant way of serving asparagus.

The easy chile sauce will keep sealed in a jar for a week in the fridge if you have any left over. It's the perfect thing to perk up all manner of dressings and marinades.

SERVES 4 TO 6

Sunflower oil, for deep-frying

A selection from:

Asparagus spears

Zucchini slices (cut on the diagonal, 1/8-inch / 3mm thick)

Broccoli or cauliflower florets

Strips of bell pepper or eggplant

Green onions or thin wedges of red onion

Sliced large mushrooms

Wide ribbons of kale (stems removed)

FOR THE TEMPURA BATTER

3/4 cup / 100g all-purpose flour

6 tablespoons / 50g cornstarch

1/2 teaspoon baking powder

1/2 teaspoon sea salt

About 1/2 cup / 200 to 225ml ice-cold sparkling mineral water

FOR THE DIPPING SAUCE

6 tablespoons / 85g red currant or crab apple jelly

2 tablespoons cider vinegar

2 teaspoons soy sauce

2 fresh red chiles, seeded and very finely chopped

2 garlic cloves, very finely chopped

A few twists of black pepper

A good handful of cilantro, finely chopped (optional)

Make the dipping sauce first. Tip all of the ingredients except the cilantro into a small saucepan and stir over very low heat until the fruit jelly has dissolved and you are left with a silky syrup. Bring it to a simmer and let it bubble gently for a few minutes – this will mellow the harshness of the garlic. Set aside to cool to room temperature. If the sauce resets to a jelly when it's cooled, simply whisk in a splash of warm water. If using the cilantro, stir it in just before serving.

Have all the vegetables prepared and ready. Before you prepare the batter, heat about a 2-inch / 5cm depth of sunflower oil in a large, deep, heavy-bottomed saucepan until a cube of white bread dropped in turns golden brown in about 50 seconds.

To make the batter, sift the flour, cornstarch, baking powder, and salt into a bowl. Begin whisking in the water, ideally with an ice cube or two, until you have a batter the thickness of heavy cream. Be careful not to overmix and don't worry if there are a few lumps.

You will need to fry the prepared veg in batches. Begin dipping them in the batter, one piece at a time, transferring them to the hot oil as soon as they are coated; don't overcrowd the pan. Fry until they are crisp and a light golden color.

Remove carefully with tongs or a slotted spoon. Drain on paper towels and serve immediately with the dipping sauce. Eat with fingers or chopsticks!

Simple globe artichokes [*]

This is more a veg starter or preamble than a meze-style dish, but I love globe artichokes so much that I want to encourage everyone to eat them. Preparing them can seem fussy at first, but it's actually pretty straightforward and they make one of the most enjoyable of all summer starters.

SERVES 6

6 medium or large globe artichokes

A squeeze of lemon juice

Remove the toughest leaves from close to the base of each artichoke and trim the stem to about 1 inch / 2.5cm long (or, on good-sized ones, remove the stem completely so the artichoke sits flat on its base).

Place in a saucepan of lightly salted boiling water with a squeeze of lemon juice, or in a steamer, and cook for 15 to 30 minutes, depending on size and freshness. Just-cut artichokes will need less cooking. If you grow your own, you'll find that cooking them within minutes of cutting reduces the cooking time dramatically – to just 7 to 8 minutes for a small one. An artichoke is cooked when a leaf from the middle pulls away easily and the heart is tender when pierced with a knife.

To eat, pull off the outer leaves, dipping them in your chosen sauce and scraping away the tender part with your teeth. Work your way down to the tiny, papery leaves near the base; discard these. Remove the hairy part of the choke with a spoon, then tuck into the delicious heart.

HOW TO SERVE YOUR ARTICHOKES

• Enjoy them simply, with melted butter and a squeeze of lemon to dip the leaves into.

• Make a cheaty hollandaise: melt 10 tablespoons / 150g unsalted butter and whisk it, a little at a time, into an egg yolk until the sauce has the consistency of mayonnaise. Whisk in a generous squeeze of lemon juice and season with a pinch of salt and some pepper.

• Make a simple vinaigrette: put a crushed garlic clove, 1 teaspoon mustard, some salt and pepper, 2 tablespoons cider vinegar, and 6 tablespoons olive or canola oil in a screw-top jar and shake to emulsify. Add 1 tablespoon of finely chopped capers, too, if you like.

• Try grilled artichokes: boil or steam, as above, then slice them in half lengthwise, tip to base. Brush with some olive oil and cook the halves, cut side down, on a hot grill for a couple of minutes. Eat each half as above, relishing that intense, smoky flavor.

Deep-fried zucchini flowers stuffed with ricotta and herbs

This has got to rank as one of the most exquisite and delicious vegetable treats ever – it's certainly among my all-time favorites. You can vary the stuffing – or even leave it out altogether – and the dish will still be fantastic.

SERVES 4

Sunflower oil, for deep-frying

8 to 12 zucchini flowers

FOR THE FILLING

3½ ounces / 100g ricotta

2 good tablespoons grated Parmesan, hard goat cheese, or other well-flavored hard cheese

A large handful of mixed herbs, such as parsley and chives with a little marjoram or thyme, or parsley and a little mint, finely chopped

Sea salt and freshly ground black pepper

FOR THE BATTER

¾ cup / 100g all-purpose flour

6 tablespoons / 50g cornstarch

½ teaspoon baking powder

½ teaspoon sea salt

About 1 cup / 200 to 225ml ice-cold sparkling mineral water

TO FINISH

Flaky sea salt

Nasturtiums or other edible flowers (optional)

For the filling, beat the ricotta until soft and smooth, then stir in the cheese, herbs, and some salt and pepper. Carefully scoop the filling into the zucchini flowers: you should get 2 to 4 teaspoons in each one, depending on size. Twist the petals gently to enclose the mixture.

Heat about a 2½-inch / 6cm depth of oil in a deep-fat fryer or deep, heavy-bottomed saucepan (to come no more than a third of the way up the pan) until a cube of bread dropped in turns golden brown in about 1 minute.

While the oil heats, prepare the batter. Sift the flour, cornstarch, baking powder, and salt into a bowl. Begin whisking in the water; stop when you have a batter the thickness of heavy cream. Be careful not to overmix and don't worry if there are a few lumps.

Dip one stuffed zucchini flower into the batter and immediately lower into the hot oil. Repeat with a couple more; do not cook more than 3 or 4 at a time. Cook for 1 to 2 minutes, until puffed up, crisp, and golden brown. Drain on paper towels while you cook the remaining flowers. Serve as soon as possible, sprinkled with a little flaky sea salt and decorated, if you like, with other edible flowers.

VARIATIONS

Zucchini and goat cheese stuffed flowers
Use goat cheese in place of the ricotta and the soft zucchini mixture from the bruschetta on page 200, mixing them together before stuffing the flowers. Continue as above.

Risotto-stuffed zucchini flowers
Stuff the flowers with leftover risotto (see pages 269–72). As the risotto will have been chilled, you'll need to fry the flowers for a little longer.

Zucchini flowers stuffed with mozzarella
Slip a thick slice of good buffalo mozzarella, lightly seasoned with pepper, inside each zucchini flower, along with a couple of basil leaves. Dip in the batter and deep-fry as above. I've even managed to stuff a whole bocconcino (mini mozzarella) inside a large zucchini flower. As you'd expect, the cheese comes out lovely and melty.

Marinated zucchini with mozzarella

If you can make this with a mixture of green zucchini and yellow summer squash, it is particularly attractive, but just one type looks – and tastes – pretty good, too.

SERVES 2

4 medium zucchini
(about 1 pound / 500g)

5 tablespoons extra-virgin
olive or canola oil

1 large garlic clove,
finely slivered

Finely grated zest of 1 lemon,
plus a little juice

Sea salt and freshly ground
black pepper

A handful of mint or basil,
coarsely torn

1 ball of buffalo mozzarella
(about 4 ounces / 125g), or other
mild, soft cheese, sliced or
coarsely torn

Top and tail the zucchini, then cut them lengthwise into thin slices, $^1/_{16}$-inch / 1 to 2mm thick. Put them in a bowl with 2 tablespoons of the oil and use a pastry brush to get them all lightly coated.

Heat a large nonstick frying pan over fairly high heat. Working in batches, sear the zucchini slices for about 2 minutes on each side until tender and golden. Transfer them to a shallow dish.

Take the frying pan off the heat and let it cool down a bit. Add the remaining 3 tablespoons of oil, the garlic, and the lemon zest. Heat very gently for a few minutes – the residual heat in the pan may be enough – you just want to take the raw edge off the garlic and infuse the flavors into the oil.

Pour the infused oil over the zucchini. Add some salt and pepper, a little squeeze of lemon juice, and the mint or basil. Toss together, cover, and leave for 1 hour at room temperature.

Strew with mozzarella and serve with good bread or, better still, warm flat breads (see page 176).

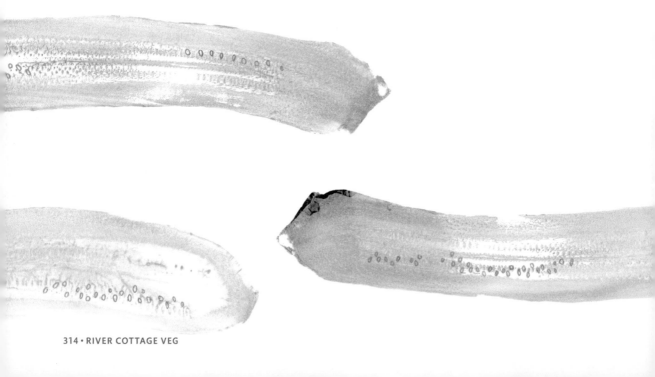

Fava beans with herbed goat cheese

*This is wonderful as part of a spread of small tapas-style dishes. It is also
a great starter or lunch, served with a hunk of bread or wedge of oily toast,
or folded into a wrap for a lunchbox or picnic basket.*

SERVES 4 TO 6

14 to 16 ounces / 400 to 500g
shelled young fava beans
(about 3 pounds / 1.5kg
unshelled)

FOR THE HERBED GOAT CHEESE

About 4 ounces / 125g soft, mild
goat cheese

4 to 5 tablespoons plain
full-fat yogurt

A good handful of mixed herbs,
such as parsley, chives, tarragon,
and thyme, chopped

A scrap of garlic, crushed

Sea salt and freshly ground
black pepper

Bring a large saucepan of water to a boil and drop in the fava beans.
Return to a simmer and cook until the beans are tender. For very
small, tender beans, this will be only a minute. Larger beans may take
2 to 3 minutes, but I wouldn't recommend using older, bigger beans
that need any longer. Drain well and slip larger beans out of their
skins; tender babies are fine as they are. Leave to cool completely.

Beat the goat cheese with the yogurt until reasonably smooth.
Mix in the chopped herbs, garlic, and some salt and pepper.

Fold the cooled beans into the goat cheese mixture. Taste and adjust
the seasoning if necessary before serving.

Broccoli salad with asian-style dressing ᵛ

*This simple salad is full of aromatic Eastern flavors, all beautifully carried by
the crunchy broccoli.*

SERVES 4

1 large head of broccoli
(about 1 pound / 500g)

½ garlic clove

1 teaspoon freshly grated
ginger

A pinch of sugar

Sea salt and freshly ground
black pepper

1 tablespoon rice vinegar or
cider vinegar

1 tablespoon toasted sesame oil

2 teaspoons soy sauce

2 teaspoons sesame seeds

2 or 3 green onions, trimmed
and thinly sliced

Cut the broccoli into small florets and steam, or cook it in some
lightly salted boiling water, until just tender but still a bit crunchy,
4 to 5 minutes.

Meanwhile, using a mortar and pestle, crush the garlic and ginger
with the sugar and some salt and pepper to a paste. Combine with
the vinegar, sesame oil, and soy sauce.

As soon as the broccoli is cooked, drain it in a colander and leave for
a few minutes so all the moisture can steam off. While still hot, toss
with the dressing and put into a serving dish. Set aside to cool.

Lightly toast the sesame seeds in a dry small frying pan until fragrant.
When the broccoli has cooled to room temperature, scatter over the
green onions and sesame seeds, and serve.

Cauliflower pakoras with tamarind raita

These irresistible morsels make a great canapé, but they are also very good before or alongside a curry. Eat them with your fingers as soon as they're cool enough to pick up: the contrast between the hot, spicy pakoras and the cold, slightly sour yogurt is delicious. If tamarind paste is not on hand, use mango chutney, or any spicy-sweet fruit chutney, instead.

SERVES 6 TO 8

1 medium-large cauliflower (about 1¾ pounds / 800g), trimmed

Sunflower oil, for frying

FOR THE BATTER

1½ cups / 150g chickpea flour

½ teaspoon baking powder

2 teaspoons ground cumin

2 teaspoons ground coriander

½ teaspoon ground turmeric

A good shake of cayenne pepper

½ teaspoon fine sea salt

FOR THE TAMARIND RAITA

6 heaping tablespoons plain full-fat yogurt

A large handful of cilantro, chopped (optional)

2 teaspoons seedless tamarind paste or mango chutney

Sea salt and freshly ground black pepper

First make the raita; mix together the yogurt; cilantro, if using; and the tamarind paste or chutney. Season with salt and pepper to taste and set aside.

Cut the cauliflower into small florets, no more than 1 inch / 2.5cm across in any direction, discarding nearly all the stalk.

For the batter, put the chickpea flour, baking powder, ground spices, and salt into a large bowl. Whisk to combine and get rid of any lumps. Slowly whisk in ¾ cup / 175ml of cold water, which should give you a smooth batter with a consistency similar to heavy cream. Add a little more water if necessary – different brands of chickpea flour will vary in how much they absorb.

Add the cauliflower florets to the batter and turn them, making sure they are all thoroughly coated.

Heat about a ½-inch / 1cm depth of oil in a large, heavy-bottomed saucepan over medium-high heat. When the oil is hot enough to turn a cube of white bread light golden brown in 30 to 40 seconds, start cooking the pakoras a few at a time, so you don't crowd the pan. Place spoonfuls of battered cauliflower – just a few florets per spoonful – into the hot oil. Cook for about 2 minutes, until crisp and golden brown on the base, then turn over and cook for another minute or two.

Drain the pakoras on paper towels, then serve piping hot with the raita for dipping.

VARIATION

Flat onion bhajis

Make the raita and batter as above, but use 3 medium onions or 2 dozen green onions instead of the cauliflower. Slice the onions fairly thinly and stir into the batter, making sure they're well coated. Heat the oil as above and fry spoonfuls of the onions in batches, being careful not to crowd the pan, for about 4 minutes, turning halfway through, until crisp and golden. Serve immediately, with the raita.

Spiced spinach and potatoes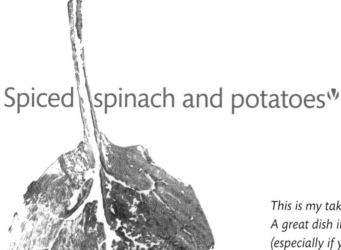

This is my take on saag aloo. A great dish in itself (especially if you add a poached egg), it also makes a lovely addition to a meze spread or a tasty side dish to serve with curries.

SERVES 4

14 ounces / 400g waxy or new potatoes

Sea salt and freshly ground black pepper

14 ounces / 400g spinach, stripped of any coarse stems

2 tablespoons canola or sunflower oil

1 onion, halved and thinly sliced

1 garlic clove, finely chopped

1 fresh red chile, seeded and finely chopped

1 good teaspoon freshly grated ginger

2 teaspoons garam masala

2 to 3 tablespoons heavy cream or coconut cream (optional)

Halve or quarter larger potatoes so that all the pieces are roughly the same size. Put into a saucepan, cover with water, add salt, and bring to a boil. Simmer for 8 to 12 minutes, until tender. Drain. (You can use leftover cooked potatoes for this dish, too.)

Wash the spinach thoroughly, then pack it, with just the water that clings to it, into a saucepan. Cover and put over medium heat until the spinach has wilted in its own liquid – just a few minutes. Drain and leave in a colander until cool enough to handle, then squeeze out as much liquid as you can with your hands. Chop the spinach coarsely.

Heat the oil in a frying pan and gently sweat the onion for 10 minutes or so, until soft. Meanwhile, thickly slice the potatoes. Add the garlic, chile, ginger, and garam masala to the onion and cook for a couple of minutes more, then add the potatoes and cook for a further couple of minutes.

Now add the chopped spinach and cook briefly to warm through. The dish is lovely like this, or you can make it a little richer and more luxurious by stirring in the heavy cream or coconut cream with the spinach. Either way, season with salt and pepper, and serve.

Patatas bravas^ⱽ

This is a classic Spanish tapa that works beautifully with a selection of other little dishes – chunks of frittata, simple salads, olives, dips, and so on – but it also makes a great starter in its own right. Add an extra chile if you want more heat. And if you have any sauce left over, save it to toss through hot pasta.

SERVES 4 TO 6

2 pounds / 1kg waxy or new potatoes, cut into 1-inch / 2.5cm cubes

5 tablespoons olive or canola oil

Flaky sea salt

FOR THE SPICY TOMATO SAUCE

2 tablespoons olive or canola oil

1 onion, finely chopped

A handful of thyme sprigs, leaves only, chopped

3 garlic cloves, finely chopped

1 small, fairly hot fresh red chile, seeded and finely chopped

1 (14-ounce / 400g) can plum tomatoes, chopped, any stalky ends and skin removed

2 teaspoons sweet paprika

A pinch of sugar

Sea salt and freshly ground black pepper

TO FINISH

A handful of parsley, coarsely chopped

First make the sauce. Heat the 2 tablespoons of oil in a saucepan over medium-low heat. Add the onion with the thyme and sweat until softened and translucent, about 10 minutes. Add the garlic and chile and cook, stirring, for a minute.

Now add the tomatoes with their juice, paprika, sugar, and some salt and pepper. Simmer for about 10 minutes, stirring occasionally and breaking up the tomatoes with a wooden spoon, until you have a nice, rich, piquant tomato sauce. Taste and adjust the seasoning if necessary and keep the sauce warm.

Bring a large saucepan of well-salted water to a boil, and add the potatoes. Bring back to a boil and cook for 5 to 8 minutes, until on the firm side of tender – that is, not quite done. Drain in a colander and leave to steam for a few minutes. Gently tip onto a clean kitchen towel and pat dry.

Warm the 5 tablespoons of oil in a large frying pan over medium-high heat and sauté the potatoes for 10 to 15 minutes, until crisp and golden. Drain on paper towels, tip into a warmed dish, and season with a scattering of flaky sea salt.

Check the consistency of the tomato sauce and thin it with a splash of hot water if necessary, then pour it over the potatoes. Scatter with chopped parsley and serve warm.

Sweet corn fritters with cilantro or mint raita

Sweet kernels of corn combine wonderfully with the earthy, fiery spices in these fritters. Serve small fritters as a meze/nibble, larger ones with a salad or two as a meal in themselves. The recipe makes 12 large or 24 canapé-sized fritters.

SERVES 4

1¼ cups / 120g chickpea flour

½ teaspoon baking powder

2 teaspoons ground cumin

2 teaspoons ground coriander

½ teaspoon ground turmeric

A shake of cayenne pepper

½ teaspoon fine sea salt

7 ounces / 200g fresh or frozen sweet corn kernels (no need to defrost if using frozen)

3 green onions, trimmed and finely chopped

A big handful of cilantro, coarsely chopped

½ to 1 small green chile, seeded and finely chopped (optional)

⅔ cup / 160ml whole milk or water

Sunflower or canola oil, for frying

FOR THE CILANTRO/MINT RAITA

¾ cup / 200g thick, plain full-fat yogurt (plus an extra ⅓ cup / 75g if not using goat cheese)

About 2½ ounces / 75g fresh, very soft goat cheese (optional)

A small bunch of cilantro or mint, coarsely chopped

Sea salt and freshly ground black pepper

First make the raita. Stir together the yogurt and goat cheese, if using. Add the chopped cilantro or mint and season with salt and pepper to taste.

For the fritter batter, sift the flour, baking powder, spices, and salt into a bowl. Mix in the corn, green onions, cilantro, and chile, if using. Slowly whisk in the milk or water until everything is well combined and there are no floury lumps.

Heat about a ½-inch / 1cm depth of oil in a heavy-bottomed saucepan over medium-high heat until a cube of white bread dropped into the oil turns light golden brown in 30 to 40 seconds. You will need to cook the fritters in batches. Drop spoonfuls of the batter (soup spoonfuls for large fritters, heaping teaspoons for canapé sized ones) into the oil, spacing them well apart; don't overcrowd the pan. Cook for about 3 minutes on each side, turning once. Remove and drain on paper towels.

Keep the corn fritters warm while you cook the rest. Serve with the cilantro or mint raita.

Spinach and thyme pasties

These tasty little parcels are very good still warm from the oven, but let them cool down and they'll pack a real punch for a picnic, a party, or a lunch box. If using ricotta, it's a good idea to add in the Parmesan, but if you're using a fairly strong goat cheese, you won't need it.

MAKES 6

FOR THE PASTRY

2 cups / 250g all-purpose flour

A pinch of sea salt

$^1/_2$ cup plus 1 tablespoon / 125g chilled unsalted butter, cut into small cubes

About 5 tablespoons / 75ml cold whole milk

FOR THE FILLING

12 ounces / 350g spinach, tough stems removed

1 tablespoon canola or olive oil

1 onion, finely chopped

1 garlic clove, finely chopped

About 4 ounces / 125g soft goat cheese or ricotta

About 1$^3/_4$ ounces / 50g Parmesan, finely grated (optional)

A pinch of freshly grated nutmeg

A handful of thyme sprigs (lemon thyme is particularly good), chopped

1 teaspoon finely grated lemon zest (optional)

1 large egg, lightly beaten

Sea salt and freshly ground black pepper

To make the pastry, sift together the flour and salt, or give them a quick blitz in a food processor. Add the butter and rub in with your fingertips, or blitz in the food processor, until the mixture resembles fine bread crumbs. Mix in the cold milk, little by little, until the pastry just comes together, then turn out onto a work surface and knead briefly to bring it into a ball. Wrap and chill for 30 minutes.

Preheat the oven to 350°F / 180°C. Line a baking sheet with parchment paper or a nonstick liner.

For the filling, wash the spinach thoroughly, then pack it, with just the water that clings to it, into a saucepan. Cover and put over medium heat until the spinach has wilted in its own steam. Drain in a colander. When the spinach is cool enough to handle, squeeze out as much moisture as you possibly can with your hands, then chop coarsely.

Meanwhile, heat the oil in a frying pan over medium heat and sweat the onion and garlic for about 10 minutes, until soft and translucent. Stir in the chopped spinach and leave to cool.

Tip the spinach mixture into a bowl and add the goat cheese or ricotta; Parmesan, if using; nutmeg; thyme; lemon zest, if using; about half of the beaten egg; and plenty of salt and pepper. Mash together thoroughly.

Roll out the pastry to a 10 by 15-inch / 26 by 39cm rectangle, about $^1/_8$ inch / 3mm thick, and cut into six 5-inch / 13cm squares. Brush the rim of each square with a little water. Divide the spinach mixture among the squares, then fold the pastry diagonally to enclose the filling and crimp the edges well to seal. Brush with the remaining beaten egg and make a slit in the top of each with a small, sharp knife.

Transfer the parcels to the prepared baking sheet and bake for 25 to 30 minutes, or until golden brown. Eat the pasties warm or at room temperature.

Roast, grill & broil

I look to roasting, grilling, and broiling to add whole new

layers of flavor to vegetables. These methods of controlled burning, if you like, caramelize the rich supply of natural sugars that most vegetables possess, giving them a resonance and character that simple boiling or steaming – useful techniques though these are – cannot.

We all know that the effect of roasting and broiling on meat is to give it a fantastic, deep, smoky-sweet taste, which comes from that browning and crisping of the exterior. What is perhaps not so widely recognized is that much the same transformation takes place when you char vegetables. Put a zucchini on the grill, get it really well cooked so the edges are almost burnt, the flesh striped with a thin layer of "vegetable charcoal," and you will create a delicious taste that simply wasn't there before. It's a pretty magical moment. It even has a name, if you want to get all scientific about it: the Maillard reaction, which describes the chemical change that occurs when sugars react, in the presence of heat, with other substances in a food, creating new molecules and thereby a new range of complex and highly appealing tastes and smells.

Vegetable cookery makes use of this flavor-generating technique all the time – when you fry and lightly brown an onion, or roast some spuds for Sunday lunch, you are pursuing just this aim – but the recipes in this chapter really bring it to the fore. And here's the big news: because the range of textures and flavors in the vegetable kingdom is so much wider than that of the animal kingdom, the charring of veg offers a far greater variety of novel tastes than the charring of meat.

I roast vegetables several times a week. The technique is so simple and so forgiving, and I've not yet met a vegetable that didn't respond well to it. (Lettuce, maybe . . .) Indeed, I hope this chapter will have you roasting things you never would have considered before: not just potatoes, parsnips, and peppers, but squash, carrots, beets, even cauliflower and brussels sprouts.

Once you've got the hang of the taste-transforming alchemy, you can develop it – with the addition of spices, perhaps some garlic and chile. What goes into the oven as a simple assembly of vegetables, oil, and seasoning becomes something else entirely: a glorious dish full of complexities and different flavor notes. The beautiful colors of browned veg shouldn't be overlooked either – this is food that tends to look incredibly appetizing.

Roasted veg is not only delicious but wonderfully versatile. It's good hot, of course – but I frequently eat the leftovers cold, in a salad, or blitzed with some stock and maybe some herbs or spices to make a soup that I can then reheat. A blended soup made with roasted veg has deeper and more resonant flavors than one made with boiled. In short, a hot oven is often, for me, the most obvious tool to use when I want to rustle up some delicious veg with very little effort.

Broiling and griddling use the same application of high heat to brown and sweeten vegetables, but these techniques are even more direct and controlled, especially because the contact is with hot metal, rather than hot air. I use the overhead broiler to turn out things like tomatoes on toast or tender, smoky eggplant slices, but the ridged grill pan is my favorite tool here. This heavy-bottomed, corrugated pan is essentially a sort of indoor barbecue. Its main marketing pitch may be the promise of those alluring char lines on your home-cooked steak, but it delivers them just as effectively to vegetables, producing zebra stripes of irresistible flavor on eggplants, zucchini, beets . . . you name it.

Of course, if it's full-on, freshly fired smokiness you're after, it's really hard to beat the outdoor grill. It can work wonders on everything from fennel to asparagus, sweet potatoes to green onions. It's true that this is something of a seasonal cooking method – but include an umbrella as well as a sun hat in your grilling kit, and you should be able to get good results for at least six months of the year. (If it's truly torrential, you can always default indoors to the aforementioned ridged grill pan.)

A platter of roasted, grilled, or broiled vegetables, of just one kind or several, is welcome on any table. Some of the recipes you'll find in the following pages, such as caramelized carrots with gremolata (see page 355) and roasted parsnip "chips" (see page 357) are definitely more side dish than centerpiece: perfect when combined with other roasted veg and/or salads, good bread, and some kind of dressing, even if it's just a trickle of good oil and a squeeze of lemon. However, others such as halloumi, new potato, and tomato kebabs (see page 334) stand as dishes in their own right, where that alluring, almost-burnt flavor can really steal the show.

One of the greatest challenges to which I've risen while exploring a life with less meat has undoubtedly been the vegetable-only summer barbecue. Thanks to some of these recipes, it was also one of the most rewarding.

Chargrilled summer veg^v

I learned the joy of chargrilling veg over twenty years ago when I was working at the River Cafe. I still come back to it every summer. Vary the vegetables as you like here, bumping up the zucchini if you have lots in the garden, or adding some quartered bell peppers, eggplant sticks, or slices of red onion. I like to toss the veg with chopped herbs, though they are very good just as they are. They're also delicious trickled with the tahini dressing on page 74.

SERVES 2 TO 4

4 zucchini

2 fennel bulbs, trimmed

A generous bunch of green onions, trimmed

4 to 6 tablespoons olive oil

1 garlic clove, very thinly sliced

Juice of 1 lemon

Sea salt and freshly ground black pepper

A small bunch of parsley or basil, plus a few sprigs of chervil, tarragon, or thyme, chopped fairly finely (optional)

1 ounce / 30g Parmesan, hard goat cheese, or other well-flavored hard cheese, to finish (optional)

Light the grill well in advance if you are cooking the veg outside. If cooking indoors, heat the griddle or grill pan over high heat until hot or preheat the broiler.

Cut the zucchini and fennel lengthwise into ¼-inch / 6mm slices and set aside with the whole green onions.

In a small bowl, lightly mix together the olive oil, garlic, and lemon juice with some salt and pepper.

Lightly brush the vegetables with a little of the olive oil mixture (try not to get any bits of garlic on the veg at this stage, as they will burn on the grill). Cook the veg in batches over a medium-hot fire, on the griddle or grill pan, or under the broiler, until marked with scorch lines on the outside and tender right through. Zucchini and fennel should take 3 to 5 minutes per side, green onions 1 to 2 minutes per side, but be vigilant, as a hot grill can burn them very quickly. As you take each batch off the grill, put into a large serving dish and toss with a little more of the oil mixture.

When everything is cooked, toss it together with the chopped herbs, if using, and finish with cheese shavings if you like. Serve either warm or at room temperature.

Halloumi, new potato, and tomato kebabs

Salty, chewy halloumi cheese is great with all kinds of grilled summer vegetables. You can adapt this recipe as you like, using zucchini, eggplants, and bell peppers as well as, or instead of, the potatoes and tomatoes.

SERVES 4

9 ounces / 250g small, waxy new potatoes

Sea salt

1 pound / 500g halloumi cheese

7 ounces / 200g cherry tomatoes

A handful of bay leaves

FOR THE MARINADE

3 tablespoons olive oil

A handful of thyme sprigs, leaves only, finely chopped

A handful of mint, finely chopped

1 teaspoon clear honey

1/2 teaspoon dried chile flakes

TO SERVE

Plain full-fat yogurt

A few mint leaves, chopped

Hummus (optional)

A little extra-virgin olive oil (optional)

A squeeze of lemon juice (optional)

Light the grill, if using – to allow time for the flames to die down and the coals to develop an even cooking heat. If you're using wooden skewers, soak 6 to 8 of them in cold water at least 30 minutes ahead of cooking.

Put the potatoes in a saucepan, cover with water, add salt, and bring to a boil. Simmer for 8 to 10 minutes, until almost tender – just a shade underdone. Drain and leave to cool slightly.

Whisk together the ingredients for the marinade in a large bowl. Cut larger potatoes into halves or quarters. Cut the halloumi into 1-inch / 2 to 3cm cubes and add to the marinade with the potatoes and tomatoes. Turn to coat well and leave to marinate for 10 minutes.

Thread the potatoes, tomatoes, and halloumi cubes onto the skewers, interspersing a few bay leaves with the veg on each one. If you are cooking indoors, preheat the broiler or heat a grill pan over high heat. If cooking on a grill, you need medium heat – you should be able to hold the palm of your hand about 6 inches / 15cm above the fire for 5 to 6 seconds.

Put the skewers on the grill, under the broiler, or in the grill pan and cook for about 10 minutes, turning from time to time, until the cheese and veg are hot and starting to blister on the outside.

For the full kebab-style presentation, serve with yogurt flavored with some chopped mint, and hummus loosened with a little extra-virgin olive oil and a squeeze of lemon. (Or try the cannellini bean hummus and paprika oil on page 300.) Accompany with warm, soft flat breads (see page 176) or pita.

Charred baby leeks with romesco ♥

Romesco, a brick-orange blend of garlic, nuts, tomatoes, and chiles, is a Catalan sauce that is great with pretty much any grilled vegetable – certainly zucchini, eggplant, and fennel.

SERVES 4 AS A STARTER

About 14 ounces / 400g baby leeks, or large green onions

1 tablespoon olive oil

Sea salt and freshly ground black pepper

FOR THE ROMESCO

1 large or 2 medium fresh red chiles (hot, but not too fiery)

3 or 4 large plum or other large ripe tomatoes (about 10 ounces / 300g)

½ red bell pepper (optional)

1 slice of sourdough or other robust bread (about 2 ounces / 60g), crusts removed

7 tablespoons / 100ml olive oil

2 fat garlic cloves, peeled and halved

½ cup / 50g hazelnuts, lightly toasted and skinned

1 tablespoon red wine vinegar

½ teaspoon sweet smoked paprika

Sea salt and freshly ground black pepper

Light the grill well in advance if you are cooking the veg outside. To make the romesco, on the grill, in a cast-iron grill pan over high heat, or foil-lined baking sheet under a hot broiler, char the chile(s), tomatoes, and red pepper, if using, until blackened all over. (Or roast at 400°F / 200°C for 25 to 30 minutes, but you'll have less of the charred flavor). Leave to cool, then peel off the skins. Cut out the stem end from the tomatoes. Remove the seeds and stem(s) from the chile(s) and pepper. Put the chile(s), tomatoes, and red pepper in a food processor.

Cut the bread into chunks. Heat the olive oil gently in a small frying pan. Add the halved garlic cloves and fry gently for a few minutes until they are just turning golden. Scoop out and add to the food processor. Add the bread cubes to the pan and fry for a few minutes until golden. Leave to cool a little, then add to the processor with the toasted nuts, wine vinegar, paprika, and some salt and pepper. Blend to a chunky purée. Taste and adjust the seasoning. If the sauce seems overly thick, you can thin it down with a little more oil and/or a dash of hot water.

Very slender baby leeks or green onions don't need precooking but leeks more than ½-inch / 1cm thick benefit from being blanched before grilling. Add to a saucepan of boiling water and blanch for 1 to 2 minutes, then drain and refresh under cold running water. Drain and pat dry.

Toss the leeks with the olive oil and some salt and pepper. If cooking indoors, preheat the broiler. Cook the leeks on a medium-hot grill or under the broiler for a few minutes, turning from time to time, until lightly charred and tender. Serve warm with the sauce.

VARIATION

Roasted leeks with romesco or cannellini bean hummus ♥
Trim 4 medium leeks, removing the outer layer, wash, and cut into 1½-inch / 3 to 4cm lengths. Toss in a roasting dish with 2 tablespoons canola or olive oil and plenty of salt and pepper. Cover with foil and roast at 350°F / 180°C for 30 minutes, until tender. Uncover and roast for a further 10 minutes. Let stand for a few minutes. Serve warm, with romesco or cannellini bean hummus and paprika oil (see page 300).

Grilled asparagus spears with lemon dressing

These can be done on a grill outdoors, or on a ridged cast-iron grill pan in the kitchen, or in a pinch, even under a broiler. When grilling, threading the asparagus spears onto skewers makes it easier to turn and cook them without losing them through the bars of the grate.

SERVES 4

20 to 30 asparagus spears, trimmed

4 tablespoons olive or canola oil

Flaky sea salt and freshly ground black pepper

Juice of 1/2 lemon

6 to 10 mint leaves, finely shredded

Parmesan, pecorino, or hard goat cheese, to serve (optional)

Light the grill well in advance if you are cooking the asparagus outside. Soak 6 wooden skewers in water for 30 minutes.

If the asparagus spears are pretty thick or perhaps not so freshly cut, it's best to blanch them first. Add to a saucepan of boiling water, blanch for 1 minute, then drain and refresh in cold water. Drain well and pat dry.

Thread the asparagus on to the skewers – you can mount 5 or 6 of them on a single skewer, pushing it through the middle of the spears. Brush the asparagus with 2 tablespoons of the oil and season with salt and pepper.

If cooking indoors, heat a grill pan over high heat or preheat the broiler until hot, then place the asparagus skewers in the grill pan or under the broiler about 4 inches / 10cm from the heat. If using an outdoor grill, you want it medium-hot, rather than super-fierce – you should be able to hold your palm about 6 inches / 15cm above the coals for a few seconds. Grill the asparagus spears for about 3 minutes on each side, depending on thickness, until tender in the center and lightly charred on the outside.

Whisk the remaining 2 tablespoons oil with the lemon juice, some pepper, and the mint to make a dressing. Remove the asparagus from the skewers, arrange on a plate and trickle the dressing over them. Sprinkle with flaky salt and shave some cheese over the top, if you like.

Broiled eggplants with chile and honey

Well-oiled eggplant slices – broiled until really soft and yielding – make a delicious, velvety sponge for the flavors of honey, lemon, chile, and thyme. Other herbs would work well here, too, giving the dish a subtly different character – try parsley, basil, mint, or cilantro.

SERVES 4

3 medium eggplants (about 1½ pounds / 750g), trimmed

Olive oil, for brushing

Sea salt and freshly ground black pepper

1 fresh red chile, seeded and finely chopped

A few sprigs of thyme, leaves only

A little clear honey

A little lemon juice

Preheat the broiler. Slice the skin off the eggplants, then cut crosswise into ½-inch / 1cm slices. Place on a foil-lined broiler pan. Brush liberally with oil and sprinkle with salt and pepper. Broil until golden brown on one side, then flip the slices over, brush with more oil, and season with more salt and pepper. Keep broiling until the slices are deep golden brown all over and very tender, flipping them again if you need to. This will take around 15 to 20 minutes.

Transfer the grilled eggplant slices to a plate or dish, layering them if you need to, and sprinkling each layer with chopped chile and thyme leaves. Trickle with a little honey and lemon juice. Leave for at least 10 minutes until tepid or, even better, 30 minutes until cooled, by which time the juices will have run and mingled a little.

Add more salt and pepper if you think it necessary, then serve as a starter, with bread, or as part of a meze spread.

Honey-roasted cherry tomatoes

These gorgeously sweet and tangy, juicy and sticky tomatoes are fantastic
served on top of a simple, saffron-infused risotto. You can also serve them
as a complement to almost any other grilled or roasted veg, but I particularly
like them piled on toast with a sprinkling of flaky sea salt on top.

SERVES 4

1 pound / 500g cherry tomatoes

2 garlic cloves

1 tablespoon clear honey

3 tablespoons olive oil

Flaky sea salt and freshly
ground black pepper

Preheat the oven to 375°F / 190°C. Lightly oil a roasting pan. Halve the tomatoes and place them, cut side up, in the dish. They should fit snugly with little or no space between them.

Crush the garlic with a pinch of salt, then beat it with the honey, olive oil, and a good grinding of pepper. Spoon this sticky, garlicky mixture over the cherry tomatoes. Roast for about 30 minutes, until golden, juicy, and bubbling.

Seared belgian endive with blue cheese

The combination of hot, tender, wilted, bittersweet Belgian endive with some bubbling,
salty blue cheese is a love-it-or-hate-it thing. No prizes for guessing which way I go.

SERVES 4

4 small or 2 large heads
of Belgian endive

3 tablespoons canola
or olive oil

Sea salt and freshly ground
black pepper

About 4 ounces / 125g blue
cheese, thinly sliced

Extra-virgin olive oil, to finish

Cut each head of endive in half lengthwise, keeping them joined at the root end. Put them into a large bowl, trickle over the oil, and add plenty of salt and pepper. Work the oil and seasoning all over the endive with your hands.

Preheat the broiler and put a large broilersafe nonstick frying pan or a ridged grill pan over fairly high heat. When the pan is hot, add the endive, cut side down. Cook for about 2 minutes, until golden brown and wilted at the base, then turn the endive halves over and cook for another minute or two.

Lay the sliced cheese over the endive and put under the broiler for a minute or two until the cheese is melted and bubbling. Trickle over some extra-virgin olive oil and serve right away, with bread.

Roasted eggplant "boats"

This is a really simple but delicious way to cook eggplants. Usually I serve them with fresh mint and yogurt, but I've also tried smearing them with a little homemade pesto, which is lovely. To make a meal of them, serve alongside a simple couscous salad, or just a green salad and some hot flat breads (see page 176).

SERVES 2 TO 4

2 large eggplants (about 1½ pounds / 700g)

3 garlic cloves, finely chopped

2 or 3 pinches dried chile flakes or ½ to 1 large fresh red chile, seeded and finely chopped

3 tablespoons olive oil, plus more for trickling

Sea salt and freshly ground black pepper

TO SERVE

4 to 6 tablespoons / 65 to 90g thick, plain full-fat yogurt, plus about 8 mint leaves, shredded or 2 to 3 tablespoons pesto (see page 256)

Preheat the oven to 375°F / 190°C. Cut the eggplants in half lengthwise. Using a small, sharp knife, make a series of deep slashes diagonally across the flesh, going about two-thirds of the way into the flesh, but not right through to the skin. You want to end up with 6 to 10 slashes, ½ inch / 1 to 2cm apart in each, depending on the size of your eggplants.

Mix the garlic and chile with the olive oil. Hold one eggplant half in your hand and squeeze it from side to side so the slashes open up a little. Spoon some of the garlic and chile oil over the eggplant with a teaspoon, using the back of the spoon to work the oil down into the slashes. Repeat with the other halves.

Put the eggplant halves, flesh side up, in a roasting pan. Sprinkle with salt and pepper, then trickle over a little more olive oil – there should be little or no unoiled flesh showing on each eggplant half. Roast for about 50 minutes, or until deep golden brown and completely tender.

Leave the eggplants to cool slightly. Serve them hot or warm, either dabbed with yogurt and sprinkled with mint and a touch more salt, or smeared with a little pesto.

Roasted squash ᵛ

Roasting is the technique I choose most often to cook squash and pumpkin: it gives such a tasty, caramelized edge to their sweet flesh. Simply done like this, they are a great side dish, but can also be used as the starting point for all sorts of fantastic meals (see below).

Preheat the oven to 375°F / 190°C. Slice the squash into quarters and scoop out the seeds with a spoon. You can leave the skin on at this stage, or peel it off if you prefer. Cut the squash into wedges or large chunks and put them in a roasting pan. Add the garlic, along with any of the optional extras you fancy, and some salt and pepper.

Trickle over the oil and toss the lot together. Roast for 40 to 55 minutes, turning once or twice during cooking, until the squash is completely soft and starting to caramelize on the corners and edges.

THINGS TO DO WITH YOUR ROASTED SQUASH

• Toss with toasted walnuts, pine nuts, or hazelnuts, or a scattering of pistachio dukka (see page 294), trickle over a little more oil and squeeze over some lemon juice before serving with a green salad.

• Combine with roasted red onion wedges, couscous, grated lemon zest and juice, lots of chopped parsley, a generous trickle of oil, and plenty of salt and pepper.

• Add to a risotto or a "speltotto" (see page 283), toward the end of cooking. Finish with some chopped sage.

• Blitz roasted squash in a food processor to make a delicious purée, or do so with some stock for a fast and satisfying soup. Finish the soup with a scattering of toasted pumpkin seeds if you like.

• Add chunks of roasted squash to vegetable curries.

Stuffed peppers with new potatoes, feta, and pesto

This is a lovely, simple way to enjoy the smoky taste of roasted peppers without any of the bother of peeling them. The potatoes, meanwhile, make this a pleasingly substantial dish. You could use a good store-bought pesto, but a homemade one will be better.

SERVES 4

7 ounces / 200g small new potatoes

4 red bell peppers

1 tablespoon olive oil

7 ounces / 200g feta cheese

1/4 cup / 55g pesto (see page 256)

Sea salt and freshly ground black pepper

A small handful of basil leaves, shredded, to finish (optional)

Preheat the oven to 400°F / 200°C. Bring a saucepan of salted water to a boil, add the potatoes, and boil for 8 to 12 minutes, until just tender. Drain and cool slightly.

Halve the peppers lengthwise and remove the seeds and ribs. Brush the outsides with the olive oil, then place in a roasting pan.

Halve or quarter the new potatoes and place in a bowl. Cut the feta into 1/2-inch / 1cm cubes and add to the potatoes. Add the pesto, season with salt and pepper, and toss until well combined.

Spoon the filling into the halved peppers and bake for 40 to 45 minutes, until browned on the top. If using shredded basil, scatter over the peppers before serving.

Roasted potatoes and eggplants ᵛ

This is a very simple dish, and one that doesn't take long to cook. You can serve it alongside a rich stew, or as part of a spread of meze-type dishes. There are various ways to finish it that subtly alter its character: stir in the finely grated zest of a lemon when it comes out of the oven, or dust with hot smoked paprika for a patatas bravas *effect. Leftovers are great in an omelet or frittata.*

SERVES 4

¼ cup / 60ml canola
or olive oil

2 medium eggplants
(about 1 pound / 500g)

About 1 pound / 500g potatoes
(any type will do), unpeeled

Sea salt and freshly ground
black pepper

2 garlic cloves, sliced

Lemon juice

TO FINISH (OPTIONAL)

Finely grated lemon zest,
hot smoked paprika, or
chopped herbs

Preheat the oven to 400°F / 200°C. Put the oil in a large nonstick roasting pan and heat in the oven for a good 10 minutes, until the oil is sizzling hot.

Meanwhile, cut the eggplants and potatoes into 1-inch / 2.5cm cubes, tip into a bowl, and season with salt and pepper. Take the roasting pan from the oven and place on a stable, heatproof surface. Add the eggplants and potatoes and turn to coat in the oil, being careful not to splash yourself. Roast for about 30 minutes, stirring halfway through.

Remove from the oven, stir in the garlic, and roast for another 10 to 15 minutes, until the vegetables are golden brown all over. Add a squeeze of lemon juice, a little more salt and pepper if needed, and any finishing touches you fancy. Serve warm or at room temperature.

VARIATION

Roasted spiced eggplants with chickpeas ᵛ
Omit the potatoes and use a total of 5 medium eggplants (about 2½ pounds / 1.2kg). Toss the cubed eggplant with ¼ teaspoon ground cumin; ¼ teaspoon ground coriander; and a small fresh red chile, finely chopped (or a good pinch of cayenne). After the initial 30 minutes' roasting time, add a drained and rinsed 14-ounce / 400g can of chickpeas, along with the sliced garlic, and return to the oven for 10 minutes. Season with salt, pepper, and lemon juice, and add the grated zest of a small lemon and lots of chopped parsley and cilantro. Serve warm or at room temperature.

Roasted brussels sprouts with shallots℣

This is a dish to convert sprout shirkers – it's a delicious, easy way to serve sprouts, and one that's likely to encourage you to dish them up more often. For a change, try a sprinkling of cumin or caraway seeds instead of thyme.

SERVES 4

14 ounces / 400g brussels sprouts, trimmed and halved (or left whole if small)

12 ounces / 350g shallots, peeled and halved, or small onions, peeled and halved or quartered

3 tablespoons canola oil

Sea salt and freshly ground black pepper

Several sprigs of thyme

A squeeze of lemon juice

Preheat the oven to 375°F / 190°C. Put the brussels sprouts and shallots or onions in a large roasting pan. Trickle over the oil, season with salt and pepper, and toss to coat, then tuck in some thyme sprigs.

Roast for about 35 minutes, giving a good stir halfway through, until everything is a bit crispy, brown, and caramelized.

Squeeze some lemon juice over the roasted vegetables, along with a sprinkling of fresh thyme if you like, and serve.

Roasted cauliflower with lemon and paprika℣

Another "veg-you-wouldn't-think-of-roasting," these cauliflower florets make a great nibble to go with drinks but they are also very good as part of a spread of tapas-type dishes. The smoky, caramelized flavor has been known to win over even the most cauliflower-skeptical.

SERVES 4

1 medium-large cauliflower (about 1½ pounds / 750 to 800g), trimmed

2 lemons

3 tablespoons olive oil

½ teaspoon hot smoked paprika

Flaky sea salt and freshly ground black pepper

Preheat the oven to 425°F / 220°C. Cut the cauliflower into medium florets and rinse, leaving some of the water clinging to the florets. Put them in a large roasting pan, squeeze over the juice from one of the lemons, trickle over the olive oil, and add the paprika and some salt and pepper. Toss the whole lot together.

Cut the remaining lemon into 6 segments and scatter these in the pan. Roast for 25 to 30 minutes, turning once, until the florets are slightly caramelized at the edges.

Squeeze the juice from the roasted lemon segments over the roasted cauliflower and serve at once, scattered with a little flaky sea salt.

Caramelized carrots with gremolata

The contrast of sweet, caramelized carrots and zesty gremolata is brilliant – and it looks great, too. But if you fancy a variation, try tossing the cooked carrots with my pistachio dukka (see page 294) instead. I like to do this with young, small summer carrots, but you can use bigger winter ones if you cut them into long, thin batons.

SERVES 4

1 tablespoon canola
or olive oil

2 tablespoons / 30g butter

1 pound / 500g young carrots,
larger ones halved lengthwise

Sea salt and freshly ground
black pepper

FOR THE GREMOLATA

½ garlic clove

A small bunch of flat-leaf
parsley, leaves only

Finely grated zest of 1 lemon

Preheat the oven to 350°F / 180°C. Put the oil and butter in a large roasting pan and place in the oven until the butter melts. Add the carrots, season generously with salt and pepper, and toss well. Cover with foil and roast in the oven for 30 to 40 minutes, until the carrots are tender.

Take the pan out of the oven, remove the foil, and give the carrots a stir. Roast, uncovered, for 20 to 30 minutes, until they start to brown and caramelize.

While the carrots are in the oven, make the gremolata. Coarsely chop the garlic on a large cutting board, then add the parsley and lemon zest. Use a large, sharp knife to chop and mix the three ingredients together until very fine and well mixed.

As soon as the carrots are ready, toss them with the gremolata and serve right away.

Roasted parsnip "chips"

*I think the top-heavy cone shape of parsnips is a vital part
of their charm. Roast them like this, in long, thin "chips,"
and they're crisp and caramelized at the thin ends, chewy
in the middle and tender and creamy at the fat ends – really,
the best of all worlds. Small or medium parsnips will give you
elegant, slender, slightly curved "chips." Sometimes I roast
some shallots or onions with them, and sometimes I don't . . .*

SERVES 4 TO 6

1¹/₂ to 2 pounds / 750g to 1kg
smallish parsnips

¹/₂ to 1 pound / 250 to 500g
small onions or shallots
(optional)

2 to 3 tablespoons canola
or olive oil

Sea salt and freshly ground
black pepper

Preheat the oven to 375°F / 190°C. Peel the parsnips, top and tail
them, and quarter lengthwise. Any very thick pieces should be cut
in half lengthwise again – you want the pieces to be no more than
1 inch / 2.5cm wide at the thickest end. Put the parsnips into a large
roasting pan, spreading them out evenly. (If using both parsnips and
onions or shallots, you'll need a pretty large pan, or two smaller ones.)

Peel the onions or shallots, if using, and trim each end, but keep
them together at the root end. Cut the onions into eighths; halve or
quarter shallots lengthwise. Add them to the pan with the parsnips.
It's important not to crowd the pan – the vegetables can be snug, but
in a single layer, not overlapping or piled on top of each other.

Trickle over the oil, sprinkle with some salt and pepper, and toss the
lot together. Roast for 40 to 50 minutes, giving the veg all a good stir
about halfway through the cooking time. The parsnips are ready when
they are tender, crispy, caramelized, and well browned. The onions will
be soft in the middle and nicely browned at the edges and ends.

Roasted new potatoes with two mojo sauces ⱴ

A mojo *is an intensely flavored, aromatic sauce that hails from the Canary Islands. It is generally served with potatoes – often boiled in very salty water so that a fine crust of salt clings to their skins. I also like them with simply roasted new spuds, as in this recipe.*

SERVES 4 TO 6

2 pounds / 1kg small new potatoes

2 to 3 tablespoons olive oil

Sea salt and freshly ground black pepper

FOR THE MOJO PICÓN

2 mild dried chiles, such as ancho

2 roasted red bell peppers (from a jar or cooked as on page 336), coarsely chopped

1 garlic bulb, cloves separated and peeled

3/4 teaspoon ground cumin

1/2 teaspoon sweet smoked paprika

7 tablespoons / 100ml white wine vinegar

3/4 cup / 180ml extra-virgin olive oil

Sea salt and freshly ground black pepper

FOR THE MOJO CILANTRO

1 garlic bulb, cloves separated and peeled

3/4 teaspoon ground cumin

Sea salt and freshly ground black pepper

7 tablespoons / 100ml white wine vinegar

A big handful of cilantro, finely chopped

3/4 cup / 180ml extra-virgin olive oil

First make the sauces, to allow time for their flavors to develop. For the mojo picón, put the dried chiles in a bowl and cover with boiling water. Leave to soak for 45 minutes, then drain, stem, and chop. If you have a good, large mortar and pestle, use it to pound the chopped chiles, red peppers, garlic, cumin, and paprika until smooth. Stir in the wine vinegar and then slowly mix in the extra-virgin olive oil until you have a thick sauce. Alternatively, you can blitz everything together in a blender, but leave it with just a bit of texture. Season with salt and pepper to taste, adding a touch more vinegar, too, if you like.

For the mojo cilantro, put the garlic cloves in a large mortar with the cumin and a good pinch of salt, then pound with a pestle until you have a smooth paste. Stir in the wine vinegar, then the chopped cilantro. Finally, stir in the oil slowly until you have a smooth, herby dressing. Alternatively, you can do this in a blender. Season with salt and pepper to taste, adding a touch more vinegar, too, if you like.

To roast the potatoes, preheat the oven to 400°F / 200°C. Bring a large saucepan of salted water to a boil, add the potatoes, and boil for 5 minutes. Drain well and leave to steam in the colander for a few minutes to drive off excess moisture. Cut any larger spuds in half or into quarters, so they are roughly the same as the smaller whole ones.

Toss the potatoes with the olive oil in a roasting pan. Season well with salt and pepper and roast for 25 to 30 minutes until golden and crisp. Serve the potatoes hot, with the mojo sauces for dipping.

Roasted roots with apples and rosemary ⱴ

This dish produces a lovely commingling of rooty, fruity, sweet, and aromatic flavors. You can include some squash or pumpkin, too, if you like.

SERVES 4

2 pounds / 1kg mixed root veg, such as parsnips, celery root, carrots, Jerusalem artichokes, and potatoes

3 tablespoons canola or olive oil

Sea salt and freshly ground black pepper

3 medium or 2 large crisp, tart eating apples, cut into eighths, core removed, skin left on

A couple of sprigs of rosemary, coarsely torn

Preheat the oven to 375°F / 190°C. Peel all the vegetables and cut into medium spears or chunks. Put into a large roasting pan with the oil and some salt and pepper. Toss well and roast for about 35 minutes, stirring halfway through, until the veg are tender and starting to brown.

Add the apple wedges and rosemary, toss with the roots, and roast for a further 15 to 20 minutes, until the apples are golden. Serve at once.

Oven-roasted ratatouille^ᵛ

*Roasting intensifies the flavors of the veg in this modern interpretation of the
classic Niçoise dish. The rich, garlicky tomato sauce that ties it all together
could very deliciously be replaced by one recipe of my roasted tomato sauce
(see page 366). Serve the ratatouille with bread and salad to make a main
course, as a side dish, or part of a spread.*

SERVES 4

2 onions, peeled

2 red, orange, or yellow bell
peppers, halved, cored, and
seeded

14 ounces / 400g zucchini

1 large eggplant (about
12 ounces / 350g)

5 tablespoons olive oil

Sea salt and freshly ground
black pepper

FOR THE TOMATO SAUCE

2 tablespoons olive oil

3 garlic cloves, slivered

2 (14-ounce / 400g) cans plum
tomatoes, chopped, any stalky
ends and skin removed

1 bay leaf

A large sprig of thyme

Sea salt and freshly ground
black pepper

A pinch of sugar

TO FINISH

A small handful of oregano
or thyme sprigs, leaves only,
chopped

Preheat the oven to 375°F / 190°C. Cut the onions into thick slices
from root to tip. Cut the peppers into 1-inch / 2.5cm pieces. If the
zucchini are very thick, halve them lengthwise before slicing them
thickly. Cut the eggplant into 1-inch / 2.5cm cubes.

Tip the vegetables into a large roasting pan, add the olive oil and
plenty of salt and pepper, and toss well together. Roast for 1 to
1½ hours, giving it all a good stir once or twice, until the vegetables
are tender, reduced, and starting to brown in places.

Meanwhile, make the tomato sauce. Heat the olive oil in a large frying
pan over medium-low heat. Add the garlic and let it sizzle gently for a
minute, without browning, then add the tomatoes with their juice, the
bay leaf, and thyme. Cook at a gentle simmer for about 45 minutes,
stirring often and crushing the tomatoes down with a fork. When you
have a thick, pulpy sauce, season with salt, pepper, and the sugar.

When the veg are cooked, add the tomato sauce, mix well, then
return to the oven for 10 minutes until bubbling and fragrant. While
still hot, stir in the chopped oregano or thyme. Serve the ratatouille
warm or at room temperature, but not chilled.

VARIATION

Dry-roasted ratatouille ^ᵛ

This is a lovely variation using oven-roasted cherry tomatoes instead
of the tomato sauce. It's great served on bruschetta, or with couscous
or rice. Arrange 1 pound / 500g of halved cherry tomatoes snugly in
a single layer in a roasting pan (slightly smaller than the one you're
roasting the veg in). Trickle with a little olive oil and season with salt
and pepper. Roast the tomatoes at the same time as the veg, on a
lower oven shelf, for at least an hour (but not as long as the veg), until
reduced, wrinkled, and lightly charred. Once the roasted vegetables
and tomatoes have cooled a little, toss them very gently together in
a bowl. Trickle with a little best-quality olive oil and serve at room
temperature.

Roasted squash and shallots
with merguez chickpeas♥

I like to cook dried chickpeas from scratch for this dish. Mixed with the spicy oil while still hot, they absorb the flavors beautifully – and home-cooked chickpeas have such a lovely, nutty texture. But this is still a sterling dish if made with canned chickpeas – use two 14-ounce / 400g cans, drained and rinsed. Actually, the merguez chickpeas are a lovely tapas dish in their own right – worth plonking on the table with any spread of veg dishes.

SERVES 4

About 2 pounds / 1kg squash or pumpkin

About 10 ounces / 300g shallots or small onions, peeled

4 or 5 garlic cloves (unpeeled), bashed

3 tablespoons olive oil

Sea salt and freshly ground black pepper

FOR THE MERGUEZ CHICKPEAS

7 ounces / 200g dried chickpeas, soaked overnight in plenty of cold water

2 bay leaves

1 teaspoon cumin seeds

1 teaspoon fennel seeds

1 teaspoon cilantro seeds

1 teaspoon caraway seeds (optional)

10 to 12 black peppercorns

1 garlic clove, finely chopped

1 teaspoon finely chopped rosemary

1 teaspoon sweet smoked paprika

A good pinch of cayenne pepper

¼ teaspoon fine sea salt

¼ cup / 60ml extra-virgin olive oil

TO FINISH

A handful of flat-leaf parsley

First, drain the chickpeas and put them into a large saucepan. Cover with lots of cold water, bring to a boil, and boil hard for 10 minutes, then lower to a gentle simmer. Skim off any scum and add the bay leaves. Simmer for 1 to 1¼ hours, topping up with more boiling water if necessary, until the chickpeas are tender and crushable.

Meanwhile, preheat the oven to 375°F / 190°C. Peel and seed the squash or pumpkin and cut into roughly 1½-inch / 4cm chunks. Halve or quarter the shallots or onions, depending on size. Put the squash, shallots, and garlic cloves into a large roasting pan. Trickle over the olive oil and sprinkle generously with salt and pepper. Toss well and roast for 50 to 60 minutes, stirring and jumbling once or twice, until the vegetables are soft and caramelized.

Meanwhile, for the chickpea seasoning, toast all the spice seeds and the black peppercorns in a dry small frying pan for a few minutes over medium heat until fragrant. Crush to a coarse powder, using a mortar and pestle or spice grinder. Combine with the garlic, rosemary, paprika, cayenne, salt, and extra-virgin olive oil in a small saucepan over low heat. Warm gently for 1 minute (the oil should barely sizzle), then remove from the heat and set aside.

When the chickpeas are cooked, drain well, return them to their still-hot pan, and toss while still hot with the seasoned oil. (If using canned chickpeas, heat them through in the oil, then leave to cool a bit.)

Divide the roasted squash and shallots among warmed plates. Top with the warm chickpeas, spooning over any oil left in the pan. Finish with a scattering of parsley leaves.

Roasted tomato sauce

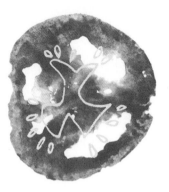

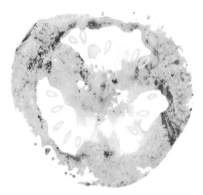

This intense tomato sauce is a River Cottage classic and an absolute mainstay of my cooking. I prepare pan after pan of it from the tomatoes I grow at home, and freeze batch after batch for use in the coming months. I make no apologies for including the recipe again here because it's such a useful and delicious thing – and elsewhere in this book you will find several new ideas for using it. The consistency of the sauce can vary quite a bit, depending on the tomatoes you use – sometimes you end up with a thick purée, and sometimes with a rich liquid. The flavor should always be good, though. Simmer the sauce to reduce and thicken it as necessary.

MAKES ABOUT 2 CUPS / 500ML

3 to 4 pounds / 1.5 to 2kg ripe tomatoes, larger ones halved

3 garlic cloves, finely chopped

A few sprigs of thyme

A couple of sprigs of marjoram (optional)

2 tablespoons canola or olive oil

Sea salt and freshly ground black pepper

Preheat the oven to 350°F / 180°C. Lay the tomatoes, cut side up if halved, on a baking sheet. Scatter over the garlic and herbs, and trickle over the oil. Season with plenty of salt and pepper.

Put the baking sheet in the oven for about an hour, maybe a bit longer, until the tomatoes are completely soft and pulpy, and starting to crinkle and caramelize on top.

Set the tomatoes aside to cool for half an hour or so. Then tip them into a large sieve set over a bowl and rub the pulp through with a wooden spoon, or use a food mill. Discard the skins and seeds. Your tomato sauce is now ready to use.

RECIPES USING ROASTED TOMATO SAUCE

Eggplant and green bean curry (page 29) • North African squash and chickpea stew (page 30) Mexican tomato and bean soup (page 138) • Beet pizza with cheddar (page 180) Tomato and mozzarella risotto (page 272) • New potato gnocchi (page 284) Oven-roasted ratatouille (page 362) • Roasted tomato ketchup (page 392)

Side dishes

The recipes in this chapter are among the simplest in the book, and many are among my oldest favorites, having done years – even decades – of service. Some of these ways of giving plainly cooked veg "a bit of a lift" were devised to nudge younger members of the family toward more avid consumption of vegetables – and they worked a treat.

Indeed, the enduring successes – steamed veg with a hint of garlic (see page 372) and creamy potato and celery root mash (see page 388) – are now perceived as a treat. And some of the newer recipes – rutabaga with onion and sage (see page 382) and leeks (and greens) with coconut milk (see page 378) – look set to achieve the same "family favorites" status.

So the term "side dishes" does not in any way diminish the recipes you will find here – it simply describes how they are usually deployed. To be honest, I often serve them beside fish or meat. And I'd be delighted to think that you'd want to do that, too, from time to time. But increasingly, I dish them up alongside other more substantial veg dishes. In this context, they seem less like side dishes, more like pass-around dishes in their own right.

While few of these dishes are sustaining enough to constitute a whole meal, they have other virtues. The simple cooking allows the flavor, texture, and color of the vegetables to shine through; they unambiguously celebrate the principal ingredients. I like that. It's a bit of a cliché of food writing these days to note that if you have some beautiful, plump, fresh leeks or some sweet, earthy, just-dug carrots – or even some very nice potatoes from the farmers' market or supermarket – doing as little as possible to them is often the best approach. But it's a cliché for good reason – because it's absolutely true. The first few recipes here prove the point – these are just very plainly cooked veg, given the merest twist of spice or the most basic of dressings to enhance their flavors and to indicate that they deserve your attention.

All that's required is a little mind-shift. I realize it might seem slightly odd to put a plate of mash on the table unaccompanied by sausage – but if it's good mash, it will go as quickly as any other dish. The same is true of stir-fried sesame cauliflower (see page 376), or a bowl of garlicky, minty mushy peas (see page 387), or golden potato rosti (see page 391). All you need is one or two complementary dishes to bring the meal together.

The recipes here are perfect foils to the more complex and often more highly seasoned ones in Meze and Tapas (pages 292–327), and many of my comments in that chapter apply here, too. These are dishes that suit that generous, communal, mix-and-match way of eating that feels so wonderfully appropriate when vegetables are at the heart of your cooking. In that sense, they pretty much have honorary meze or tapas status anyway.

The reason why I've called them "side" dishes is that they can also do sterling service as the single extra element that rounds out a "big dish" meal. You might, for example, consider runner beans with tomatoes and garlic (see page 375) alongside a creamy potato dauphinoise (see page 60), or big baked mushrooms (see page 385) with a hearty frittata (see pages 232 and 234).

The chapter ends with a quirky flourish, which I'll happily admit is a bit of an indulgence. A handful of sweet recipes whose primary ingredients are also vegetables feels like a fun way to finish. They are not side dishes, I'll grant you, they're definitely "afters." But they are not afterthoughts, nor are they mere novelties. On the contrary, they are lovely examples of the way in which vegetables can find their way into every corner of our diet.

We are all familiar with the carrot cake, and those of you who are familiar with my other work may be *au fait* with the chocolate and beet brownie, and the mashed potato lemon trickle cake. The treats with which I've chosen to round off this book fall into the same category: indulgent sweet recipes that just happen to be based on veg. And, I promise you, the duo of vegetable ice creams is an absolute revelation. Maybe even a revolution.

So, perhaps surprisingly, this is the broadest chapter in the book, ranging from the very simplest dish of garlicky, buttered green veg, through a selection of luxurious, creamy root veg purées, to a splendid dessert tart that you might choose to serve with a glass of sweet sherry. What it demonstrates again, I hope, is just how adaptable vegetables can be. Whether you are tired and pushed for time, or you have an entire afternoon free to spend pottering about in the kitchen, vegetables – delicious, wholesome, enticing, and infinitely various and versatile – are perhaps the most useful and rewarding of all ingredients.

Steamed veg with a hint of garlic

This is possibly the simplest recipe in the book, but it's one I turn to often.
It's an easy way to take any green veg up a notch. I've found it particularly
successful for encouraging younger family members to eat their greens.

SERVES 4

14 to 16 ounces / 400 to 500g
green veg (peas, beans, broccoli,
cauliflower, cabbage, etc.)

2 tablespoons / 30g butter

1 tablespoon canola
or olive oil

1 fat garlic clove, crushed

Sea salt and freshly ground
black pepper

Prepare the veg: peas are fine as they are, of course. Trim the beans (removing the strings from the sides of runner beans, if using, with a potato peeler), then cut into 1½-inch / 4cm lengths. Cut broccoli or cauliflower into small florets. Remove tough stalks from cabbage, greens, or kale and shred their leaves.

Now steam the veg over boiling water until just done – tender but with a bit of crunch left. The time taken depends on the vegetable.

While the vegetables are cooking, heat the butter and oil in a saucepan over low heat. Once the butter is melted, add the garlic. Cook very gently for a couple of minutes, letting the fat fizz just slightly and taking care that the garlic doesn't color. Remove from the heat.

Toss the hot with steamed vegetables with the garlicky butter, along with some salt and pepper, and they're ready to serve.

VARIATIONS

Garlic and caraway greens
Steam greens, kale, cabbage, or brussels sprouts as above, or wilt in a drizzle of water and drain well. Add ½ teaspoon lightly bashed caraway seeds to the butter and oil at the same time as the garlic.

Garlic and cumin roots
For lightly steamed carrots, parsnips, or beets: peel and cut the veg into slices or batons before steaming, and add ½ teaspoon lightly toasted and ground cumin seeds to the butter and oil with the garlic. (If you haven't time to toast and grind cumin seeds, ground cumin is still good.)

Garlic and mint peas and beans
For lightly cooked, just-picked peas or green or runner beans: prepare as above, adding 1 tablespoon finely chopped mint and 1 teaspoon balsamic vinegar right at the end. Toss the peas/beans thoroughly with the minty, piquant butter.

Runner beans with tarragon and lemon^v

This is a lovely, fresh-tasting way to prepare runner beans – or green beans.

SERVES 4

1 pound / 500g runner beans

2 tablespoons canola
or olive oil

2 shallots or 1 small onion,
finely chopped

1 small garlic clove,
finely chopped

Juice of 1 lemon

A handful of tarragon,
finely chopped

Sea salt and freshly ground
black pepper

Use a potato peeler to remove the stringy fibers from the sides of the beans, top and tail them, then cut into 1-inch / 2.5cm pieces.

Heat the oil in a large saucepan or casserole over medium heat. Add the shallots or onion and sweat down for about 10 minutes, until soft.

Add the garlic and beans. Cover the pan, lower the heat, and sweat for another 10 minutes. Add about 1/2 cup / 100ml water and continue to cook, uncovered, for another 10 minutes or so, stirring from time to time. You want the beans to be just tender but still with a bit of crunch, and just a little liquid to remain at the end of cooking.

Remove from the heat and stir in the lemon juice, tarragon, and some salt and pepper. Serve warm or at room temperature.

Runner beans with tomatoes and garlic^v

Grating tomatoes is an easy way to peel them – as you rub the halved ripe tomato firmly against a box grater, the skin will remain in your hand while the pulp and juices fall into the bowl. This dish works well with green beans, too. Eat it hot as an accompaniment or at room temperature as a part of a selection of meze.

SERVES 4 TO 6

1 pound / 500g runner beans

1 pound / 500g large, ripe
tomatoes

2 tablespoons olive oil

1 onion, finely chopped

1 large garlic clove,
finely chopped

Sea salt and freshly ground
black pepper

A small handful of basil
(or a mix of parsley and basil),
finely shredded

Use a potato peeler to remove the stringy fibers from the sides of the beans, top and tail them, then cut into 2 1/2-inch / 6cm pieces.

Halve the tomatoes. Using the large-holed side of a box grater, grate the tomatoes into a bowl. Discard the skins.

Heat the olive oil in a large frying pan over medium-low heat, add the onion, and sauté gently, until soft, about 10 minutes. Add the garlic and sauté for a further minute.

Stir in the beans, then the tomato pulp and some salt and pepper. Bring to a simmer over medium heat, cover, and cook for 10 minutes. Add the herbs and simmer for another 5 minutes, until the sauce has thickened and the beans are tender. Check the seasoning and serve hot, warm, or at room temperature.

Stir-fried sesame cauliflower🌱

Cauliflower takes strong seasonings exceptionally well, and this easy stir-fry – flavored with chile, garlic, and ginger – is a good example. This is a great side dish, but you can also serve it with rice or noodles as a supper in itself.

SERVES 2 TO 4

1 medium cauliflower
(about 1½ pounds / 700g),
trimmed

2 tablespoons sesame seeds

2 tablespoons sunflower oil

1 onion, halved and thinly sliced

2 garlic cloves, sliced

1 or 2 green chiles, seeded
and thinly sliced

2 teaspoons freshly grated
ginger

1 teaspoon toasted sesame oil

2 teaspoons soy sauce, plus
extra to serve

A small handful of cilantro,
chopped, plus sprigs to finish

Break the cauliflower into small, neat florets. Place in a bowl of cold water and leave to soak for 10 minutes.

In a dry small frying pan, toast the sesame seeds for a minute or two until toasted and fragrant. Tip onto a plate and set aside.

Heat the sunflower oil in a large frying pan or wok over medium heat and add the onion. Sauté until pale golden, then add the garlic, chile(s), and ginger and fry, stirring, for a minute.

Drain the cauliflower. Raise the heat under the frying pan, then tip in the cauliflower and ½ cup / 100ml of water. Cook, stirring, for 5 to 10 minutes until the florets are browning around the edges, adding a splash more water if they start to stick. Stir in the sesame seeds, sesame oil, soy sauce, and chopped cilantro.

Serve scattered with cilantro sprigs, and with soy sauce for people to add as they choose.

Leeks (and greens) with coconut milk♥

*I've been cooking this a lot recently – with and without greens. It's great
with spicy roasted roots or squash, rice, and maybe some dal (see page 238)
on the side. In early summer, when leeks are out of season, I sometimes
make it with young green onions instead.*

SERVES 4

4 or 5 medium leeks, trimmed
of tough ends

About 8 ounces / 250g kale,
Swiss chard, or cabbage
(optional), tough stalks
removed

2 tablespoons sunflower oil

3 garlic cloves, sliced

1 teaspoon curry powder

1²/₃ cups / 400ml coconut milk

2 ounces / 60g roasted peanuts
or cashews, coarsely chopped
or crushed, to finish (optional)

Cut the leeks into ½-inch / 1cm slices on the diagonal. If using greens,
shred into ½-inch / 1cm ribbons and set aside.

Heat the sunflower oil in a large frying pan over medium-low heat
and sweat the garlic for a couple of minutes, being careful not to let
it burn.

Add the leeks and sauté for a few minutes, then add the curry powder
and cook, stirring occasionally, for another couple of minutes, until
the leeks are becoming tender but still have a bit of bite.

Add the greens, if using, and sweat down for 3 minutes or so, until
wilted but still slightly crunchy.

Pour in the coconut milk and heat through, letting it bubble for just
a minute. Serve at once, sprinkled with peanuts or cashews if you like.

Cheat's cauliflower cheese

*There's no need to make a béchamel for this quick and easy cauliflower
gratin, yet it's still delicious and filling. A good distribution of the cheesy,
crumby topping is the key to success. Serve as a side dish or alone.*

SERVES 2 TO 4

1 large cauliflower (about
2 pounds / 1kg), trimmed

1 generous tablespoon /
20g butter

1 tablespoon cream (optional)

Sea salt and freshly ground
black pepper

3½ ounces / 100g mature
cheddar or other flavorsome
hard cheese, grated

1½ to 2 ounces / 40 to 60g
bread crumbs

Cut the cauliflower into very small florets. Put into a saucepan, cover
with lightly salted water, bring to a boil, then simmer for about
5 minutes, or until al dente. Drain well and toss with the butter, the
cream if you like, and plenty of salt and pepper.

Preheat the broiler. Tip the cauliflower florets into a gratin dish or
shallow ovenproof dish in which they fit snugly in one layer. Combine
the cheese and bread crumbs and scatter thickly and evenly over the
top. Place under the broiler until golden brown and nicely toasted.
Serve right away.

Celery gratin

It's easy to think of celery as a mere "flavoring" vegetable, crucial to soups and stocks, and not a star in its own right. This deeply flavored dish shows how delicious it can be when given center stage. Try it with dressed lentils (see page 237), or even a simple frittata (see pages 232 and 234).

SERVES 4

1 bunch of celery

1 bay leaf

1 sprig of thyme

2 tablespoons / 30g butter

Sea salt and freshly ground black pepper

A scant ½ cup / about 100ml heavy cream

2½ ounces / 75g bread crumbs

1 ounce / 30g Parmesan, Gruyère, hard goat cheese, or other well-flavored hard cheese, finely grated

Preheat the oven to 325°F / 160°C. Separate the bunch of celery into stalks, and if the outer stalks look coarse or a bit hollow, set them aside to use for vegetable stock (see page 130). Cut any leaves from the remaining stalks and save these for stock, too (they would go brown in the oven). Cut the stalks into 4-inch / 10cm lengths.

Put the celery into a shallow ovenproof dish and tuck the bay and thyme among the pieces. Pour over 3 tablespoons of water, dot with the butter, and sprinkle on some salt and pepper. Cover with foil and bake for about 40 minutes or until the celery is tender. Take the dish out of the oven and turn up the oven temperature to 400°F / 200°C.

Discard the bay and thyme and carefully pour off the liquid from the celery into a liquid measuring cup. Add enough cream to amount to ⅔ cup / 150ml and whisk together. Taste the liquid and add more salt and pepper if needed, then pour over the celery in the dish.

Mix the bread crumbs with the grated cheese, sprinkle over the celery, and return to the oven for 15 to 20 minutes, until the crumb topping is golden brown and crispy. Grind over some black pepper and serve.

VARIATION

Gratin of chard stalks

If you've used chard leaves in a recipe, this is an ideal way to serve up the delicious, tender-crunchy stalks. Cut the stalks from a 2-pound / 1kg bunch of chard into roughly ½-inch / 1cm slices. Heat 1 tablespoon oil and 1 tablespoon butter in a large frying pan over medium heat and sauté the chard stalks with some chopped garlic, stirring often, for 10 to 15 minutes, until tender. Stir in the chopped leaves from a handful of thyme sprigs, some salt and pepper, and a scant ½ cup / 100ml of heavy cream. When bubbling, transfer to a gratin dish and scatter over 1 ounce / 30g grated Parmesan or Gruyère mixed with 1 ounce / 30g bread crumbs. Put under a hot broiler until golden brown. Serve as a side dish, or with dressed French green lentils (see page 237), or perhaps some new potatoes as a supper.

Rutabaga with onion and sage

This is a delicious way to serve rutabaga: the sweetness of the onions softens its pungency and the sage adds an extra layer of flavor.

SERVES 4

3 tablespoons / 45g butter

About 1 pound / 500g rutabaga, peeled and cut into ½-inch / 1cm cubes

1 large onion, chopped

About 12 sage leaves, finely shredded

Sea salt and freshly ground black pepper

Heat the butter in a large frying pan over medium heat. Add the rutabaga, onion, half of the sage, and some salt and pepper. Stir well. When the vegetables are sweating nicely, cover the pan and lower the heat a little.

Cook, stirring from time to time, for 40 to 45 minutes, until the rutabaga is tender and the onion is sweet and caramelized.

Stir in the remaining shredded sage, taste and adjust the seasoning if necessary, and serve.

Jerusalem artichoke frying pan gratin

Jerusalem artichokes make an excellent gratin. For a less substantial dish, you can just simmer them with the onions and thyme, but the addition of crème fraîche and cheese turns this into a really luxurious treat.

SERVES 4

2 tablespoons / 30g butter

1 tablespoon canola or olive oil

1 large onion, cut into thin wedges

1 pound / 500g Jerusalem artichokes, peeled and cut into ⅛-inch / 3mm slices

A handful of thyme sprigs, leaves only, chopped

Sea salt and freshly ground black pepper

4 tablespoons crème fraîche

About 1½ ounces / 40g mature cheddar, grated

Heat the butter and oil in a large broilersafe frying pan over medium heat. Add the onion and sweat for about 10 minutes, until soft and just beginning to color.

Add the sliced Jerusalem artichokes, thyme, some salt, and lots of black pepper. Pour in a scant ½ cup / 100ml of water, bring to a simmer, then cover and turn down the heat to low. Simmer, stirring from time to time, for about 20 minutes, until the artichokes are nice and tender throughout, adding a little more water if you need to. Remove the lid and simmer for a further few minutes if necessary to reduce the liquid to a thick glaze.

Preheat the broiler. Check the seasoning of the Jerusalem artichokes, then dollop the crème fraîche over them evenly. Scatter over the cheese and broil for a few minutes until bubbling. Serve right away.

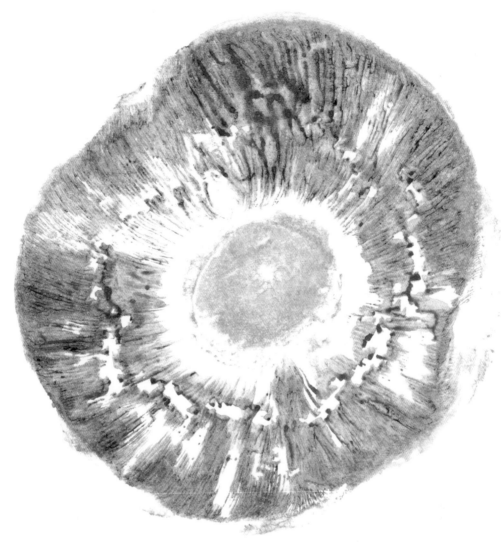

Big baked mushrooms

This is such an easy way to cook big, flat fresh mushrooms, and they make a surprisingly "meaty" accompaniment to anything from a potato gratin to a spelt salad. You could serve them with the cheesy topping as a starter, but they are very good just as they are.

SERVES 2

4 large, portobello mushrooms

1 tablespoon /15g butter

1 garlic clove, finely chopped

1 ounce / 30g well-flavored cheddar or hard goat cheese, grated (optional)

Sea salt and freshly ground black pepper

Preheat the oven to 375°F / 190°C. Put the mushrooms, gill side up, into a small, lightly oiled roasting pan. Dot with the butter, scatter on the garlic, then dust with some salt and pepper. Bake for about 15 minutes, until the mushrooms are tender and juicy.

Serve the baked mushrooms as they are, or sprinkle over the grated cheese and return to the oven for another 5 minutes or so, until the cheese is golden and bubbling.

Garlicky, minty mushy peas

*This is another one of those highly seasoned, blitzed vegetable purées that I am
so fond of. They are great as a side dish, or as part of a meze spread, or they
can be eaten as a snack or starter with some toast fingers or flat bread wedges.*

SERVES 4

4 teaspoons / 20g butter

3 shallots or 1 medium onion,
finely chopped

3 or 4 garlic cloves, finely
chopped

A good handful of mint, finely
chopped, plus a sprig

1 pound / 500g fresh or frozen
shelled peas

Sea salt and freshly ground
black pepper

A handful of chives (optional)

Melt the butter in a saucepan over low heat. Add the shallots or
onion and sauté for 15 to 20 minutes, until very soft. Add the garlic
and sauté for a couple more minutes, then set aside.

In a separate saucepan, cook the peas with a sprig of mint in enough
lightly salted boiling water to cover them by 1 inch / 2.5cm, until
tender. Drain, saving some of the cooking water.

Using a food processor, blender, or an immersion bender, blitz the
peas with the shallots, garlic, chopped mint, and a twist of pepper,
adding just a little of the pea cooking water, to obtain a coarse purée.

Taste and adjust the seasoning. Serve warm, scattered with chopped
chives, if you like.

Salsify purée

*Salsify is a root vegetable with a delicate earthy flavor. It's lovely just boiled
and tossed with butter and pepper, but this recipe turns it into something rich
and comforting. Scorzonera, which is closely related, would work well here, too.
Serve as a side dish, or with flat breads (see page 176), or toast as a starter.*

SERVES 4

About 1 pound / 500g salsify or
scorzonera

Sea salt and freshly ground
black pepper

2 tablespoons / 30g butter

3 tablespoons heavy cream

A handful of thyme sprigs,
leaves only, chopped (optional)

Peel the salsify, dropping the roots directly into a saucepan of water
(they discolor extremely quickly on exposure to air). Chop the peeled
roots into large chunks and return to the pan. Add salt to the water –
which, for cooking, should cover the roots by ½ inch / 1cm or so. Bring
to a boil, lower the heat, and simmer for 15 to 20 minutes, or until the
salsify is completely tender. Drain, reserving the cooking water.

Transfer the salsify to a blender and add the butter, cream, thyme
if using, and a generous few twists of black pepper. Process to a thick
purée. You can add a splash of the cooking water to loosen it if you
like, but it's best when thick enough to hold its shape. Check the
seasoning. Serve right away.

Creamy potato and celery root mash

This makes a gorgeous smooth and velvety mash – worth the little extra effort of passing the cooked potatoes through a ricer or food mill. Don't be tempted to blitz them in a processor, as this makes them gluey and will spoil the texture of the mash.

SERVES 6

2 pounds / 1kg starchy potatoes, peeled and cut into even-sized chunks

3 cups / 700ml whole milk

14 ounces / 400g celery root, peeled and cut into 1-inch / 2.5cm chunks

3 tablespoons / 45g unsalted butter, plus extra to taste

Sea salt and freshly ground black pepper

A few gratings of nutmeg

Add the potatoes to a large saucepan of salted water, bring to a boil, and cook until tender, about 20 minutes. Drain well and leave to steam in a colander for a few minutes to drive off excess moisture.

While the potatoes are cooking, bring the milk to a boil in a separate saucepan. Add the celery root and simmer until very soft, about 20 minutes. Drain, reserving the milk and keep it warm. Purée the celery root in a food processor with the butter and about ²/₃ cup / 150ml of the hot milk. Place the celery root purée in a warmed large bowl.

Press the potatoes through a potato ricer or pass through a food mill into the bowl with the celery root. (If you don't have a ricer or food mill, mash them separately until they're very smooth.)

Using a wooden spoon, beat the celery root purée with the potatoes until smooth and well combined, adding a little more of the hot milk and/or some more butter until you get the consistency you like. Season with salt, pepper, and nutmeg to taste and serve immediately.

Potato rosti ᵛ

A simple rosti – well-seasoned grated potato, fried until golden and crunchy – is hard to beat. Sometimes, rather than making individual rosti, I put all the mixture in the pan at once to form a single giant rosti cake. Serve as a side dish, or with a poached egg (see page 210), or a pile of dressed lentils (see page 237), or beans.

**MAKES 6 SMALL
OR 4 LARGE ROSTI**

1 pound / 500g starchy potatoes

Flaky sea salt and freshly ground black pepper

Canola oil, for frying

Peel the potatoes. Leave small ones whole, halve medium ones, and quarter large ones. Put into a saucepan, cover with water, add some salt, and bring to a boil. Lower the heat and simmer for just 5 minutes – they should be just underdone. Drain and leave to cool completely (otherwise they will crumble as you grate them), then grate coarsely. Season generously with salt and pepper, tossing thoroughly to mix.

Heat enough oil in a nonstick frying pan to cover the bottom by about 1/16 inch / 1mm and place over medium heat. Form handfuls of the grated potato into thin cakes, no more than 1/2 inch / 1cm thick. Don't worry if they are prone to falling apart at this stage – the cooking will sort that out.

Add the potato cakes in batches to the hot pan and fry without moving them for about 5 minutes, so they form a golden brown crust underneath. Carefully flip them over. Continue to cook until golden brown and crisp on the second side, turning once or twice more if you need to. One batch will take about 12 minutes in all. Remove the rosti to paper towels to drain off any excess oil. Sprinkle over a little salt and serve on warmed plates.

VARIATIONS

Potato and onion rosti ᵛ

Fry 1 thinly sliced onion in 1 tablespoon of canola oil for 10 minutes, or until soft. Stir into the grated potato and continue as above.

Potato and seaweed rosti ᵛ

Simmer a good handful of fresh dulse seaweed in water for about 10 minutes until tender, drain well, and chop coarsely. (Or, soak about 1/2 ounce / 15g dried seaweed, such as dulse, wakame, or arame according to the package instructions, usually about 10 minutes, then squeeze out excess liquid and chop coarsely.) Fry 1 sliced onion in 1 tablespoon canola oil for about 10 minutes, until soft. Mix the seaweed and onion with the grated potato and some salt and pepper before forming the rosti. These are good sprinkled with a little soy sauce before serving.

Roasted tomato ketchup^ᵛ

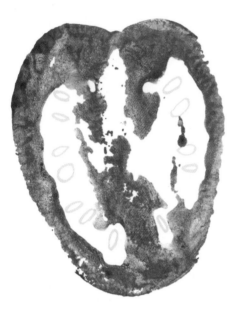

This is a lovely, loose ketchup with a deep, rich flavor acquired from roasting the tomatoes. For a bit of heat and a smoky tang, include the smoked paprika. Use this sauce whenever you might think of using ketchup – it's perfect with French fries.

MAKES 1¼ TO 2 CUPS / 300 TO 500ML

1 quart / liter roasted tomato sauce (see page 366)

3½ tablespoons / 50g brown sugar

3½ tablespoons / 50ml cider vinegar

¼ teaspoon ground mace

A pinch of ground cinnamon

A pinch of freshly grated nutmeg

A pinch of ground cloves

1 teaspoon hot smoked paprika (optional)

Sea salt and freshly ground black pepper

Put the roasted tomato sauce into a fairly large, heavy-bottomed saucepan and add all the rest of the ingredients, except salt and pepper. Bring to a merry simmer, stirring occasionally.

Cook down over medium-low heat for 20 to 40 minutes, maybe longer, stirring regularly to prevent it from sticking to the bottom of the pan. You'll want to reduce the sauce by at least half, or up to three-quarters, depending partly on how loose the sauce was to start with, and partly on how thick and intense you want your ketchup to be. So when you think you're pretty much there, take a teaspoon and blob some on to a cold plate, leave it to cool, and then taste it. Season the sauce with salt and pepper to taste.

The finished ketchup will keep in a sealed jar in the fridge for a couple of weeks.

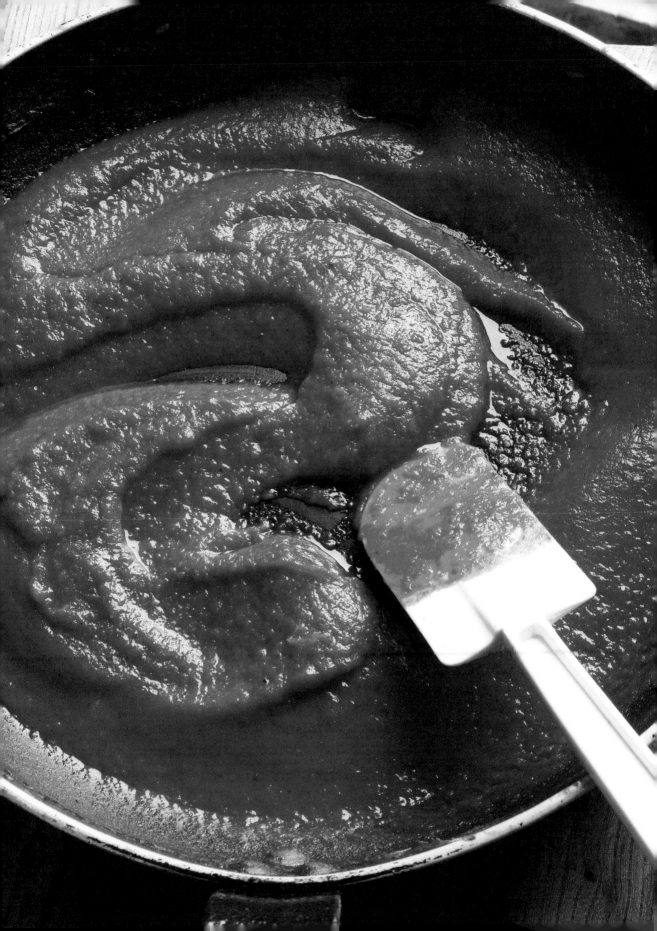

Pumpkin and raisin tea loaf

This delicious tea loaf is rich and sweet, but also quite light because it doesn't contain any butter or oil.

MAKES 1 LOAF CAKE

1 cup / 200g light muscovado sugar

4 large eggs, separated

7 ounces / 200g finely grated raw pumpkin or squash flesh

Finely grated zest and juice of 1 lemon

3½ ounces / 100g raisins

3½ ounces / 100g ground almonds

1½ cups / 200g self-rising flour

A pinch of fine sea salt

1 teaspoon ground cinnamon

A generous grating of nutmeg

Preheat the oven to 325°F / 170°C. Lightly grease a loaf pan, about 8 by 4 inches / 20 by 10cm, and line with parchment paper.

Using an electric mixer, beat together the sugar and egg yolks for 2 to 3 minutes, until pale and creamy. Lightly stir in the grated pumpkin or squash, lemon zest and juice, raisins, and ground almonds. Sift together the flour, salt, and spices over the mixture and then fold them in using a large metal spoon.

In a large, clean bowl, beat the egg whites until they hold soft peaks. Stir a heaping tablespoonful of the beaten egg whites into the batter to loosen it a little, then fold in the rest as lightly as you can.

Tip the batter into the prepared loaf pan and gently level the surface. Bake for about 1 hour, or until a skewer inserted into the center comes out clean.

Leave to cool in the pan for 10 minutes, then transfer to a wire rack to cool completely before slicing.

VARIATIONS

Zucchini, carrot, or beet tea loaf
Replace the pumpkin with 7 ounces / 200g finely grated raw zucchini, carrot, or even beets (which produces a striking purple-marbled effect).

Chocolate-beet ice cream

This pairing works brilliantly in an ice cream. Once you're in the swing of vegetable ice creams, try the variation. It's a stunner – cool, minty, and gorgeous.

MAKES ABOUT 3½ CUPS / 800ML

10 ounces / 300g red beets

1¼ cups / 300ml whole milk

A generous ¾ cup / 200ml heavy cream

4 large egg yolks

½ cup / 100g superfine sugar

3½ ounces / 100g dark chocolate, broken into small pieces

Preheat the oven to 400°F / 200°C. Put the beets in an ovenproof dish, add a ½-inch / 1cm depth of water, cover with foil, and roast until tender – at least 1 hour. Let cool. Peel the beets, chop coarsely, and purée in a blender with one-third of the milk. Measure the purée. You should have about 1¼ cups / 300ml; it does not matter if there's a little less, but you don't want more. Set aside.

To make the custard, heat the remaining milk and the cream in a saucepan to just below boiling. Cool a little. Whisk together the egg yolks and sugar in a bowl, then pour in the hot milk and cream, whisking until smooth. Return to a clean saucepan. Cook gently, stirring all the time, until the custard thickens. Don't let it boil or it will "break." Remove from the heat and leave to cool until tepid, stirring often to stop a skin forming.

Meanwhile, melt the chocolate in a heatproof bowl placed in a larger bowl filled with just-boiled water, stirring from time to time. Stir the melted chocolate into the custard (don't worry if it looks a bit grainy at this point). Stir in the beet purée. Pass the mixture through a fine sieve into a pitcher, leave to cool, then chill.

Once cold, churn the mixture in an ice cream maker until soft-set, then transfer to a suitable container and freeze until solid. (If you don't have an ice cream maker, freeze in a shallow container, mashing with a fork after every hour for 3 hours, or until the mixture is solid.) Transfer to the fridge 20 to 30 minutes before serving, to soften a little.

VARIATION

Pea and mint ice cream

Make the custard as above, but use all 1¼ cups / 300ml of milk with the cream. Strain the cooked custard into a bowl, cover with plastic wrap and cool, then chill. Simmer 12 ounces / 350g shelled peas with 2 mint sprigs until just tender. Drain, rinse under cold water, and discard the mint. Blitz the peas in a blender with 4 tablespoons finely shredded mint and 2 tablespoons crème fraîche until smooth, adding a dash of milk if necessary. Stir together the chilled custard and pea purée. Taste and add a little confectioners' sugar if necessary – freezing will diminish the sweetness. Chill, then churn or freeze as above.

Tourte de blettes

Based on a traditional Niçoise recipe, this sweet pie makes a lovely dessert, and it's a great way to use Swiss chard. You only need the leaves; use the stems for another dish, such as a gratin of chard stalks (see page 380).

SERVES 8

FOR THE SWEET PASTRY

2¹/₃ cups / 300g all-purpose flour

A generous ¹/₃ cup / 50g confectioners' sugar

A pinch of fine sea salt

³/₄ cup / 175g chilled unsalted butter, cut into cubes

1 large egg yolk

About 5 tablespoons / 75ml cold milk (or water)

A little milk or beaten egg, for brushing

FOR THE FILLING

2 ounces / 60g raisins

3 tablespoons apple brandy

Leaves from 2 pounds / 1kg Swiss chard

2 large eggs, lightly beaten

¹/₃ cup / 50g pine nuts, lightly toasted

Finely grated zest of 1 lemon

2¹/₂ tablespoons / 35g superfine sugar

2 dessert apples, such as Cox's or Ashmead's Kernel (about 8 ounces / 250g)

Confectioners' sugar, to dust

For the filling, combine the raisins and brandy in a small bowl and leave to soak for a few hours.

For the pastry, put the flour, sugar, and salt in a food processor and blitz briefly to combine (or sift into a bowl). Add the butter and blitz (or rub in with your fingertips) until the mixture resembles bread crumbs. Add the egg yolk and mix in enough milk or water to bring the dough together in large clumps. Tip out onto a lightly floured surface and knead lightly into a ball. Wrap and chill for 30 minutes.

Preheat the oven to 400°F / 200°C. Wash the chard and put into a saucepan with just the water that clings to the leaves. Cover the pan and cook over medium-low heat until the leaves have wilted in their own steam, about 5 minutes. Tip into a colander and leave to drain. When cool enough to handle, squeeze out all the liquid from the leaves, then chop them.

Combine the chopped chard with the beaten eggs, pine nuts, lemon zest, superfine sugar, and raisins, plus their soaking liquid. Peel and grate the apples, avoiding the core, squeeze out as much liquid as you can from them with your hands, then stir the shreds into the mixture, too.

On a floured surface, roll out two-thirds of the pastry fairly thinly and use to line a 9¹/₂-inch / 24cm springform pan. Trim the excess pastry away from the edge. Spread the chard mixture in the pastry. Brush a little milk or beaten egg around the rim of the pastry. Roll out the remaining pastry to form the lid, place over the pan, and press the edge down lightly to seal. Trim off the excess pastry.

Make a couple of slits in the pastry lid for steam to escape. Bake for 30 minutes, or until golden brown on top. Leave to cool for a few minutes in the pan, then lift out the tart, keeping it on the pan bottom, then slide the tart off the pan bottom onto a wire rack. Dust the surface generously with confectioners' sugar. Serve warm.

Pantry

Many of these ingredients are hugely useful for on-the-fly veg-based cooking, and you'll find all of them referred to several times, at least, throughout this book. Some, I think, are pretty essential if you're looking to go meat-free at least some of the time. Others are perhaps not quite so crucial, but extremely useful.

Oils for cooking For frying, I like sunflower (*not* cold-pressed) and canola oil; both can be heated to a high temperature. I sometimes also use an inexpensive (generally refined) olive oil, but it's not suitable for very high temperature frying. For salads, extra-virgin canola oil and a good, peppery, extra-virgin olive oil are my usual choices, although intense, grassy hempseed oil makes a welcome change.

Vinegars Organic cider vinegar is my default option here, while apple balsamic is my favorite when a slightly sweet, rich vinegar is called for. I use red and white wine vinegars, too, and brown rice vinegar for Asian salad dressings and marinades.

Mustards Occasionally, I dabble in fancy, seedy mustards but I always have a good, strong English mustard on hand.

Nuts I like to have at least one or two of the following standing by: walnuts, pine nuts, almonds, pistachios, cashews, and peanuts.

Seeds I'm never without pumpkin, sesame, and sunflower seeds at the very least.

Flour Between them, organic white bread flour, all-purpose white flour, and whole-wheat cake flour cover most of my needs, though I do like to try out different flours when bread-making, including spelt and rye flours.

Yeast These days, I mostly use instant dried yeast – the kind that goes straight in with the flour – as I find it gives very good results. However, I do sometimes pick up fresh yeast when I'm visiting the local health food shop.

Canned legumes Chickpeas, some kind of white bean such as cannellini, and canned brown lentils (which can be used to make a very quick dal) are pantry essentials for me.

Dry lentils I keep French green lentils, mostly for using "whole" in salads and soups, and red (actually orange) lentils for cooking to a purée, or dal.

Canned tomatoes I never have fewer than four cans in the pantry. I prefer whole plum tomatoes, rather than chopped, because I think you get more tomato for your money and a better, richer flavor.

Spices It's lovely to have a whole range of spices in your cupboard, but inevitably a lot of them stand idle for months on end. In my kitchen, the ones that get used pretty much every week are cumin seeds, coriander seeds, cayenne pepper, smoked paprika (sweet and hot), caraway seeds, black peppercorns, dried chile flakes, dried whole chiles, and a good blended curry powder (I keep a mild blend handy and spike it up with extra chile if I want more heat).

Salt A good, fine-grained, free-flowing sea salt for salting cooking water and for instantly seasoning dishes is a must. For finishing dishes and to have on the table, I favor a good, flaky British sea salt, such as Cornish, Maldon, or Halen Môn.

Vegetable stock cubes I favor the organic, yeast-free ones produced by Kallo, which are not overly salty. Marigold bouillon granules are also worthwhile.

Lemons and bay leaves Although not exactly pantry items, I'd say never be without either of these, if you can help it.

Excellent extras

You might not have all of these items in your pantry (or freezer) all of the time, but I like to have most of them, most of the time. They all place you that much nearer to a truly satisfying, relatively fuss-free veg-based meal.

- Couscous
- Pasta
- Noodles
- Basmati rice
- Risotto rice
- Pearled spelt and/or pearled barley
- Quick-cooking polenta
- Quinoa
- Coconut milk
- Oil-preserved artichoke hearts
- Tomato purée
- Capers
- Olives
- Frozen puff pastry
- Tahini
- Peanut butter

Veg on the go

Meat-free midday sustenance doesn't have to mean endless cheese sandwiches. Think outside the (lunch)box when it comes to packing up a portable meal and you'll find workday lunches can be just as exciting as your evening repast. All of these recipes will serve well . . .

Dips, spreads and sandwich or wrap fillings These are so versatile – in a straight-up sandwich or wrap, maybe with a few crunchy salad leaves, or in a sealed jar or box as a portable dip for crudités, tortilla chips, or even a bag of potato chips. If you're making flat breads for wraps (using the recipe on page 176), remember to wrap them immediately after cooking in a clean kitchen towel and they will stay soft as they cool. Try the following tasty fillers:

- Garlicky fava bean purée, ricotta, and mint (page 196)
- Carrot hummus (page 296)
- Beet and walnut hummus ♥ (page 300)
- Cannellini bean hummus ♥ (page 300)
- Baba ganoush ♥ (page 303)
- Artichoke and white bean dip (page 303)
- Caponata ♥ (page 307)
- Fava beans with herbed goat cheese (page 316)
- Oven-roasted ratatouille ♥ (page 362)

Big salads Most of the recipes in Hearty Salads (pages 68–95) will be delicious eaten cold from a tub, but my lunch box favorites are:

- Herby, peanutty, noodly salad ♥ (page 71)
- Spelt salad with squash and fennel (page 72)
- Summer spelt salad ♥ (page 72)
- Tahini-dressed zucchini and green bean salad ♥ (page 74)
- New potato, tomato, and boiled egg salad (page 76)
- New potato salad "tartare" (page 79)
- Arugula, fennel, and green lentil salad ♥ (page 82)
- Fish-free salad niçoise (page 85)
- Couscous salad with herbs and walnuts ♥ (page 89)
- Summer couscous salad ♥ (page 89)
- Roasted baby beets with walnuts and yogurt dressing (page 92)
- Green beans, new potatoes, and olives ♥ (page 222)
- Quick couscous salad with peppers and feta (page 231)
- Tomato and olive couscous ♥ (page 231)
- Moroccan-spiced couscous ♥ (page 231)
- White bean salad with tomatoes and red onion ♥ (page 240)
- Broccoli salad with asian-style dressing ♥ (page 316)

Raw salads and coleslaws When you take a leafy salad in a lunch box, you'll want to take the dressing separately and dress it just before you eat, as dressed leaves are inclined to wilt as your lunch box sits around. As the following are not leafy, they can be taken predressed. You may lose a little crunch in some cases, but the dressing has a marinating effect on the ingredients, which is rather nice. Try these tasty options:

- Fennel and goat cheese (page 102)
- Carrot, orange, and cashews ❦ (page 107)
- Celery root with apple, raisins, and parsley ❦ (page 107)
- Cauliflower with toasted seeds ❦ (page 108)
- Red cabbage, parsnip, orange, and dates ❦ (page 110)
- Beets with walnuts and cumin ❦ (page 113)
- Asian-inspired coleslaw (page 115)
- Marinated cucumber with mint ❦ (page 122)

Tarts, pasties, pies, and frittatas All of these sustaining choices are highly portable when cold:

- Lettuce, green onion, and cheese tart (page 44)
- Beet greens (or chard) and ricotta tart (page 47)
- Rutabaga and potato pasties (page 52)
- Frittata with summer veg and goat cheese (page 232)
- Oven-roasted roots frittata (page 234)
- Spinach and thyme pasties (page 326)

Cold, cooked veg These are a really satisfying addition to a lunch box, along with a lubricating dip or hummus, or something a little "saucy" such as a coleslaw. Try a sprinkle of seeds or dukka (page 294) as well . . .

- Dressed green lentils ❦ (page 237)
- Spiced spinach and potatoes ❦ (page 321)
- Broiled eggplants with chile and honey (page 340)
- Honey-roasted cherry tomatoes (page 343)
- Roasted squash ❦ (page 346)
- Roasted potatoes and eggplants ❦ (page 351)
- Roasted cauliflower with lemon and paprika ❦ (page 352)
- Roasted parsnip "chips" ❦ (page 357)
- Roasted new potatoes with two mojo sauces ❦ (page 358)
- Roasted roots with apples and rosemary ❦ (page 361)
- Roasted squash and shallots with merguez chickpeas ❦ (page 365)

And, of course . . .
- DIY pot noodles (page 248)

index

❦ denotes vegan recipes

Acknowledgments

A huge amount of work has gone into *River Cottage Veg* and I am indebted to the many dedicated and talented people who've made it happen.

Among the skilled cooks who contributed to this book was Philippa Corbin – "Pip" to all of us – a highly valued member of the River Cottage team and a dedicated advocate of local, seasonal food. She tragically died before it was completed. She is greatly missed by us all.

I want to thank Gill Meller, who has led the River Cottage kitchen from the start and from the front, and has always been a great pleasure to work alongside. I'm grateful not just for his delectable recipe ideas, but also for the immense work he has put into preparing the dishes for photography. He has been ably supported by the whole River Cottage kitchen team and I'd especially like to thank Neil Matthews, Oliver Gladwin, and Bryan Johnson. Thanks also to Tim Maddams, James Whetlor, and their kitchen team, for upping the veg ante at the River Cottage Canteen.

And of course it's the images generated by the extremely talented Simon Wheeler that bring all these dishes to life on the page. Simon and I have now celebrated our tenth anniversary, and our seventh book together. I say "celebrated" – I guess I mean that metaphorically, but it's high time we did it literally. Thank you so much, Simon.

I would not have been able to pull all these dishes together without the hard work and inspiration of two dedicated and knowledgeable writers, Debora Robertson and Nikki Duffy. Their work in brainstorming, developing, testing, and editing recipes has been invaluable. Nikki's thoroughness and enthusiasm in "bringing this book home" has been unrelenting and highly professional.

Away from the kitchen, there are many people who've put in a huge amount of effort to bring this book to fruition. To my truly wonderful PA, Jess Upton, a thousand thanks for working her cool, calm, level-headed organizational magic on everything from photo shoots to the sourcing of ingredients, to the seventh circle of hell that is my schedule. And a big thanks to all the other members of the team at Park Farm (and beyond) who have worked with and supported me during the making of this book, including Lucy Brazier, Cat Bugler, Sally Gale, Liz Murray, Steve Lamb, Mark Diacono, Victoria Moorey, Ali Thomson, Kate Colwell, Pam Corbin, John Wright, Murry Toms, and Simon Dodd. Particular thanks to Rob Love, for his continuing partnership, support and encouragement in all things River Cottage.

For providing some lovely extra veg for the photo shoots, thanks to all at Trill Farm, Fivepenny Farm, Washingpool Farm, and Millers Farm Shop. And a special thanks to Mary Hugill for helping us to nurture all the wonderful vegetables here at home.

At Bloomsbury, my heartfelt thanks go to my editor Richard Atkinson for his continuing commitment to all my book projects, and superb editing and guidance from start to finish. Huge thanks to Natalie Hunt and Janet Illsley who have put so much careful thought – and so many hours – into honing the text from raw to nicely done. Lawrence Morton's clever design work and Mariko Jesse's beautiful illustrations make an elegant and witty marriage, which has truly done the recipes and text proud – it's been great fun working with you both. I'm grateful also to Penny Edwards who has guided the book so efficiently through the production stages.

To the team at Keo Films, especially Claire Lewis, Callum Webster, Kim Lomax, Aidan Woodward, Sancha Starkey, Jade Miller Robinson, Mark Davenport, Maria Norman, Tom Zynovieff, and, of course, my Keo partners Andrew Palmer and Zam Baring, a big thank you for *River Cottage Veg* TV.

To Antony Topping, my agent, and the third member of the "ten years and counting" club, a million thanks for your amazing work behind the scenes, on this and every other project I'm involved in.

Last, and the opposite of least, thank you to the people who continue to inspire, nourish, and support me (and share wonderful food with me, mainly vegetables) every single day: my wife Marie and our fantastic children Chloe, Oscar, Freddie, and Louisa.